W9-CEG-471

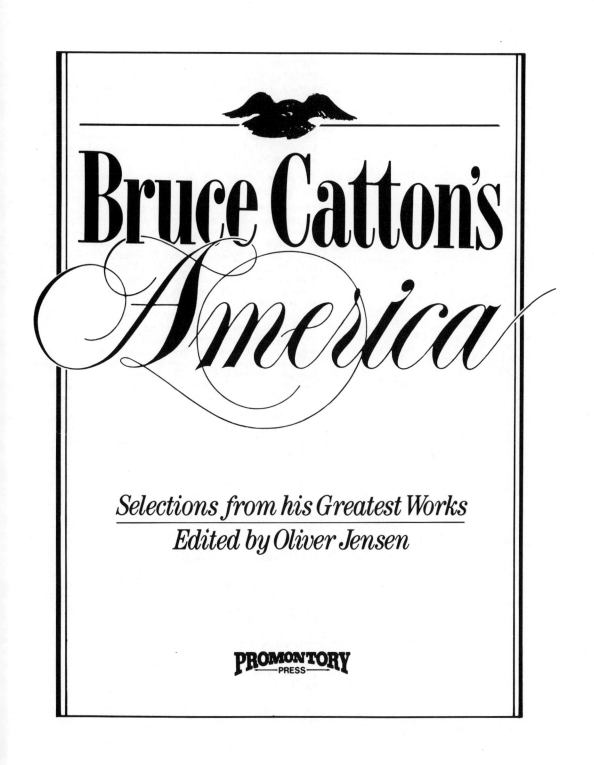

Bruce Catton's *America*

Selections from his Greatest Works

Edited by Oliver Jensen

PROMONTORY PRESS

PICTURE CREDITS
Pages 12, 34, 71, 80, 93, 101, 119, 124, 149, 151, 166, 177, 180, 212, Library of Congress; 56, 61, 74, 111, 136, 141, 175, 204, National Archives; 27, Benzonia Public Library, Benzonia, Michigan; 43, Library of the Boston Athenaeum; 68, Chicago Historical Society; 106, Cook Collection, Valentine Museum, Richmond, Virginia; 96, 218, David Plowden; 114, Colorado Historical Society; 144, National Library of Medicine; 191, Minnesota Historical Society; 198, New York Public Library.

The editor is grateful for permission to reprint from the following copyright material:

From *The War Lords of Washington*, copyright 1948, 1976, by Bruce Catton. Reprinted by permission of Harcourt Brace Jovanovich, Inc.
From *Mr. Lincoln's Army*, copyright 1951, by Bruce Catton; *Glory Road*, copyright 1952, by Bruce Catton; *A Stillness at Appomattox*, copyright 1953, by Bruce Catton; *This Hallowed Ground*, copyright 1955, 1956, by Bruce Catton; *Never Call Retreat*, copyright 1965, by Bruce Catton; *The Coming Fury*, copyright 1961, by Bruce Catton; *Terrible Swift Sword*, copyright 1963, by Bruce Catton; *Waiting for the Morning Train*, copyright 1972, by Bruce Catton. Reprinted by permission of Doubleday & Company, Inc.
From *U. S. Grant and the American Military Tradition*, copyright 1954, by Little, Brown & Company, Inc.; *Grant Moves South*, copyright 1960, by Little, Brown & Company, Inc.; *Grant Takes Command*, copyright 1968, 1969 by Little, Brown & Company, Inc. Reprinted by permission of the publisher.
From *Michigan: A Bicentennial History*, copyright 1976, by Bruce Catton. Reprinted by permission of W. W. Norton & Company.

The editor would also like to thank the University of Wyoming for permission to quote from a speech whose transcript is contained in the Bruce Catton Collection in the University's American Heritage Center.

Copyright © 1979 by American Heritage Inc.

All rights reserved. No part of this work may be reproduced or transmitted in any form or by any means, electronic or mechanical, including photocopying, recording, or any information storage and retrieval system, without permission in writing from the publisher.

Published in 1987 by

Promontory Press
166 Fifth Avenue
New York, NY 10010

By arrangement with American Heritage, a Division of Forbes, Inc., and Doubleday & Company, Inc.

Library of Congress Catalog Card Number: 86-83359
ISBN: 0-88394-070-1

Printed in The United States of America

TABLE OF CONTENTS

Introduction

No one ever wrote American history with more easy grace, beauty and emotional power, or greater understanding of its meaning, than Bruce Catton. The purpose of this memorial volume is, very simply, to demonstrate that fact. Its selections, some long and some fragmentary, are drawn from an immense body of work, comprising eighteen books, all but one produced after the author was fifty years old, and countless essays, articles and speeches. Some of the passages are familiar, but many are not, and several have not previously been published. Most but not all deal with the central American tragedy of the nineteenth century, the Civil War; and it is perhaps not too much to say that Catton was its Homer. In his hands the conflict becomes a truthful epic, told with the kind of philosophical insight and sweeping narrative power required of that artistic form. And if Catton wrote in prose, he could on many occasions verge on something else. Consider, for example, this glimpse of Grant's army just before the slaughter in the Battle of the Wilderness:

"It was the fourth of May, and beyond the dark river there was a forest with the shadow of death under its low branches, and the dogwood blossoms were floating in the air like lost flecks of sunlight, as if life was as important as death; and for the Army of the Potomac this was the last bright morning, with youth and strength and hope ranked under starred flags, bugle calls riding down the wind, and invisible doors swinging open on the other shore. The regiments fell into line, and the great white-topped wagons creaked along the roads, and spring sunlight glinted off the polished muskets and the brass of the guns, and the young men came down to the valley while the bands played. A German regiment was singing 'John Brown's Body.' "

I shivered when I first read that passage twenty-five years ago, in a review of *A Stillness at Appomattox*, my first encounter with Catton's work. But although time, that ever-rolling stream, has long since borne away all the young men who stood on that battlefield, and their sons as well, and now Bruce Catton himself, I still shiver as I copy out the words. I suppose I do because they are so poetic, and also because what the passage foretells is so terribly sad, but there is more to it than that. There is a near-magic power of imagination in Catton's work; it almost seemed to project him physically onto the battlefields, along the dusty roads and to the campfires of another age. He made these scenes live, and he took spellbound readers with him. Arthur Schlesinger, Jr. has compared this remarkable ability of Catton's to identify himself with his subject to Walt Whitman's, and Catton may have been aware of it himself. He once turned off a serious question about it with a kind of half-joke. How could he know so very much about what it was really like? his friend and research collaborator, E. B. Long, once asked.

"I don't know," replied Catton. "Maybe I was there."

There is a thoroughly rational explanation for this supposedly supernatural reality in his books: He had read about all he could lay hands on in a huge literature—the regimental histories, the biographies and memoirs, the general histories, the government records, the commentaries, the letters and manuscripts. He had been immersing himself in them for years before he first wrote about the Civil War. He pored over contemporary pictures until, he confessed, he would have recognized more faces on the streets of Washington in the 1860's than in the 1960's.

Some years ago when he was away for the summer at his home in Michigan I happened to ask him in a letter how he had developed such enthusiasm for that war, and got a typically self-deprecatory reply: "That question always reminds me of the old gag about 'How did a nice girl like you ever get into a business like this?' "And he went on to say, "I grew up amidst a regular flower-bed of Civil War veterans. In the small town that I infested as a lad I used to hear the old gentlemen tell war stories until I felt as if the whole affair had taken place in the next county just a few years ago. I remember especially on Memorial Day when I was small there'd always be a meeting in the town hall, with the Grand Army of the Republic veterans on the platform, with songs and speeches: then everyone would troop out to the village cemetery, to lay lilacs on the graves of the departed veterans. . . . Incidentally, our cemetery was built on a low ridge looking out over pleasant rolling country, and one or another of the G.A.R. vets told me it was not unlike the famous, much-fought-over cemetery at Gettysburg. That's how direct the line was to the Civil War, in those days. . . ."

The town he infested was Benzonia, Michigan, described by Catton himself in the selections in the first chapter of this book. It is near Lake Michigan, on the state's lower peninsula, and about one hundred miles south of the resort and camp-meeting town of Petoskey, where he was born on October 9, 1899. He left Benzonia in 1916 for Oberlin College, then brief service in the Navy during World War I. He returned for a while to college, but never took his bachelor's degree—not a notable lack, it turned out later, for he eventually collected well over a score of honorary ones.

Such honors were yet to come during Catton's long career as a newspaperman. In the 1920's and '30's he was variously a reporter, editorial writer, interviewer, book reviewer and columnist, working for the Cleveland *News*, the Boston *American*, and the Cleveland *Plain Dealer*. By 1939 he was in Washington, writing a syndicated column.

When the United States entered World War II, Catton went to the War Production Board as a director of information, which gave him a close view of battles between his chief, Donald Nelson, and the Army: the old struggle of the civilian with the military arm of government. Out of these bureaucratic follies and missed opportunities Catton drew his first book, *The War Lords of Washington*, written at times with white heat but received with calm if not silence when it was published in 1948. Wars have to be seasoned before they can be written about. For several years, Catton continued in government, writing speeches and acting as director of information in the Department of Commerce. But the Civil War still lurked in his mind.

His first attempt, Catton said long afterward, was to try a novel about the war. But, disliking the result, he tore up the manuscript and decided to go at things straight. And his first subject was that great, vanished, blue-clad host—by turns overconfident, defeated, valiant and triumphant—the Army of the Potomac. *Mr. Lincoln's Army*, the first volume of what became a trilogy, had trouble finding a publisher. Turned down at several noted houses, it was published by Doubleday in 1951, with the second volume, *Glory Road*, following a year later. The reception was modest until, with the publication of *A Stillness at Appomattox* in 1953, all the trumpets sounded.

It was at the height of his new fame that, less than a year later, in mid-1954, Bruce Catton, urged on by such eminent friends as the late Allan Nevins, consented to join the small group who were organizing the new hardcover magazine of history, *American Heritage*. The magazine had existed before, to be sure, for five modest years as the quarterly of the American Association for State and Local History; but this was a new, bigger, and riskier enterprise. Before meeting him I wondered whether our proposed first editor would be a little flamboyant—in the newspaper tradition of *The Front Page*—or perhaps a big-time bureaucrat; but what appeared was a tall, quietly dressed, and unassuming man with the courtly good manners of the old Midwest. He put on no airs, and made no demands. As his editor Samuel Vaughan of Doubleday once wrote of him, "Many popular or distinguished writers receive (in the post-office phrase) special handling, but Mr. Catton, who is both distinguished and popular, earns much special handling and never demands any."

It would be idle to deny the fact that Catton had been invited, certainly in part, to lend tone to the new enterprise, but he turned out to be a thoroughly professional editor as well. His knowledge of history, it was soon clear, was immense and by no means confined to the Civil War. He had perception, taste, and an unerring ear for good writing by others. He seemed to have at command a fact or an anecdote to back up (or, if necessary, refute) any point, in conversation or on paper, and he indulged other interests as varied as the Mayans and baseball. There was nothing pedagogical or academic about him.

A magazine like *American Heritage*, heavily illustrated but carrying no advertising, is necessarily designed throughout. That part of the job Catton largely left to others, reserving his enthusiasm for the business of all editors, getting articles and performing the necessary rites (and rewrites) that precede publication. Years as a newspaperman had taught him the art of speedy revision, as well as the other art of knowing when to leave things alone. He was the best cutter I have ever encountered. Seven thousand words, say, would come down to five; yet many an author, going over his prose in print afterward, could not understand why, somehow, it was even better than he had thought.

Reading through manuscripts circulating among the editors for opinions, he could be blunt in the little comments he would attach to the memo sheets. Blunt to the point of annihilation, as a few quick samples from the files will indicate: "This can't be repaired and wouldn't be much good if it were." Of a piece on Coolidge: "Almost as insubstantial and uninspiring as Coolidge himself, about whom it is easy to read too much." Or: "The high-water mark of this piece comes at the bottom of page one, where the naked Indian nymph offers the hero strawberries. Unfortunately this level is not maintained."

Actual dealings with authors, whether through the mails or in person, are another matter. To be rejected by Catton was like landing in a pile of pillows.

The Catton kindness was so great that it could come back to haunt him later. Very occasionally a magazine will buy a badly written article because the subject or the information it contains is new or compelling, and someone will rewrite it. Once I saddled us with an execrable manuscript on an amusing Civil War topic by a writer I will call Mr. Brown. Would Catton repair it? He liked the subject too, but regarded me with a sigh after reading it. A few hours later he emerged from his office with a pile of yellow foolscap, his favorite writing paper, on which nothing of the original had survived but the author's by-line. So it appeared in print. Some months later Catton received a call from a publisher who was considering employing Brown to write a company history. "Brown gave you as a reference, Mr. Catton," said the caller. "He showed me an article he wrote for you. What do you think of him?"

"Oh, Brown," replied Catton, seized by panic and searching to combine truth with kindness. "It was a good subject. Yes, indeed, a great subject." A year or two later the bird came home to roost in the form of a perplexed and outraged call from the publisher. Brown's book was a disaster. Catton came quivering into my office, saying, "I finally told him I touched up that fellow's work a little. Why do I get into scrapes like this?"

He was not only kind but approachable, which is not always the hallmark of editors. His door was open and he was interruptible by any head poked in. Would he look over this map, or tell us whether this photograph really showed Fitz-John Porter, or this other General Burnside? Did he have a minute to meet so-and-so? He could, and he did, but you were only halfway out the door before his fingers were flying again at the old-fashioned, non-noiseless typewriter.

His book writing continued at the same time, along with the lectures, the articles and reviews, the roundtables, the prefaces for other authors, the prize givings and receivings (among them his receipt of the Medal of Freedom from President Ford), and all the other rewards and penalties of literary success. He doggedly endured them. In these years he published eleven more books on the Civil War, including *This Hallowed Ground*, two volumes on Grant in the war (to complete a series commenced by the late Lloyd Lewis), the three-volume *Centennial History of the Civil War*, and the narrative of *The American Heritage Picture History of the Civil War* (which won a special Pulitzer citation). Several books of his collected pieces and talks appeared, and a one-volume biography of Grant called *U.S. Grant and the American Military Tradition*. Then there was the memoir of his early life, *Waiting for the Morning Train*; a history of Michigan; a juvenile called *Banners at Shenandoah*; and, *The Bold and Magnificent Dream: America's Founding Years, 1492-1815*, a collaboration between Bruce and his son, William B. Catton, Professor of History at Middlebury College in Vermont. Somehow in this vast body of work he never flagged, although he did step back somewhat from the job of editor in 1959, to become senior editor—taking what he called "vacations" in Michigan. But he usually came back from them with another book manuscript under his arm. And he continued to write for the magazine.

Concentration was no doubt the secret, that and getting an early start. For many years Catton was always the first person in the office, so early that most of the staff never knew when he did arrive. On his desk the little piles of yellow sheets grew slowly, with much larger piles in the wastebasket. A neat and orderly man, he preferred to type a new page than correct very much in pencil. By the time the rest of the staff had ordered coffee and hung up their coats, he was ready for the day's business. At home Catton and his wife, Hazel, who died in 1969, lived an intensely private life, at least in the big cities where fortune took them. He saw his friends at lunch, and he loved good restaurants with a former country boy's zest. "Thank God for the Army of the Potomac," he would tell his Doubleday editor as his royalty statements were delivered over the delicacies in the comfortable precincts of the Oak Room of the Plaza Hotel in New York. A man who has beaten the birds out of bed and done his stint is hungry and thirsty and enjoys his midday break among friends. He joined several clubs, some convivial and some august, although his favorite watering place was no doubt his corner table at the old-fashioned Algonquin Hotel, then a few steps from his office.

Of all the folkways of business and city life, I believe meetings pleased him the least. He never called one in my memory, although he would loyally attend those of others, sitting through them quietly with every sign of alert attention, sometimes making what I first thought were notes on a small white pad. It was quite a while before I discovered that these supposed notes, which he regularly dropped in the wastebasket on leaving, were mainly doodles, or cartoons. I discovered this after he once passed me a note, like a boy in a schoolroom, seeking to be released at twelve o'clock. On the other side I found a cartoon of a train of the Civil War era with a tiny shack coupled on the end. You looked twice to see that it was an outhouse, with a little half-moon cut over the door. I began collecting Catton, the comic artist, out of wastebaskets. There was broad humor in him, too. It occurs to me now that Catton possessed much the same mix of melancholy and rough wit that characterized Mr. Lincoln.

On August 8, 1978, the night train, his metaphor for death, stopped for Catton at Frankfort, Michigan, and carried him off into the national inheritance. His services to history were prodigious and will live, I hope, for generations. As he once said, to a graduating class at the Loomis School.

"It is the noble dreams of men which live the longest . . . Shakespeare was a cynic when he remarked that the evil men do lives after them. The evil is of short life. It is the good that survives. It survives in brick and stone, in human institutions that go on working long after the men who founded them have been gathered to their fathers. It survives in the hearts of men who . . . re-examine their debt to the past."

My aim in this collection has been to select what I think are examples of Bruce Catton's best work without necessarily including chapters, articles or speeches in their entirety. Explanatory notes and comment are provided only where they seem necessary or helpful. The photographs are for remembrance. The majority of the material naturally deals with the Civil War, but the first chapter and the last are autobiographical, and Chapters XI and XII offer glimpses of Catton as a biographer, an essayist, a journalist, and a storyteller. It is impressive to realize that he wrote *something*, if only one of his compelling book reviews, in nearly every issue of *American Heritage* for twenty-four years, and contributed constantly to other periodicals.

I am deeply obliged to Doubleday & Company, publishers of the bulk of Mr. Catton's books, and to American Heritage Publishing Company, for making this book possible, and also grateful to Little, Brown & Company, W. W. Norton & Company, and Harcourt Brace Jovanovich for permission to reprint copyright material. The University of Wyoming Archives of Contemporary History kindly allowed me to use part of a speech Mr. Catton gave in Galesburg, Illinois in 1958.

I would also like to thank Geoffrey Ward, Tim Hill, Murray Belsky, Kate Slate, Donna Whiteman, Beverley Hilowitz, and Richard Snow of American Heritage Publishing Company; Professor William B. Catton; Professor E. B. Long; and Mr. Catton's principal publisher, Samuel S. Vaughan of Doubleday & Company.

Oliver Jensen

I

The Morning Train

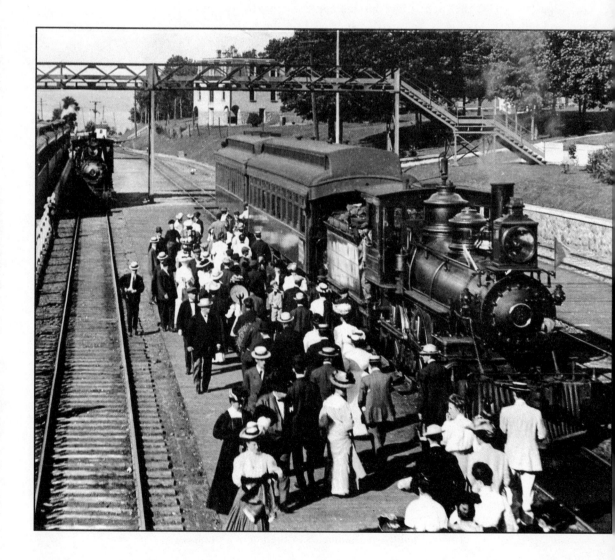

Morning train, Petoskey, Michigan, about 1908

Bruce Catton loved railroads, their puffings and clankings, their mournful whistles, their far wanderings; whenever possible he did his traveling on them. In the memoir of his own boyhood, Waiting for the Morning Train, *they serve as a metaphor of life, from the cars that carry a man off into the world at the end of childhood to the night sleeper that bears him away at the finish. All the selections in this chapter are taken from that enchanting book, which was first published in 1972.*

Although Catton was born in Petoskey, Michigan, a shore resort where his grandparents lived, on the northern, Lake Michigan side of that state's lower peninsula, his boyhood was spent in the little town of Benzonia, about one hundred miles southwest. The hopeful institution mentioned here—Grand Traverse College, later Benzonia College—had declined by 1900 into a preparatory school, Benzonia Academy; but it was no less aspiring and earnest. Its hard-working, underpaid principal was George R. Catton, the father, eventually, of three sons and two daughters. Bruce, the middle son, born October 9, 1899, was the only boy who did not become a minister.

According to the Bible, a city that is set upon a hill cannot be hid. We used to repeat that text often, and I suppose we were a bit smug and self-righteous about it; our city was built upon a hill, and if it was visible to all men it had been meant from the first to be sign and a symbol of a better way of life, an outpost of the New Jerusalem sited in backwoods vacancy to show people the way they ought to go. To be sure, it was not exactly a city. It was in fact the tiniest of country villages, containing probably no more than three hundred and fifty inhabitants, and it has grown no larger to this day. And the hill on which it was built was not really much of a hill. It was a small flat plateau rising less than two hundred feet above the surrounding country, with a placid lake to the north, a narrow valley containing an insignificant creek to the east, and gentle slopes coming up from a broad river valley to the west and south. It was not impressive to look at, although it commanded some pleasant views and it was high enough to get a cooling breeze on all but the hottest summer days.

The name of this town was Benzonia, and when we tried to tell strangers about it we usually had trouble because most people refused to believe that there was any such word. Like the town itself, the name had been self-consciously contrived. The story we were always told—and as far as I know it was perfectly true—had it that this name was a Greek-Latin hybrid put together by learned men who wanted a word that would mean "good air." . . .

The town had been founded as an act of faith. In a two-hundred-mile radius it was probably the only town that had not been established by men who wanted to cash in on the lumber boom. All around the state the little settlements were springing up, and the reason for their existence was always the same—cut the pine trees down, float the logs down the rivers, put a sawmill at the river mouth to turn the logs into boards, load the boards on schooners or sway-backed steamboats, ship them off to Chicago or to Buffalo, and keep it up as long as the timber lasted. Once the trees are gone, dismantle the mills and move on, and if some of the people cannot get away they may stay on and try hardscrabble farming among the stumps. Life in lumber towns had an active present but no future to speak of. The lumber town was much like the mining camp. It was not going anywhere.

But our town was different. It was put there by men who believed that there was going to be a future, and who built for it. When they looked about them they saw people instead of trees; what was going on, as far as they were concerned, was not so much the reduction of pine logs to sawn timber as the foundation of a human society. They believed in the competence and benevolent intent of Divine Providence, and with certain reservations they had faith in the men through whom the purpose of Providence was to be worked out. We were all put on earth to serve that purpose; therefore it was all-important to show everyone what that purpose was and how it could best be served. People had to be educated. They needed a light for their feet, and the light could come only from a Christian education. Benzonia was founded by people who thought that the fringe of a boundless forest was just the place to start a college. A college town it was, from the beginning, laid out and built at a time when the entire county in which it was situated contained no more than five hundred inhabitants.

This happened in 1858, and the nation was unconsciously nerving itself for the first of the prodigious shocks the next hundred years were to bring, the American Civil War. The founding fathers were men from Oberlin College. They brought with them Oberlin's characteristic discontent with the things that are and its impassioned belief in the things that some day will be. They also had another trait instilled at Oberlin—a conviction that faith without works is of small account. Their faith was in the revealed religion as expounded by the Congregational Church, although they suspected that the revelation might be modified here and there by godly men who took prayerful thought, and by this faith they wholeheartedly lived. . . .

These men were intensely logical. They believed in the perfectibility of human society, and a man who held that belief must of course do what he could to bring perfection about. It was not enough to exhort people to lead a better life; you had to lead a better life yourself, and do it in such a way that all men would see it. If society was to lift itself by its bootstraps, your place to begin was with your own bootstraps. Life in a community dedicated to this belief is apt to be rather special, and it was so in our town. Growing up in Benzonia was just a bit like growing up with the Twelve Apostles for next-door neighbors. You never could forget what you were here for. . . .

We were, I suppose, annoyingly conscious that we were the sons of light, and now and then we were disturbed because the children of darkness seemed to be in the majority. I remember once when there was some sort of county election: local option, I suppose, in which the voters were asked to say whether the sale of alcoholic liquors should be prohibited. Benzonia supported the measure, but most of the rest of the county opposed it, and in the election Benzonia was roundly beaten. A few days afterward a citizen met my father on the street and asked him how he felt about the way the election had gone.

"I feel like Lazarus," said Father.

Like Lazarus?

"Like Lazarus," Father repeated. "According to the Bible, Lazarus was licked by dogs."

So much for the opposition.

So there was an especial flavor to life in our town, and it remained at full strength for generations. Probably this was inevitable, inasmuch as we felt that the eye of God was constantly upon us. The knowledge that the God of the Old Testament was watching every act and recording every word was sobering, and it could lead an impressionable child (or an impressionable adult, for that matter) to strange thoughts. . . .

The Bible is fairly strong medicine for a small child, and it can touch off diverse chains of thought and emotion. It occurs to me that I ought to mention an event that took place in the same year that I got religion. Some six months before that glad occasion I crucified a doll.

The Easter season had recently passed, and of course we had been reading and hearing about the crucifixion. One day I was looking through the bookshelves in my father's study, and I came on somebody's commentary on the New Testament. Why I should take that book out and look through it I cannot say, but I did, and in the book I found a chapter on crucifixion—not *the* crucifixion, just crucifixion as practiced by the Romans in the old days. It was an oddly bloodless chapter, saying nothing about the sufferings of the condemned but going into a good deal of detail about the process by which they were executed, and it struck me as most interesting. I went out of doors, after a while, and in the barn I found a very old rag doll, long since abandoned. This seemed to be grist for my mill. I dug up a couple of laths, a hammer, and some shingle nails, made a cross, crucified this lopsided doll, and planted the burdened cross on a sandhill back of the barn. Then I went on about my business—back to fill the woodbox, as likely as not—in a that's-that frame of mind. The next time I went back of the barn, cross and doll had vanished. I never heard a word from my parents about it, although they must have known that I was responsible. I sometimes wonder what they said to each other about it.

Waiting for the Morning Train

IN THE MORNING AT THE JUNCTION

Early youth is a baffling time. The present moment is nice but it does not last. Living in it is like waiting in a junction town for the morning limited; the junction may be interesting but some day you will have to leave it and you do not know where the limited will take you. Sooner or later you must move down an unknown road that leads beyond the range of the imagination, and the only certainty is that the trip has to be made. In this respect early youth is exactly like old age; it is a time of waiting before a big trip to an unknown destination. The chief difference is that youth waits for the morning limited and age waits for the night train.

Benzonia was a good place to wait for the morning train. Life was unhurried and unworried. The daily routine was wholly uneventful, and yet there was always a lot to do. We probably had all of the ordinary problems of childhood but we were never bored. There was a boy of my own age who lived in Chicago, and his parents brought him to our town every summer, and he used to protest bitterly when it was time for him to go back home. In Benzonia, he said, there was always something going on, but "in Chicago nothing ever *happens*." His parents chuckled at this, but we children knew exactly how he felt.

So the slow years passed, and we had nothing to do but taste the special flavor of each day. In the spring the south wind carried the scent of apple blossoms and lilacs, and the summer was warm, timeless and peaceful, with clear water for swimming, and fish to be caught. Autumn was somewhat sad, because it was a reminder that even a friendly changeless world had to show a different face now and then; yet the flaming maple leaves glowed through the October haze with an implicit promise that in the end everything would be all right, and even though the winter was long and cold it offered coasting and skiing and skating, and its white fields glittered under the sunlight and caught the glint of the big stars at night. There was nothing to do but grow up, and we could take our time about it. Let that morning train come whenever it chose. We could board it at the proper time with confidence.

Part of this attitude came no doubt because we lived in a hopeful middle-class society that was adrift in a quiet backwater, seemingly removed from the current of change that swept down the mainstream. Knowing very little about the outside world, we accepted it without questioning it; we understood that much was wrong with it, but it was easy to suppose that the wrong was being worked out. I used to hear grown-ups repeat that timeworn, stupendously false sentence of reassurance: Whatever is, is right. I have not heard anyone say that for more than half a century, and it is certain that no one will ever say it again, so that it is hard now to believe that any sensible adult ever felt that way; yet it passed for distilled wisdom at that time. When I was about twelve years old I had a private suspicion that the world might actually come to an end in my lifetime. Why not? The big wrongs were all being righted, the world was steadily getting better, and it probably would not be long before all of the necessary reforms had been made; then the universe, the fullness of God's time having arrived, would be rolled up like a scroll, and as the revival hymn said, time would be no more. It figured.

It may of course be true that only a backward child would have had such a daydream. Yet it was characteristic of my time and place. Our town was a tiny fragment of the American whole, sliced off for the microscope, showing in an enlarged form the inner characteristics of the larger society, and my boyhood in turn was a slice of the town, with its quaint fundamentals greatly magnified. On the eve of the terrible century of mass slaughter and wholesale collapse, of concentration camps and bombing raids, of cities gone to ruin and race relations grown desperate and poisonous, of the general collapse of all accepted values and the unendurable tension of the age of nuclear fission—on the very eve of all of this, it was possible, even inevitable, for many people to be optimistic. The world was about to take off its mask, and our worst nightmares did not warn us what we were going to see.

Waiting for the Morning Train

THE HUNTER AND HIS PREY

In 1909 our family moved into Mills Cottage . . . it was the girls' dormitory and the central dining hall, and it provided living quarters for the principal of the academy, who was my father. When I went out of the back door of this building I was less than one hundred yards away from what I could easily imagine to be the deep woods—second-growth timber, half a century old or more, its beeches and maples tall and robust enough to give any small boy the feeling that he had gone far into the untracked wilderness. The equipment needed for a venture of this kind was of the simplest. Take an old broomstick, and to one end nail a slim triangle of wood, suitably whittled; you then have a Kentucky rifle, as good as anything Daniel Boone had, and if you can get a fragment of an abandoned cigar box and cut out something vaguely resembling a trigger and hammer, and fasten it loosely to the breech of this weapon with a brad, so much the better. All you have to do is crook your finger and say, "Bang!" loudly, and you have killed a moose, or a grizzly bear, or a redskin.

If you preferred to be an Indian the same shooting iron would serve. There were enough dead sticks lying around in the woodlot to build a wigwam, and if the wigwam was not weatherproof, and was so small that you had to huddle in a cramping squat when you got inside of it, that did not matter; when it rained you went back in the house anyway, and besides the wigwam was just part of the stage setting. As an Indian, of course, you were never shot by Daniel Boone; instead, you shot him, and with a wooden knife whittled out of any stray piece of a packing box you could dash in and lift his scalp. . . .

Now and then we fought the Civil War. The woods were not so good for this, unless we elected to do the Battle of the Wilderness, but in the center of town there was a twelve-acre park, officially the academy's West Campus, and it was open enough for any battle. It was not possible to do the Civil War properly with just two actors; at least half a dozen were needed, and it was not always possible to find half a dozen boys who all felt like playing the Civil War game at the same time. We got along without officers, because nobody was willing to take orders, and the enemy of course was always imaginary. We were invariably the Union army, and we never lost. Johnny Reb died by the platoon and the battalion before our unerring musketry. . . .

Somewhere along the line my older brother, Robert, acquired an air rifle. It was not exactly a rifle, really—it fired BB shot, one at a time, it was grossly inaccurate at any distance greater than about twenty feet, and at that distance it did not hit hard enough to be dangerous to anything much bigger than a butterfly—but it was a real gun firing real pellets, and one day Robert and I went hunting. . . . We were not playing Daniel Boone now; we were actually hunting, questing for game, and we crept through the woods looking for a victim. At last we saw one; a perky little chipmunk, capering about on an old stump, sitting up now and then to pose, chipmunk-fashion, with his tail flicking.

We approached with proper stealth, and at a distance of perhaps eight feet my brother steadied his gun against the side of a sapling, took careful aim, and pulled the trigger. Somewhat to our surprise the chipmunk fell over, lifeless, drilled through the head. We went up to the stump and examined our prey.

At that moment the fun went out of it all. The chipmunk had been so lively and engaging, and now he was dead, looking pathetic, and we did not know what to do with him. It was unthinkable to take him home, haggle the skin off, clean the carcass and ask our mother to cook it for us; her sympathies, we knew, would be all with the chipmunk, and anyway who wanted to *eat* him? We wound up at last by burying him in the earth at the base of the stump, and we went off home soberly. We had had our big moment as hunters only to learn that success was worse than failure. As an adult I once slew a rabbit with a shotgun, and I have hunted, steadfast but unsuccessful, for pheasant, but from that day to this chipmunks have been safe in my presence.

Waiting for the Morning Train

IN THE STEAM CARS

This is how it was in the old days. A family that wanted to go from here to there went by railroad train because there was no other way to do it. If the distance was short, ten or a dozen miles only, you might hire a rig at the livery stable and let the horses do the work, and if you lived on deep water you might go all or part of the way by steamboat, but as a general thing to make a trip meant to take a ride on the cars. The process was slow by later standards, the journey was apt to be bumpy and dusty, and there were inflexible schedules to keep, but it was exciting, especially for children past the time of actual babyhood. It differed from modern travel in that the mere act of departure was a great event. . . .

We always began by going to the railroad station at Beulah. Mr. Benner had a wagon that left the Benzonia post office in time to meet all the trains, under contract to receive and deliver the mail; he carried our baggage, and his wagon had crosswise seats for passengers, who could ride for a modest fee, so he usually carried us as well. The trip to Beulah was unexciting—no driver in his senses drove down that hill at anything but a plodding walk—but once we reached the depot the atmosphere changed and we began to understand that we were really going somewhere. Actually, we already understood it. Mother felt that her children ought to be presentable if they were going on the cars, so the night before we all had to take baths, even though it was not Saturday night—a gross violation of custom that led us to make vain protests—and when we got dressed on the morning of departure we had to put on our Sunday suits, so that the special quality of the event had already been impressed on us. But when we reached the station platform the reality of the whole business came home to us.

For all that Beulah and Benzonia together made no more than a decidedly small town, this seemed like a busy place at train time. Somebody would be wheeling a platform truck down to the spot where the head-end cars were to stop: empty ice-cream freezers going back to the distributor at Cadillac, ice-packed containers from the Beulah creamery bound for assorted destinations downstate, a traveling salesman's sample cases, somebody's trunk, a few suitcases, a mysterious cardboard-bound parcel or two, and so on. People who were going to get on the train stood about looking expectant, while behind the platform teams waited for passengers or packages coming down from Frankfort. The station agent was out, keeping an eye on the platform truck while he assured some anxious woman that this train would infallibly reach Copemish in time for her to catch the Manistee and Northeastern going southwest. Miss Marshall, who collected personal items for the weekly newspaper, would be moving about with pad and pencil, asking people where they were going and when they would be back, and there was always the usual assortment of men and small boys who had nothing in particular to do and had just sauntered over to watch the train go through.

Then at last, just as the tension was almost more than we could take, we could hear the train as it rounded Outlet Point and came along the lake shore, the clear notes of its whistle sounding across the water, and finally it would drift around the last curve and swing up to the platform, smoking and hissing and clanking, with the locomotive putting on its characteristic act of looking and sounding like something alive. A few passengers would get off, and the conductor would call a long-drawn "All abo-o-o-a-r-d!" and we would scramble up the steps and into one of the cars, racing down the aisle for a pair of facing seats. By the time Mother arrived to settle the inevitable argument as to which of three boys would occupy the two places next to the windows the train would be moving again. Wisps of smoke and steam would whip past the windows as we took the first curve and left Beulah behind; then came the familiar East Hill crossing, and Will Case's sawmill with men putting lumber into a boxcar, and we were really on our way. In some ways the mere act of leaving was the high-water mark of the whole trip.

The next big moment came fourteen miles down the track when we reached Thompsonville, where we changed cars. No matter where we were going, we almost always began by changing cars at Thompsonville, where our Ann Arbor railroad crossed the north-south line of the Pere Marquette. The Ann Arbor went all the way to Toledo, two hundred and eighty miles away, but somehow our affairs never seemed to take us in that direction; we usually were going to visit Grandfather in Petoskey, a hundred miles to the north, although once in a while we went south, around the foot of Lake Michigan to Chicago, and in either case we got off at Thompsonville, lugged our suitcases across the tracks to the Pere Marquette station, and went through the whole platform routine all over again. If there was time we strolled down the main street to see the sights. These were not numerous or startling—after all, Thompsonville was a mere village—but in those days it was a busy place, with two hotels, two railroads, a saloon or two and several sawmills, and it struck me as decidedly metropolitan. Compared with Benzonia, almost every town was metropolitan; and anyway this was the gateway to the outer world, bound to the great cities by steel rails, definitely though remotely in touch with the main currents of life from which our city on the hill was so completely insulated. One thing puzzled me: one of the mills at Thompsonville announced itself as a clothes pin factory, and that seemed odd; how could there possibly be a demand for the unutterable quantities of clothes pins that could be produced by an entire factory working ten hours a day, six days a week? It just did not seem reasonable.

Sooner or later the northbound train arrived, and again we sat by the windows to enjoy the delights of travel. It must be confessed that after a while these began to wear a bit thin. We had to stay in our seats—Mother refused to let us roam up and down the aisle, annoying our elders—and presently we began to get somewhat bored. We never admitted this, because we knew that traveling by the cars was exciting, but it was there just the same and we resented it. What we could see out of the windows took on a monotonous sameness: acres and acres of stumps, low hills covered with uneven second-growth, usually aspens packed so tightly together that you could not imagine playing Indian among them, and weedy farms with tired-looking houses that had lost all their paint and most of their prospects. It was nice to go through a town, because we could see people hanging about and we could reflect in a superior way that we were traveling while they were mere stay-at-homes, but most of these places were dying lumber towns and they were depressing to look at. It was always a relief when we finally reached Petoskey and took the carriage up the hill to Grandfather's house. The trip was a great experience, but it was nice when it ended.

It was even better when we took the night train, because to ride in a sleeping car was to touch the summit of human experience. This did not happen often, but every other summer or thereabouts Mother took us children to Minneapolis for a visit with her sister and the sister's husband, Aunt Vade and Uncle Ed. Aunt Vade's given names, by the way, were Sierra Nevada; Grandfather had quite a few daughters, and he gave the rest of them workaday names like Emma and Kate and Ida and Belle and Adella, but when this girl came along he spread himself. As an aunt, she was as dignified and in many ways as impressive as the mountain chain she was named for, although she was not at all icy; on the contrary, she was warm and affectionate, and although I was a little bit scared of her I was a little bit scared of all adults, including my own parents—they lived in a different world and seemed to be accountable to strange gods, and it was necessary for a small boy to watch his foot in their presence. I realize now, although I did not know it at the time, that my aunt probably sent Mother the money to pay for these trips to Minneapolis, because the academy paid starvation salaries and Father could not possibly have financed them.

In any case when we went to Minneapolis we usually went by way of Chicago, which meant that we got to Thompsonville late in the afternoon and waited there for the night train, and sometimes we had supper in a Thompson-ville hotel, which to my mind was another bonus. . . .After supper we went over to the Pere Marquette station, to wait in the darkness, looking up a track spangled with green switch lights, watching for the far-off glow of the engine's headlight, listening anxiously for the first haunting note of the whistle, which came in like an echo of all the horns of elfland.

This train arrived, I suppose, somewhere around ten o'clock, mysterious and magnificent, long shaft of light shining down the track ahead, red glow from the cab if the fireman opened the firebox to shovel in coal, baggage man lounging in the open door of a baggage car, smoker and day coaches brightly lit with passengers drowsing in their seats . . . and then the Pullmans, vestibule doors open, thin strips of light coming out from below the green curtains here and there, porters swinging down to the platform when the train stopped, planting footstools in front of the steps and chanting quietly: "Pullman car for Chicago . . . Pullman car for Detroit . . ." It was almost too much to bear.

Getting undressed in the berth of an old-style twelve-section sleeping car meant that you almost had to be a contortionist. Getting your pants off, for instance, required you to lie on your back, arch yourself until you were supported by your heels and your shoulders, and start fumbling. I always shared a berth with one of my brothers, and how the two of us managed it I do not quite know, but we always made it, wadding our discarded clothing in the hammock netting over the car window, getting into our pajamas somehow, and then sliding down beneath the covers and turning off the light. Nothing on earth today is quite as snug and secure as a Pullman berth used to be once you were fairly in it, and it seemed to me at the time that to lie there feeling the swaying and jiggling of the car's motion, listening to the faraway sound of the whistle, getting up on elbow now and then to peer out the window when we reached a station, and at last drifting off to sleep, was to know unadulterated happiness. It was best of all if one happened to wake up when the train reached Grand Rapids, which it did along in the small hours. Here there was a cavernous train shed, with cars on other tracks, a switch engine puttering about, people coming and going—none of your small-town depots, where the station agent doused the lights, locked the door and went home after the last train went through: this place was in action all night long. From the car window you could see the station dining room, with its gleaming silver coffee urns, doughnuts stacked under glass domes on the counter, belated travelers here and there having a final snack before going off about their business, and it looked so inviting I used to want to be there myself—except that it was so cozy in the berth, and it would be even cozier when the train began to move again, and it was sheer heresy to wish to be anywhere else.

Waiting for the Morning Train

"GIVE IT TO HIM!"

My sixth birthday was a special occasion. We were staying with Grandfather in Petoskey just then, and for a birthday celebration my parents took me to the theater for the first time in my life. There was no theater to go to anywhere near Benzonia, and in any case most people in our town considered the theater more or less sinful, and spoke against it in prayer meeting. My parents were less strait-laced than that, and anyway the show I was taken to was highly moral—*Uncle Tom's Cabin*, no less, complete with tossing ice floes, bloodhounds, and the transfiguration of Little Eva; all very edifying and painfully exciting as well. I enjoyed every minute of it, rising in my seat once to scream, "Give it to him!" when the forces of right closed in on (I think) the villainous lawyer, Marks. I was just a bit disillusioned when I heard my elders say, on the way home, that Little Eva was not really a small child but a grown woman; they had seen her in the lobby after the performance, selling photographs of herself.

Waiting for the Morning Train

A MONKEY'S HAND

I entered [Benzonia Academy] as a freshman in the fall of 1912. I had finished the seventh grade in our village school, and for some reason Father concluded that I ought to skip the eighth grade entirely and go into the academy without further delay. Whether he had a poor opinion of the kind of work our grade school was doing, or felt that it would be good for me to get on a slightly higher level and move at a more demanding pace, I do not know, but I made the move and I was delighted to do so. I felt that I was really growing up—my thirteenth birthday lay just ahead—and classroom work suddenly took on a new aspect. It was no longer just one of the unavoidable drudgeries of boyhood; it was a time of preparation, and I felt obliged to consider what I was going to do with my life. It was taken for granted that when I left the academy I would go on to college, but what was I going to do after that? It was stimulating to look so far ahead and to feel that I was about to make a decision that would affect my entire life.

You never know where the road is going to fork. That summer of 1912 Father read to us certain magazine articles by a political expert, Samuel G. Blythe, dealing with the Republican National Convention in Chicago, at which Theodore Roosevelt felt boxed in and moved out to run for the presidency as nominee of his own Bull Moose Party. Father was a consecrated Roosevelt man, and he read Blythe's analyses of the situation with a deep interest that rubbed off on me. Finishing one of these articles, Father remarked that these reporters certainly did get around, see interesting things and have interesting experiences, and apparently the remark took root in my mind. A year or two later I spent several hours a day, during the summer vacation, working for a retired minister who had a chicken farm on the edge of town, and during a pause in the work the old gentleman turned to me and asked: "What are you going to make of yourself when you grow up, Bruce?" As far as I can remember I had not consciously made any choice, but now that the question was asked I replied unhesitatingly: "I am going to be a journalist." I finally did, too—although I must say that that was the only time in my life that I ever applied the word "journalist" to myself. I have never known a newspaperman who used it. Anyway, I had made up my mind. Whether I would ever have gone in that direction if Father had not read those Samuel G. Blythe stories, and made the comment he did make, I have no idea. Maybe the moral is that fathers ought to be careful what they say to growing sons.

If I had made up my mind at such an early age I did not know it for quite a time. Indeed, there was a period—during which I must have been a trial to my elders—in which I imagined that I was going to be a violinist.

It was not as if I had any especial talent. I liked music, I had a sensitive ear, and the sounds that can be drawn from a violin stirred me deeply, so when I was asked if I would like to take violin lessons I said I would like it very much; but of the deep, instinctive, all-consuming response a born musician makes at such a time I had not a trace. I wanted to play the violin, but it was not something that I wanted more than I wanted anything else. The music world lost nothing of any consequence when, in the course of time, I let the dream die and went off in another direction.

Still, some sort of desire was present. Underneath everything else, I suppose, was the notion that a violinist was a romantic figure. I wanted to be a violinist in much the same way that I wanted to be a locomotive engineer, a cavalry officer or a star pitcher for the Detroit Tigers. I needed to see myself performing to the admiration of everyone, including myself, in some very public place. These other roles were clearly beyond my reach, but apparently the violinist goal was attainable—and after all a concert hall was just as fine a stage as a locomotive cab, a battlefield or a big league ball park. So for a number of years I nursed the idea that I was destined to be a musician. I never quite took the dream seriously, but it was a nice thing to play with. It gave me a fine role to enact in the theater of the imagination. I noticed also that some of the loveliest academy girls used to listen, all entranced, with a faraway look, when they heard the right kind of music.

The facilities for developing a virtuoso in Benzonia were limited. There was an estimable lady in town, a Mrs. Flanner, who gave violin and piano lessons, and I was entrusted to her care. She did her best with me, but I had not progressed much beyond the sawing-and-scraping stage when she moved away and my training lapsed. Then, just as my parents were saying that it was a shame I could not go on with my music, Mr. Bucholz came to town.

Mr. Bucholz was far and away the best violinist I had ever heard. The concert stage in the early 1900's did not lead musicians of even the third or fourth rank into our part of the state, and here was a man who, by our standards at least, was straight from the big time. He was not, to be sure, a soloist, as the word would be understood in Chicago or Boston or New York, but he was no backwoods fiddler either. He had played for years in the first violin section of the Minneapolis symphony, and now some freak of fate had brought him to earth in Thompsonville, the railroad junction town a dozen miles east of Benzonia. (I have often wondered how a man like that got to our county in the first place, and how he stood it there—for a professional musician it must have been like the heart of the Sahara—but I never did find out.) He came to Benzonia to give a concert, and for the first time I heard what my chosen instrument could do when the right man was using it; and afterward he let it be known that he would come over from Thompsonville every Saturday to give violin lessons. My parents immediately signed me in as a student.

My first meeting with him was an experience. He had taken over one of the classrooms in Barber Hall—it was a Saturday, so the building was not in use—and when I came in he was striding up and down, violin under his chin, performing what seemed to me the most dazzling pyrotechnics, just as you can see two dozen violinists do backstage in a symphony hall half an hour before concert time. He laid his violin down, shook hands, and invited me to produce my own violin. I did so, wondering how it was to be tuned because there was no piano; and I immediately learned that Mr. Bucholz needed no piano for this job. Once the instrument was in tune he ordered me to tuck it under my chin and play something.

I made no music that first day. It was given over to basic training: how to stand, how to hold the violin, how to get my left arm in position, how to grip the violin with my chin. Nothing that I did was right, and Mr. Bucholz obviously felt that I needed rebuilding from the ground up. He pointed out that you did not hold the violin with your left hand; you held it with your chin and shoulder, leaving the left hand free for more important tasks, and to prove it he put his own violin under his chin, dropped his hands to his sides, and ordered: "Now—take it away from me." I hesitated, because I understood that a violin was fragile, but he insisted and I grabbed the neck of the instrument and tugged. Nothing happened: he had it clamped in place, and I was much impressed. Then he spent a long time showing me how to apply that sort of grip to my own violin, and when I began to catch on he tried to get my left hand into the proper position. It seemed to me that he was going to dislocate my wrist, but he kept at it, explaining why things had to be done his way; and while he was at it he took my hand away from the instrument, studied it carefully, flexed my fingers, and then for the first time looked at me with approval.

"You are very fortunate," he said. "You have a monkey's hand."

The ordinary hand, Mr. Bucholz said, was not really designed for the violin, and before he could make music the violinist had to conquer his own anatomy, forcing his hand and wrist into an unnatural position. The monkey's hand was different—in its shape, in the way it was attached to the wrist, and in other ways which I do not remember—and it could be put into the proper stance without strain. The rare human being who had a hand like a monkey's had a profound advantage when he undertook to play the violin. He could do easily what the ordinary mortal could do only by constant effort.

I was tempted to ask if that meant that monkeys could be better violinists than people can be, but I refrained. Mr. Bucholz was much in earnest, and besides I was somewhat impressed with myself. I had an asset other people did not have. Perhaps I really was meant to be a violinist. My opinion of myself rose, although it did seem too bad that I owed it all to a monkey.

I took music lessons from Mr. Bucholz for perhaps six months. I say "took music lessons" rather than "studied," because that expression is more accurate. Mr. Bucholz grew disillusioned; the Lord had given me as fine a left hand as any violinist could want, and I did not rise to my responsibility. I wanted to be a violinist, but I did not want to do all of the hard work that was necessary. He caught on, and became somewhat bitter. Apparently he had thought, at first, that something could be done with me, but I was just another teen-age fiddler and I suppose he had seen more than enough of them. I will not forget our last meeting.

Mr. Bucholz was leaving, getting out of Benzie County and going somewhere out-of-state to resume his professional career. He told me this, and then ordered me to run through the exercises he had prescribed at our last lesson. Unfortunately I had not been practicing much. This thing and that had come in the way; as Harry the odd-job man would have said, I had had so much to do and everything else. This became self-evident in a short time and Mr. Bucholz shook his head and told me to put my violin away. He looked at me sternly, and when he spoke his German accent was mildly intensified. "You haff a monkey's hand," he said. Then his look became a glare, and he added harshly: "But you also haff a monkey's head!"

Well, that was that, and I went away. I never saw Mr. Bucholz again, but wherever he went and whatever he did I hope nice things happened to him.

Waiting for the Morning Train

LONG DISTANCE

I became active in our church's Christian Endeavor society, which was a sort of teen-agers' prayer meeting, and sometime during the winter I was sent as our society's official delegate to a Christian Endeavor convention, or rally—I do not know what they did call it—at Traverse City. I realized that to be chosen thus was an honor, it was stimulating to spend an entire day and night away

Main Street, Benzonia, around 1910

from home without parental guidance, and it was nice to meet so many other young people; among them, a pleasant young woman from our neighboring village of Thompsonville, who was the night telephone operator there and seemed most personable. I can remember just about nothing at all of what happened at the convention; indeed, the only clear picture I brought back was of the final afternoon when, the sessions having ended and there being two hours to spend before train time, this telephone operator and I slipped away and went to a vaudeville show. I suppose Traverse City at that time was on the bottom rung of the vaudeville circuit, but that made no difference; nothing in our County was on any rung at all, I had never seen vaudeville in my life, and the afternoon was memorable. We caught our train properly enough, the girl got off at Thompsonville, and I continued on to Benzonia, vastly pleased with life. And that was that.

Except for an incident that came two or three nights later. . . . We were just sitting down to supper when the telephone rang. My father went to answer it—the instrument was in the hall, outside the dining room door—and he returned in a moment, cast a speculative eye on me, and said that there was a long distance call for me.

Long distance calls were not common, in that time and place. I had never received one in my life, and never expected to; such calls commonly grew out of some dire emergency, like a death in the family, and that I should be receiving one was the wonder of the year. My parents were very human, and my younger brother and sister were even more so, and as I clumped out to the hall to take up the telephone I was much aware that everybody was going to be hanging in breathless suspense on every word I uttered. (Who on earth can be calling *him*? What in the world is this all about?) It did not occur to me to close the door before I picked up the receiver.

The caller, of course, was my friend in Thompsonville. She was on duty at the village switchboard, nothing whatever was going on, and it seemed to her to be the most natural thing in the world to insert a plug, flip a key and chat with this boy she had just met. So she began to chat. Had I got home all right? How was I feeling? Didn't I think the convention had been most interesting? Had she thanked me properly for taking her to the theater? And wasn't it funny when that man played the violin with a frying pan? (Yes, there had been an act in which that happened, but I can't go into it now.) This went on for some time. I fumbled for answers, well aware that every word I said was being absorbed by the dear ones in the next room; I do not think I have ever been so deeply embarrassed in my life, and my remarks grew more and more laconic. It dawned on the girl, at last, that something was wrong, and finally (may Heaven bless her) she said that it had been nice to know me, and rang off. She had learned ahead of her years, I suppose, that the effervescent, carefree male met at a convention tends to be self-conscious and reserved when tackled in the bosom of his family. I never saw or heard from her again, and I was sorry. . . .

I got back to the dining room eventually. My parents undoubtedly were brim-full of questions which they forbore to ask, but my brother and sister had no forbearance at all and they asked many questions all in a moment. I answered them with what I hoped was chilling dignity, and at last managed to eat the meal of dust and ashes which had been set before me. I acquired that evening a dread of the telephone which has never entirely left me. I also learned that when explanations are in order, consciousness of total innocence in act and in intent does not help at all.

Waiting for the Morning Train

BORN FOR OTHER THINGS

It all happened many years ago, and distance puts a deceptive haze on things remembered. As I look back on my final year in the academy I seem to recall the brief spring of 1916 as a time when life was extremely pleasant and singularly uneventful. The cataract might lie just ahead, but at the moment the river was lazy, without eddies or ripples. Europe was a long way off, and the echoes from its war reached us faintly, unreal and haunting, like the cries Canada geese make when they circle over Crystal Lake in the autumn, lining up the order of flight for their southbound squadrons. It was undeniable, of course, that soon we would leave our little campus and go to whatever was waiting for us in the outside world, but that knowledge simply added a vibrant expectancy to life. Everything imaginable was going to happen tomorrow, but right at the moment nothing was happening; if the time of waiting was almost over its final moments had an uncommon flavor. Although we knew that we ought to think long and hard about what we were going to do, once the spring ripened into Commencement Week and then sent us off into unguided summer, most of the time we were undisturbed. The present moment was like a six-measure rest that had been inserted into the score just as the composition was supposed to be coming to its climax.

Naturally, when I try to recall that time I remember hardly anything specific. I remember the spring sunlight lying on the campus, and the academy buildings taking on dignity and looking as if they were going to be there forever—which, alas, they were not; I remember the band practice, and the orchestra practice, and the long, aimless walks we took on Sundays, tramping off the last vestiges of childhood, seeing things for the last time without realizing that it was the last time, unaware that once you leave youth behind you see everything with different eyes and thereby make the world itself different. We would go across country to the power dam on the Betsie River, or along the shore of Crystal Lake to the outlet; and sometimes we went down the long hill to Beulah and then crossed the low ground to go up Eden Hill, a big shoulder of land that defined the horizon to the east . . . Eden Hill and Beulah Land, named by godly settlers for the Paradise where the human race got into the world and the Paradise it will enter when it goes out; or so people believed, although we lived then in the present and asked for no Paradise beyond what we had then and there.

From the summit of Eden Hill you could look far to the north and west, across the Platte Lakes to the limitless blue plain of Lake Michigan, with Sleeping Bear crouched, watchful, in the distance and the Manitou Islands on the skyline. Beyond the green weeded country to the east, hidden by the rolling easy ridges, was the lumber town of Honor, and if we felt like making a really long walk out of it we could go on over to Honor, walk around the mill and its piled logs—they were still carving up some last allotment of first-growth wood, although most of the county's mills were stilled—and then we could tramp the long miles home by way of Champion's Hill. This was a plateau which had been named half a century earlier by some Civil War veterans who made farms there; they had served in Sherman's corps in the Vicksburg campaign and something about the shape of this land reminded them of a great battlefield in that campaign and so they had put this Mississippi name in the heart of Northern Michigan as a reminder of what they had seen and done. And we youngsters walked across it, all unthinking, on our way home to Sunday night supper.

Spring is a short haul in our part of Michigan, and we were kept fairly busy once the snow was gone making preparation for the exercises that would attend our graduation, which would be a big moment. For all that it was so small, Benzonia Academy crowded Commencement Week as full of events as the State University itself; and the graduating class was so small—just eleven of us, when fully mustered—that everybody had something to do. Which reminds me that by ancient custom, running back fully five years, the graduating class was supposed to present a play as the final event of its academic life. Our class elected to do something called *Peg o' My Heart*, and of course nobody in the class had a vestige of acting ability, but somehow we got through the thing alive.

I remember practically nothing about the performance except that I was the leading man and, as such, was called upon by the script to kiss the leading woman, who was a most attractive classmate, just as the final curtain came down. Miss Ellis, who was directing the performance, made it clear that it would not be necessary or even permissible actually to kiss the girl; I could lay my hands gently upon her shoulders and incline my head slowly, and the curtain then would descend rapidly and action could be broken off with no casualties. I do recall that when the great night came and this portentous moment arrived we discarded Miss Ellis's instructions completely. I walked the girl home afterward so bedazzled by all that had happened that I was unable to muster the nerve to try to kiss her again. I think this puzzled her slightly, although I do not believe that she felt that she had missed anything much. Now that I think of it, she was the only member of the class I ever did kiss, it took what amounted to a convulsion of nature to bring that about, and there was no repeat performance. I suppose I was born for other things.

Waiting for the Morning Train

UNDERNEATH THE LILACS

One of the pleasantest holidays of the year was Memorial Day, universally known then as Decoration Day because it was the day when you went out to the cemetery and decorated graves. This day of course belonged to the Civil War veterans, although as years passed it more and more became a day to put flowers on the grave of any loved one who had died, and when it came just about everyone in town went to the cemetery with a basket of lilacs. Lilacs grow like weeds in our part of the country, and most farmers planted a long row of lilacs as windbreaks around their houses; in town almost every house had lilacs in the yard, and in late May the scent of them lay on the breeze. To this day I never see lilac blossoms without remembering those Decoration Day observances of long ago.

The Civil War veterans were men set apart. On formal occasions they wore blue uniforms with brass buttons and black campaign hats, by the time I knew them most of them had long gray beards, and whatever they may have been as young men they had an unassuming natural dignity in old age. They were pillars, not so much of the church (although most of them were devout communicants) as of the community; the keepers of its patriotic traditions, the living embodiment, so to speak, of what it most deeply believed about the nation's greatness and high destiny.

They gave an especial flavor to the life of the village. Years ago they had marched thousands of miles to legendary battlefields, and although they had lived half a century since then in our quiet backwater all anyone ever thought of was that they had once gone to the ends of the earth and seen beyond the farthest horizon. There was something faintly pathetic about these lonely old men who lived so completely in the past that they had come to see the war of their youth as a kind of lost golden age, but as small boys we never saw the pathos. We looked at these men in blue, existing in pensioned security, honored and respected by all, moving past the mounded graves with their little flags and their heaps of lilacs, and we were in awe of them. Those terrible names out of the history books—Gettysburg, Shiloh, Stone's River, Cold Harbor—came alive through these men. They had *been* there . . . and now they stood by the G.A.R. monument in the cemetery and listened to the orations and the prayers and the patriotic songs, and to watch them was to be deeply moved.

The G.A.R., of course, was the Grand Army of the Republic, the veterans' organization of those days. The Benzonia local of this organization was officially the E. P. Case Post Number 372, and it had been named for Edward Payson Case, a Benzonia man who died in 1886, a year before the post was organized. He must have been quite a man; he had enlisted in 1864, in the artillery, and his unit had been sent to Cumberland Gap on garrison duty and had finished out the war there, never getting into combat. Almost to a man, our G.A.R. members had been in violent action during the war, and they never would have named the local post after a noncombat soldier if he had not been an impressive sort of person. The monument they built, sometime in the late 1880's or early 1890's, was completely homemade. It was a fat column of field stone and mortar, no more than four or five feet tall, capped by a round slab of rock that was just a little wider than the supporting column; it looks like an overgrown toadstool, and it would be funny if it were not so unmistakably the work of men who were determined to have a monument and built one with their own hands because they could not pay for a professional job. The spirit that built it redeems it; it stands today as the most eloquent, heart-warming Civil War memorial I ever saw.

I remember the G.A.R. men as a group, rather than as individuals, although a few do stand out. There was Elihu Linkletter, a retired minister when I knew him, who had lost his left arm in the Wilderness. I never looked at him without thinking (in bemused small-boy fashion) how proud he must be to carry this visible sign of his sacrifice for all to see. Mr. Linkletter was devoted to birds, and he waged unceasing war on red squirrels on the ground that they robbed birds' nests and ate fledglings. He used to tramp about with a .22 rifle, shooting every red squirrel he saw; he could use it one-handed and he was a remarkably good marksman with it. There was John Van Deman, who once told me how he had been wounded in some battle in West Virginia; like all the other veterans he pronounced "wounded" to rhyme with "sounded," which somehow made it more impressive. There was Lyman Judson, who had served in the cavalry under Phil Sheridan and who had been invalided out of the service when, his horse being shot out from under him, he had fallen heavily on the base of his spine so that he suffered thereafter from a weak back. Forty-five years later, in Benzonia, he slipped on the ice and again fell heavily on the base of his spine. In some unaccountable way this cured him, and for the rest of his life his back was as sound and as pain-free as anyone's. And there was Cassius Judson (no relation) who in 1916 went down to Manistee to see *The Birth of a Nation.* When he got back I asked him if he had not been impressed by the picture's portrayal of the Battle of Atlanta. Mr. Judson, who had been in that battle personally, smiled faintly and said: "Well, it wasn't much like the real thing."

Then, finally, there was John Morrow, who had been an infantryman in an Ohio regiment and who had once exchanged words with General William T. Sherman himself. ("Exchanged" probably is not the word, because Sherman did all of the talking.) Anyway, during the Atlanta campaign Morrow and some comrades were out on patrol, and they came to a stream where there was a grassy bank with trees to cast a pleasant shade, and the day was mortally hot, and so they all stacked arms and stretched out for a breather. Just then Sherman and some of his staff rode up, and Sherman came over to find out what these soldiers were doing. When he found out, as Morrow remembered it, he "used language that would make a mule driver blush" and in no time the boys were back on patrol in the hot sun. They did not hold this against General Sherman, figuring that it was just part of the fortunes of war.

By the time I knew them these veterans were in their seventies, or very close to it, and a hale and hearty lot they were. There was one man, whose name I do not remember, who lived on a farm a few miles south of town. He had fought at Gettysburg, and in 1913 there was a big fiftieth anniversary celebration of that battle, with surviving veterans invited to attend. This old chap went to Gettysburg, enjoyed the three days' activities, and then came home by train, and when he finished the trip, at Beulah, he found that the friend who was to have met him with a buggy to drive him out to his farm had somehow failed to make it. Quite undaunted, the seventy-year-old veteran picked up his carpetbag and hiked the five miles home. He could see nothing remarkable in this, because he had had many worse hikes during the war.

In their final years the G.A.R. men quietly faded away. Their story had been told and retold, affectionate tolerance was beginning to take the place of respectful awe, and in Europe there was a new war that by its sheer incomprehensible magnitude seemed to dwarf that earlier war we knew so well. One by one the old men went up to that sun-swept hilltop to sleep beneath the lilacs, and as they departed we began to lose more than we knew we were losing. For these old soldiers, simply by existing, had unfailingly expressed the faith we lived by; not merely a faith learned in church, but something that shaped us as we grew up. We could hardly have put it into words, and it would not have occurred to us to try, but we oriented our lives to it and if disorientation lay ahead of us it would come very hard. It was a faith in the continuity of human experience, in the progress of the nation toward an ideal, in the ability of men to come triumphantly through any challenge. That faith lived, and we lived by it. Now it is under the lilacs.

Waiting for the Morning Train

II

Sowing the Wind

Senator Charles Sumner of Massachusetts

The coming of the Civil War is a kind of dreadful pageant whose tragic finale is known. Inevitability hovers over its every scene; yet every moment is full of drama, even suspense. It has "if only's" by the dozen and, as we read Catton's volumes, characters of immense interest stride the boards. They step forward, vivid, almost palpable, at the very beginnings of his books and we see history through them—as, indeed, did the people who lived in those times. It is the heart of Catton's gift. The following passage begins his one-volume story of the Union side of the war, This Hallowed Ground.

The Senator was tall and handsome, with wavy hair to frame a proud ravaged face, and if hearty feeding had given him the beginning of a notable paunch he was erect enough to carry it well. He had the easy grace of a practiced orator—his speeches, according to spiteful enemies, were carefully rehearsed night after night before a mirror in his chambers, while an awed colored boy stood by with a lighted candle—and there was a great humorless arrogance about him, for he had never been blessed with a moment of self-doubt. He liked to say that he was in morals, not in politics. From this the logical deduction was that people who opposed him, numerous though they undoubtedly were, must be willfully wrong.

Such a deduction Senator Charles Sumner was quite capable of drawing for himself. He would draw it today in the Senate chamber. In his speech, he had told a friend, he would "pronounce the most thorough philippic ever uttered in a legislative chamber."

It was an ominous promise. The date was May 19, 1856, and although there was still a little time left it was running out fast, and angry words might make it run faster. Yet angry words were about the only kind anyone cared to use these days. Men seemed tired of the reasoning process. Instead of trying to convert one's opponents it was simpler just to denounce them, no matter what unmeasured denunciation might lead to.

The point at issue was, at bottom, simple enough: how to legislate so that Kansas might someday become a state. But Kansas was a symbol rather than a territory. Men saw what they feared and hated, concentrated on its wide empty plains, and as they stared they were losing the ability to see virtue in compromise and conciliation. The man on the other side, whatever one's vantage point, was beginning to look ominously alien. He could not easily be dealt with, and perhaps it was best simply to lash out at him. In the charged atmosphere thus created the lightest act could be fateful. All of the things that were slipping beyond hope of easy solution—sectional enmities, economic antagonisms, varying interpretations of the American dream, the tragic unendurable race problem itself—all of these, somehow, might hinge on what was done about Kansas, so that the wrong phrase in an enacting clause could mean earth's best hope lost forever.

In Senator Sumner's view the wrong phrase was on the verge of adoption. The bill which the Senate was about to pass would, as he saw it, mean that Kansas must eventually become a slave state. In addition, it would give a great deal of aid and comfort to slavery's advocates, wherever they were. It was not to be thought of calmly; it was not merely wrong, it was an actual crime. Furthermore, it was no common crime; it was (he solemnly assured the Senate) a fearful thing, "the crime against nature, from which the soul recoils, and which language refuses to describe." Yet if language could not describe it the Senator could, and he would do so.

He was a man of breeding and education, given to much study of the classics; and he stood now in the Senate chamber, looking imperiously about him as one who has glimpsed the tables of the law on the mountaintop, and he dwelt extensively on "the rape of a virgin territory, compelling it to the hateful embrace of slavery." The South, he said, was guilty of a "depraved longing for a new slave state, the hideous offspring of such a crime." Force had been used, he declared, "in compelling Kansas to this pollution."

The desk in front of Senator Sumner was empty. It belonged to Senator Andrew Butler of South Carolina, and when Sumner first became a Senator, white-haired Butler had been pleasant and cordial—so much so that Sumner wrote to a friend that he had learned, from the old gentleman's kindness, "to shun harsh and personal criticism of those from whom I differ." But that had been years ago, when men from Massachusetts and South Carolina could still exchange courtesies in the Senate chamber; and in any case Sumner was always ready to denounce even a close friend, and in the most unmeasured terms, if he suspected that the friend had fallen into error. Butler was a spokesman for slavery, he had had his part in the crime against nature, and the fascinating exercise of discussing political opposition in terms of sexual depravity could be carried on—by this bookish man, still unmarried at forty-five—with Butler as the target. Sumner addressed himself to the absent Butler.

The South Carolina Senator considered himself a chivalrous knight, but Sumner had seen the truth: "He has chosen a mistress to whom he has made his vows, and who, though ugly to others, is always lovely to him; though polluted in the sight of the world, is chaste in his sight—I mean the harlot slavery. For her his tongue is always profuse with words. Let her be impeached in character, or any proposition made to shut her out from the extension of her wantonness, and no extravagance of manner or hardihood of assertion is then too great for this senator."

There was quite a bit more of this, ranging all the way from Senator Butler to the ancient Egyptians, "who worshipped divinities in brutish forms," with due mention of the "obscene idols" to which the Aztecs had made human sacrifices; the connection of these latter with the harlot slavery not being of the clearest. At one stage Sumner interrupted himself to cry: "Mr. President, I mean to keep absolutely within the limits of parliamentary propriety"; and then he went on, his speech still unfinished at the session's end.

The Senator managed to reach his conclusion the following day, reminding the presiding officer (perhaps unnecessarily) that "an immense space has been traversed," and in closing he came back from brutish idols and obscene Aztecs to Senator Butler, from whom he had learned not to let political arguments get personal. There was not, he said, "any possible deviation from the truth" of which Butler was innocent, although fortunately these deviations were made in the heat of such passion "as to save him from the suspicion of intentional aberration." Still, there it was: "The senator touches nothing which he does not disfigure—with error, sometimes of principle, sometimes of fact."

A philippic, as he had promised. No single vote had been changed by it; the Senate would decide, at last, precisely as it would have done if he had kept quiet. But he had not been trying to persuade. No one was, these days; a political leader addressed his own following, not the opposition. Sumner had been trying to inflame, to arouse, to confirm the hatreds and angers that already existed. In the North there were men who from his words would draw a new enmity toward the South; in the South there were men who would see in this speaker and what he had said a final embodiment of the compelling reasons why it was good to think seriously about secession.

At the very end Sumner had a gloomy moment of insight.

The fight over Kansas, he said, spreading from the western plain to the Senate chamber, would spread still farther; would go to a nationwide stage "where every citizen will be not only spectator but actor."

There is a rowdy strain in American life, living close to the surface but running very deep. Like an ape behind a mask, it can display itself suddenly with terrifying effect. It is slack-jawed, with leering eyes and loose wet lips, with heavy feet and ponderous cunning hands; now and then, when something tickles it, it guffaws, and when it is made angry it snarls; and it can be aroused much more easily than it can be quieted. Mike Fink and Yankee Doodle helped to father it, and Judge Lynch is one of its creations; and when it comes lumbering forth it can make the whole country step in time to its own frantic irregular pulse-beat.

Senator Sumner had invited it out with his fine talk. So had the eminent clergyman, the Reverend Henry Ward Beecher, who had told the world that a Sharps rifle was a greater moral agency than a Bible, as far as Kansas was concerned. Yet these men need not have bothered. Rowdyism was coming out anyway, having been invited by men of the South as well as by men of the North, and the spirit of rowdyism was talking in the spirit of Sumner's and Beecher's exhortations without the fancy trimmings. It was saying now, south of the slavery line, that "we will continue to tar and feather, drown, lynch and hang every white-livered abolitionist who dares to pollute our soil," and in Kansas it had legislated that anyone who denied the legality of slave ownership in the territory should get five years in prison.

In Kansas there was a town called Lawrence. It had existed for two years, and although it was so new, it was solid and substantial, with buildings of brick and stone, including a hotel that was massive enough to serve as a fort. (In point of fact, the hotel had been built with that end in mind.) The town was a piece of New England set down in the prairie, but it was a New England all distorted, as if someone were seeing bizarre dream-shapes that were slipping into nightmare. In place of white steeples and colonial doorways it had grim buildings and men who carried "Beecher's Bibles"—Sharps rifles, named with a cynicism matching that of the reverend clergyman himself—and it was expressive of the stern New England purpose that had planted it there. It was named for a Massachusetts millowner who had given money to fight slavery, and it was the stronghold and rallying point of all Kansas settlers who believed that the extension of slavery must be stopped at the Missouri line.

As such, it became a focal point for hatred. The tension had been building up for months. There had been arrests and shootings and all manner of bloodthirsty threats and shouts of defiance, for nothing could be more hateful just then, to a certain attitude of mind, than the simple belief that one man ought not to own another man. A territorial grand jury with pro-slavery leanings had asked that the town's leading citizens be jailed for treason, and it had added a rider to the effect that both of the town's newspapers ought to be suppressed as public nuisances and that its fortress hotel should be torn down.

Now, on May 21—one day after Senator Sumner had finished his excellent speech—there was a posse on hand to see that the grand jury's thoughts were properly embodied in action. This posse numbered perhaps a thousand men. A great many of them came from Missouri, for Lawrence was not far from the state line, and they rejoiced in the collective title of Border Ruffians. They owed dim allegiance to a United States marshal who had certain arrests to make in Lawrence and they were heavily armed. Unlike most posses, they dragged along with them five cannons.

For once the people of Lawrence were on their good behavior. They offered no resistance when the marshal came in, and the arrests he wanted to make were made. The marshal thereupon dismissed his posse, which was immediately called back into service by a Kansas sheriff, a cover-to-cover believer in slavery, who announced himself as a law-and-order man and who said that he had a job of his own to do in Lawrence. The transformed posse was addressed briefly by former Senator David R. Atchison of Missouri, the great spokesman for slavery in the West, who cried: "Be brave, be orderly, and if any man or woman stand in your way, blow them to hell with a chunk of cold lead." The sheriff then led the posse into town and the fun began.

Various rounds from the cannon were fired at the hotel. It had been well built—and the cannon, perhaps, were aimed and served inexpertly—and nothing in particular seemed to happen. The sheriff's helpers then swarmed all over the town, setting fire to the hotel, raiding the two offending newspaper offices and dumping press and type into the river, ransacking homes and getting drunk and in general having a high old time. The home of a man who presumed to call himself the free-state governor of Kansas was burned, two men who apparently stood in the way were killed by flying pellets of lead, a certain amount of lesser damage was inflicted, various female free-staters were scared half out of their wits (though not, it would appear, actually harmed), and there was a great round of shouting and speechifying and wobbly-legged parading and rejoicing. If rowdyism could settle the matter, it had been demonstrated beyond recall that Kansas was slave territory and would someday be a slave state and that the writ that made it treason to doubt the legality of the pro-slave government of the territory would run henceforth without interference.

Lawrence was sacked by men with a genius for putting the worst foot forward. There were in Lawrence—and would arrive in droves in the next few days—certain newspaper correspondents who wrote from deep abolitionist conviction and who had access to the front pages of some of the country's most infuential newspapers. These men had something to write about now, and they would make the most of it. And there stood on the record now one more indication that the disagreement between sections might not finally be settled by the ordinary processes of reason, debate, and compromise.

Next day was May 22, and Senator Sumner sat at his desk in the Senate chamber, the Senate having adjourned for the day. The Senator was large, the fixed chair under his desk was high, and the base of the desk itself was screwed to the floor. The Senator sat all hunched over, ankles hooked behind chair legs, intent on his correspondence. As always, he was serious, concentrating on the job at hand. He once told a friend that he never left his apartment to go to the Senate without taking a last look around, to make certain that everything he owned was just as he would wish it to be if the slave power should suddenly strike him down and he should never return to the place. Presumably he had taken such a look today.

The chamber where the Senate met was nearly empty. A few Senators lounged about near the doorways, chatting, or worked at their desks. Sumner scribbled away, and then he realized that someone was standing beside him, trying to get his attention.

"I have read your speech twice over, carefully," this man was saying. "It is a libel on South Carolina and on Senator Butler, who is a relative of mine."

Then the man raised a walking stick high in the air and brought it down as hard as he could on Senator Sumner's head.

The man with the cane was a South Carolina Congressman, Preston Brooks, nephew to Senator Butler; a youthful six-footer of robust frame, sometime cavalryman in the Mexican War. He struck again and again with a full-arm swing, and a man who saw it said that he came down with the cane like a dragoon using his saber and striking to kill. Caught between the chair and the immovable desk, Sumner tried desperately to get up. He was heard to gasp: "O Lord!"—and then, with a great convulsive heave, he wrenched the desk loose from its fastenings and reeled to his feet. Brooks struck again; the cane broke, and Brooks went on clubbing him with the splintered butt.

Now Sumner was on the floor, blood on his head and clothing, and men were running down the aisle to him. Brooks stopped beating him and strolled away, remarking: "I did not intend to kill him, but I did intend to whip him." Sumner was helped to his feet and made his way to the lobby, where he fell on a sofa, half unconscious. A doctor came and dressed his wounds—the scalp was badly cut, the doctor said afterward, but beyond that the wound did not seem very severe—and someone helped Sumner to a carriage and got him back to those rooms that were always maintained in perfect order in anticipation of some violent incident.

Sumner disrobed, found his clothing saturated with blood, and sent for his own doctor—who, after examination, took a much graver view of his injuries than the doctor in the Senate lobby had done. He pronounced Sumner's condition most serious and ordered him to get into bed and stay there.

Concerning which there was much argument, then and later—the idea perhaps being that to pound a Senator into speechlessness was no especial threat to the processes of democratic government unless the man's life was actually endangered. The doctor who had treated him in the lobby declared contemptuously that as far as he could see Sumner might have ridden by carriage all the way to Baltimore without ill effect if he had wanted to—his wounds were not critical. But Sumner's own doctor disagreed violently, and so did all of Sumner's friends, and so for the matter of that did Sumner himself. For three years he did not return to the Senate chamber. He traveled to England and France for medical treatments, some of which were agonizing; his spine had been affected, the foreign specialists told him, and for a long time he walked and talked like a man who had had a partial stroke.

Thus there would be many who would consider Sumner a tragic martyr, just as others would call him a faker who had been properly beaten for loose talk; and young Brooks would be a hero in the South, the recipient of innumerable gifts of canes, one of which bore a plate with the inscription: "Hit him again." He did not have long to live, this impulsive young Congressman; within a year he would die of a bronchial infection, clawing at his throat for the air his lungs could not get; and in the days that were left to him he grew heartily sick of the kind of fame he had won, for he did not like to be considered a bully. He was a friendly, warmhearted man of good family, and he had grown up in a society in which a man might be held to render a physical account for any words he had used. He would have challenged Sumner to a duel, he said, if he had had any notion that the man would accept, but since he knew that he would not he had felt obliged to use either a cane or a horsewhip. He had chosen the cane, and undeniably he had done what he set out to do—that is, he had worked off his own anger and he had compelled Sumner to shut up—but the final effect was wholly disastrous.

For this particular method of replying to Sumner's speech was the one method above all others most certain to make many folk in the North overlook the provocation that the speech had contained. The slave power (it would be said) could not be reasoned with; the man who tried it would be bludgeoned almost to the point of death.

Violence in Kansas, violence in the Senate chamber; the infection was spreading.

The week was not over. One day there had been an elegantly phrased appeal to hatred, the next day a Kansas town had been sacked, the day after that a Senator had been beaten to insensibility. Now it was May 24, forty-eight hours after the grim scene in the Senate chamber, and men with drawn swords were climbing through the shadows of early night in the ravines bordering Pottawatomie Creek in Kansas.

As weapons go, these swords had an odd history. They were shorter than cavalry sabers, straight in the blade, and some forgotten armorer had made them originally to government order as artillery broadswords. (In the old days all gunners wore swords for defense against attack by charging dragoons.) Then, in a sale of surplus property, the swords had been bought by a harebrained secret society in Ohio which called itself the Grand Eagles and which fuzzily imagined that one day it would attack and conquer Canada. The society's plans came to nothing, and when a cranky, hard-mouthed farmer-turned-sheep-trader came through the state muttering that the way to keep slavery out of Kansas was to go out there and "meddle directly with the peculiar institution," the swords had been turned over to him. They were made of good steel, and the society which had had such grand plans for them had had ornamental eagles etched on the blades.

Tonight the swords would be used, for the lanky Ohio farmer who proposed to meddle with the peculiar institution lived with strange fever-haunted dreams and felt an overwhelming compulsion to act on them. He was a rover, a ne'er-do-well, wholly ineffectual in everything he did save that he had the knack of drawing an entire nation after him on the road to unreasoning violence. He climbed the wooded ravines in the darkness this night, seven men at his heels—four of them were his own sons—and the naked metal of the swords glimmered faintly in the starlight. The man and his followers were free-state settlers from the town of Osawatomie. The grim farmer in the lead was named John Brown.

They had taken up arms two or three days earlier, along with other men, in a dimly legal free-state militia company, to go to the defense of Lawrence. By good or evil chance they got there too late, and all of the company but Brown and his chosen seven disbanded and went home. But Brown was obsessed. He declared that "something must be done to show these barbarians that we too have rights," and he and the seven turned a grindstone and ground their broadswords to a fine cutting edge. Some other militia leader saw and came over to warn Brown that he had better behave with caution.

"Caution, sir!" growled the old man. "I am eternally tired of hearing that word caution. It is nothing but the word of cowardice."

The eight men headed for Pottawatomie Creek, where pro-slavery settlers lived; and as they went they met a man who had seen late dispatches from Washington, and this man told them how Bully Brooks had beaten Senator Sumner. One of the party wrote of this news long afterward: "The men went crazy—*crazy*. It seemed to be the finishing, decisive touch."

For John Brown no more than a touch was needed. In some shadowy way the old man had got the idea that five free-state men had been killed at Lawrence, and he felt bound to balance the account. An eye for an eye, a life for a life; if five had been killed, five more must die; the logic that would kill an abstraction by striking at living men is direct, unthinking, and grisly.

John Brown and his band went stumping along through the night. They were in pro-slavery land now, and any man they saw would be an enemy. They came to one lonely cabin, saw lamplight gleaming under the door, and pounded for admittance. There was a noise as if someone were cocking a gun and sliding the muzzle through a chink in the logs, and the men slipped away from there—it was not precisely open combat that they were looking for. They went on, and after a time they came to a cabin occupied by a family named Doyle.

The Doyles were poor whites from Tennessee. They had come to Kansas recently, and although they believed in slavery—as men counted their beliefs in those days—they did not like to live too close to it; it appears that they had migrated in order to get away from it. Brown hammered on the door. It was opened, and he ordered Doyle and Doyle's two grown sons to come outside. The three men obeyed, the door was closed behind them, and Brown's band led the three away from the cabin. Then there were quick muffled sounds, brief cries, silence and stillness and darkness, and Brown and his followers went off down the road. In the morning the bodies of the three Doyles were found lying on the ground, fearfully mangled. They had been hacked to death with the Grand Eagle swords, which were to have been employed in the conquest of Canada but which had found strange other use. The father had been shot in the head.

Next the men went to the home of one Wilkinson, a noted pro-slavery leader.

John Brown

Knock on the door again: Wilkinson, ready for bed, came and opened up without bothering to put on his boots. The threat of death was in the very look of the terrible old man who peered in from the night, and Mrs. Wilkinson—sick in bed with measles—cried and begged that her husband be spared. No pity: Wilkinson was taken out into the yard, the door was shut, and again the swords came down with full-arm swings—like the cane of Bully Brooks, only heavier and sharper. The men left Wilkinson dead in his dooryard and went on to another cabin.

Here they found William Sherman, Dutch Bill, known as one of the Border Ruffians. Dutch Bill, like the others, was dragged out into the darkness for the fearful work of darkness. In the morning he was found lying in a stream, his head split open, a great wound in his chest, one hand cut off—apparently he had put up a fight for his life.

It was past midnight now. Old Brown had planned to get five, and five he got. He and his men washed their swords in Pottawatomie Creek and went off to their homes.

There were these things that happened in one week in the month of May 1856. The wind was being sown, and the hurricane would come later; and yet, all in all, these things were not so much causes as warnings—the lightning flashes that set evil scarlet flares against the black clouds that were banked up along the horizon. Somewhere beyond the lightning there was thunder, and the making of a great wind that would change the face of a nation, destroying much that men did not want destroyed. A doom was taking shape, and it seemed to be coming on relentlessly, as if there was nothing that anyone could do to prevent it. The republic that had been born in an air so full of promise that it might have been the morning of the seventh day was getting ready to tear itself apart.

This Hallowed Ground

A TIME FOR GOOD-BYS

In the long months between Lincoln's election and his inauguration on March 4, 1861, the United States—presided over but scarcely governed by a lame duck chief executive, James Buchanan—began to fall apart. On December 20, South Carolina seceded, and, following New Year's in 1861, the lower cotton states followed her example one by one. South Carolina fired on a ship sent in vain to relieve a lonely Federal garrison at Fort Sumter, and the Southern states seized forts, government arsenals and other property. It was not exactly peace—nor was it really war. It was rather a time of polite, painful, and sometimes tear-stained leave-takings, like this one in the Senate.

The Senate chamber was crowded on the morning of January 21. People had started moving toward the Capitol at daybreak, and by nine o'clock there was hardly standing room in the galleries or in the cloakrooms; there were foreign ministers in the diplomatic gallery, and when the doors to the outer halls swung open, the expectant faces of women, "like a mosaic of flowers," could be seen. As the routine business of the morning hour was disposed of, the chamber grew hushed, simple human curiosity blending with a tragic feeling that a long era in the nation's life was today being brought to a close. The Senators from the seceding cotton states were to speak their good-bys this morning; most notably, Senator Jefferson Davis, of Mississippi, gaunt and haggard, coming for the last time to this room where he had helped to make so much history.

Davis had been ill. He was tortured by agonizing migraine headaches that had kept him in bed for a week, and this morning his doctor had not thought him able to go to the Senate at all. Yet there was a fire in this man, a thin flame burning on the edge of darkness, and by its light he would follow the path of duty despite any imaginable physical weakness. He came in now, erect and deliberate, taking his final look at the Senate of a dissolving nation. His wife, Varina Howell Davis, watching from the gallery, felt that he gazed about him "with the reluctant look the dying cast on those upon whom they gaze for the last time." When he began to speak, his voice was low and he seemed to falter, but he gained strength as he went on and presently his words rang out firmly.

He had received satisfactory evidence, he told the Senators, that his state had formally declared its separation from the United States. His functions here, accordingly, were terminated; he concurred in the action of his people, but he would feel bound by that action even if he did not concur. He was offering no argument today. He had argued for his people's cause before now, had said all that he could say, and nothing had come of it. A conservative who loved the Union, he had cast his lot with his state, and he still hoped that there might be in the North enough tolerance and good will to permit a peaceful separation; but if there was not, "then Mississippi's gallant sons will stand like a wall of fire around their State; and I go hence, not in hostility to you, but in love and allegiance to her, to take my place among her sons, be it for good or for evil."

So it was time for good-bys, and the hush deepened as Davis spoke his valedictory:

"I am sure I feel no hostility to you, Senators from the North. I am sure there is not one of you, whatever sharp discussion there may have been between us, to whom I cannot now say, in the presence of my God, I wish you well. . . . Mr. President and Senators, having made the announcement which the occasion seemed to me to require, it only remains for me to bid you a final farewell."

That night Davis prayed earnestly: "May God have us in His holy keeping, and grant that before it is too late peaceful councils may prevail." To a friend he wrote that his farewell had been wrung from him "by the stern conviction of necessity, the demands of honor"; his words "were not my utterances but rather leaves torn from the book of fate." To another friend he wrote, in more bitterness: "We have piped but they would not dance, and now the Devil may care." And to former President Franklin Pierce, in whose cabinet he had served, Davis confessed a deep pessimism and said bluntly that the Buchanan administration had mishandled the situation so badly that war was likely to be the result: "When Lincoln comes in he will have but to continue in the path of his predecessor to inaugurate a civil war, and leave a *soi-disant* democratic administration responsible for the fact." He himself would go at once to Mississippi, and he did not know what the future might hold: "Civil war has only horror for me, but whatever circumstances demand shall be met as a duty and I trust be so discharged that you will not be ashamed of our former connection or cease to be my friend."

It was over. With Davis, the other cotton-state Senators took their departure and a few more of the frail threads that bound the Union together were snapped.

The Coming Fury

"THE MAN AND THE HOUR HAVE MET"

On February 4, 1861, the seven states that had thus far seceded opened a convention in Montgomery, Alabama. In four days they adopted a constitution for a provisional Confederate government, and on the fifth day they selected as provisional President and Vice President Jefferson Davis and Alexander H. Stephens. The new President, a West Point graduate, would rather have been in the army.

His dismay at being made President was genuine. Varina Davis told how she and her husband were in the garden of Brierfield, their plantation home in Mississippi, making rose cuttings, when a messenger brought Davis the telegram announcing that he was to be President of the Confederacy. He read it with an expression that made her feel that some dreadful personal calamity had taken place, and when he told her what the message said, he spoke "as a man might speak of a sentence of death." The news in truth came to Davis as no surprise, letters from the Mississippi delegates at Montgomery having kept him posted about the drift of things, and he felt that he had no option but to accept. "The trial was too great and the result too doubtful to justify one in declining any post to which he was assigned, and therefore I accepted." It took one day to set his affairs in order, to say farewell to his slaves, and to take a last look at the plantation home which meant so much to him. Then Jefferson Davis left for Montgomery.

At Montgomery, Confederate capital until Virginia seceded and the new government moved to Richmond, Davis and the fire-eating William L. Yancey spoke from a balcony to an expectant crowd.

"It may be," cried the new President, "that our career will be ushered in in the midst of a storm; it may be that as this morning opened with clouds, rain and mist, we shall have to encounter inconveniences at the beginning; but as the sun rose and lifted the mist it dispersed the clouds and left us the pure sunshine of heaven. So will progress the Southern Confederacy, and carry us safe into the harbor of constitutional liberty and political equality. We fear nothing . . . because, if war should come, if we must again baptize in blood the principles for which our fathers bled in the Revolution, we shall show that we are not degenerate sons, but will redeem the pledges they gave, preserve the rights they transmitted to us, and prove that Southern valor still shines as bright as in 1776. . . . I will devote to the duties of the high office to which I have been called all that I have of heart, of head, of hand."

Then, thinking of the armies that would march, and responding to his own inner longing, Davis added: "If, in the progress of events, it shall become necessary that my services be needed in another position—if, to be plain, necessity require that I shall again enter the ranks of soldiers—I hope you will welcome me there."

The crowd cheered mightily; then Yancey stepped forward, to pay his own tribute to "the distinguished gentleman who has just addressed you." In Davis, said Yancey, the South had found "the statesman, the soldier and the patriot," and the South was thrice fortunate: "The man and the hour have met."

It was Yancey's odd fate that he would be remembered by remote generations chiefly for that one remark: "The man and the hour have met." He was a passionate, intense person who had labored for years to create this new nation, one of the principal authors of a great drama which other men would enact; and he would go on into the shadows leaving little enduring trace of his own taut humanity except that on the balcony of a hotel in a little Southern city he had found the words to sum up, perfectly, the nobility and the tragedy of the Southern Confederacy and Jefferson Davis.

The man and the hour had been approaching each other by unlikely channels. The hour grew out of everything that a proud, self-centered, insecure society had been striving for in its attempt to ward off unwelcome change. The long argument over slavery in the territories, the resentment aroused by abolitionist taunts and by Northern aid for fugitive slaves, the fear and fury stirred by John Brown's raid and by the realization that many folk in the free states looked on Brown as a saintly martyr, the desperate attempt to preserve a pastoral society intact in a land being transformed by the Industrial Revolution—all of these had led to this hour in Montgomery, with banners waving and words of brave defiance shouted into the winter air. And the man who was meeting the hour, tense and erect, lonely and dedicated, looking without fear into a clouded future, was perhaps greater than the cause he embraced. He came from the Ohio Valley, cradle of a leveling democracy, born within a few months and a few miles of another Kentuckian, Abraham Lincoln, coming to manhood by a different course. He was a Mississippi planter at a time when the Mississippi planter was a hard man on the make rather than the exemplar of a cultivated pillared aristocracy, and yet somehow he transcended the limitations of his background and represented, once and for all, the nobility of the dream that his fellows believed themselves to be living by. Of all the men the Confederacy might have summoned, he was the man for this hour and for the hours that would follow.

The Coming Fury

A WINTER OF LONG JOURNEYS

At just about the same time that Jefferson Davis set out for Montgomery, Lincoln was beginning a similar journey from Springfield, Illinois, to Washington.

Like Davis, Lincoln had to say farewell to much; he was moving away from his own personal existence, he would belong from now on in every word and thought and deed to something larger than himself, and everything that had happened to him until now was no more than preparation for the years that lay ahead. He would meet, as he traveled eastward, flags and music and crowds of people eager to look and to cheer, just as Davis had met them; and although he and Davis would never come face to face, they would confront one another now through tumult and wind-driven smoke, the rival leaders of two nations in a land that could hold only one.

Early in February Lincoln closed his home, selling or storing his household furnishings, moving to Springfield's Chenery House for his last days in Illinois. Shortly after daybreak on February 11 he drove to the Great Western railroad station through a cold drizzle, and in the waiting room there he spent half an hour bidding farewell to friends. There was a crush of people all about, and Lincoln was pale, apparently gripped by deep emotion. He said little as men and women pumped his hand, and when he spoke, his voice seemed almost ready to break. After half an hour of it the train was ready, and the President-elect and his party went out to go aboard.

There were three cars—baggage car, smoker, and coach, with "a powerful Rogers locomotive" in front; the railroad time card warned that "it is very important that this train should pass over the road in safety." With Lincoln there was his son Robert, already dubbed "the Prince of Rails" by newspaper correspondents; his youthful secretaries, John G. Nicolay and John Hay; and Elmer Ellsworth, the slightly unreal amateur soldier who had drilled gaily dressed militia units and who had somehow won a place in the older man's heart; he would be killed in three months, and his body would lie in state in the White House. Also present were four professional soldiers, detailed by the War Department to be an escort and to look out for the safety of the President-elect. One of these was Colonel Edwin Vose Sumner, gruff and white-haired, who became an army officer before Lincoln entered his teens, an old-timer who would not survive the war. Others were Major David Hunter, Captain George Hazard, and energetic Captain John Pope, who would live to meet responsibilities too heavy for him. There were reporters, and political characters, and the New York *Herald* man noted that the cars were well stocked with "refreshments for the thirsty." Mrs. Lincoln, with the younger sons, Willie and Tad, would board the train at Indianapolis.

The crowd surged out of the waiting room as the party got on the train. Lincoln went to the rear platform, his tall hat in his fingers, and his fellow townsmen fell silent. He faced them, a somber, brooding figure, seemingly as reluctant as Davis had been to meet the incomprehensible burdens of the presidency. He spoke, finally, the last words he would ever speak in Springfield, not so much making a speech as thinking out loud.

"No one, not in my situation, can appreciate my feeling of sadness at this parting," he said. "To this place, and the kindness of these people, I owe everything. Here I have lived a quarter of a century, and have passed from a young to an old man. Here my children have been born, and one is buried. I now leave, not knowing when, or whether ever, I may return, with a task before me greater than that which rested upon Washington. Without the assistance of that Divine Being, who ever attended him, I cannot succeed. With that assistance I cannot fail. Trusting in Him, Who can go with me and remain with you and be everywhere for good, let us confidently hope that all yet will be well. To His care commending you, as I hope in your prayers you will commend me, I bid you an affectionate farewell." . . .

This was a winter when Americans began long journeys, moving from the West toward the East, from the known to the unknown, going separately and independently but somehow making part of one great, universal journey. Jefferson Davis had set off on his travels, and Abraham Lincoln had started his; and before either man reached his goal, Robert E. Lee also began to move, pulled east by the same force that was pulling the other two. For a brief time all three men were on the road at once, each of them deeply troubled in spirit, knowing that duty might require him to do hard and painful things which he would prefer not to do.

In a singular way, Lee began his journey more in the mood of Lincoln than in the mood of Davis. Davis had fewer doubts than either of the others. He knew, broadly, what he was supposed to do, and he knew how to set about it, and he neither knew nor cared what it might cost him. Lincoln and Lee took more doubts with them—doubts not only about the future but about the precise parts they themselves might have to play. Each man would say things, in the early stages of this journey, that he would not have said later. Each man would find the dimensions of the crisis enlarging as he came closer to it, his own probable role growing as the crisis grew; and each man would grow with the crisis itself, shaped by it but at the same time giving shape to it, becoming finally larger than life-size, a different man altogether than the one who began the journey.

As lieutenant colonel of the 2nd regular cavalry, Lee was stationed at Fort Mason, Texas. The commander of the Department of Texas, Brigadier General David Emanuel Twiggs, had passed along orders just received from the War Department: Lieutenant Colonel Lee was detached from his command and was to report to the general-in-chief, in Washington, for orders. On February 13 Lee put himself and his worldly goods in an army ambulance and set out on the first leg of the trip, heading for San Antonio, site of department headquarters.

Lee's orders were slightly out of the ordinary. A regular reassignment to routine duty would call on him to simply report to the War Department and would not involve a personal call on Winfield Scott. It seemed probable that the general-in-chief had a special assignment for Lee, and this would almost certainly have something to do with the government's military plans regarding the Southern Confederacy. Lee frankly told a brother officer that if this were the case he would resign. Under no circumstances could he draw his sword against Virginia and her sons. (He was assuming, obviously, that Virginia would eventually find herself in the Confederacy.) To another officer who asked bluntly what Lee proposed to do, he replied: "I shall never bear arms against the Union, but it may be necessary for me to carry a musket in defense of my native state, Virginia, in which case I shall not prove recreant to my duty." How he could bear arms in Virginia's defense without bearing arms against the Union was not clear, but the situation itself was not clear either. Earlier, Lee had coldly written that "secession is nothing but revolution," but he had felt obliged to add that he saw no charms in "a Union that can only be maintained by swords and bayonets"; he apparently clung to a dim hope that he and his state could in some way manage to be neutral in the approaching conflict, and to an even dimmer hope that in the end there would be no war at all.

This latter hope grew noticeably weaker before he even got out of Texas. If Virginia had not yet seceded, Texas had, and when Lee entered San Antonio, the revolution that he disliked so much was visible all over town in the form of marching men, excited crowds, and an unmistakable air of general hostility to the government of the United States. Lee discovered, in fact, that he might be a prisoner of war before he left San Antonio, even though no war existed. General Twiggs had surrendered his entire department to the recently seceded state of Texas. . . .

Poor Twiggs! To his repeated telegraphic requests for instructions, the War Department made no reply, and finally merely sent him orders to turn over his command to another officer. This communication—sent by mail—*arrived late on February 15. The relieving officer was away, out of reach, and the next morning a tough Texas State force, led by an old frontiersman and friend of Davy Crockett named Ben McCulloch, surrounded Twiggs's command, demanding that he give up the post and the public property there.*

Twiggs made only a token resistance. He had been given no instructions, he was heart and soul with the South, to reject the demand would have meant bloody fighting in the streets of San Antonio, and in any case he was seventy and in poor health, not ideally fitted to become a martyr for a cause in which he did not believe. By the middle of the day he gave up, signing an agreement under which his troops would collect their weapons, clothing, and camp equipment and march out of Texas unharmed. Orders were prepared and sent out along the 1,200-mile line where the army's frontier posts and forts were scattered—there were more than 2,600 Federal soldiers in Texas, dispersed in small detachments all along the frontier—and the troops in San Antonio got under way at once, moving out of their quarters with flag flying and band playing, to make their first camp that evening on the edge of town. San Antonio contained a number of Unionists, who watched the little procession in impotent indignation, but most of the people were enthusiastic secessionists.

In the midst of all of this excitement the ambulance containing Colonel Lee came into town and pulled up in front of the Read House, where Lee was to stop. As Lee got out of the wagon he noticed that the street was full of armed men, some of them wearing strips of red flannel on their shoulders to show that they were officers. A friend met him, the Unionist-minded Mrs. Caroline Darrow, whose husband was a clerk in army department headquarters. Lee asked her who these men might be.

"They are McCulloch's," she said. "General Twiggs surrendered everything to the state this morning and we are all prisoners of war." Lee stared at her, and she wrote afterwards that his lips trembled and his eyes filled with tears as he exclaimed: "Has it come so soon as this?"

Lee's position was embarrassing. If Mrs. Darrow's story was right, he himself might at this moment be some sort of prisoner, although technically, since he had been detached from his command and ordered to Washington, he was no longer on duty in Texas, and hence should not be included in any list of officers who had been surrendered. He entered the hotel, changed his uniform for unobtrusive civilian clothing, and went to department headquarters. There he found that the story was all too true. The state of Texas was in control, and its representatives intimated that Lee might not be given transportation to get out of Texas unless he immediately resigned his commission and joined the Confederacy. This proposal he instantly rejected. He was an officer in the army, his orders were to report in Washington, and those orders he would obey—and, on consideration, the Texans decided not to try to stop him.

. . . A fascinating "if" develops at this point. A few months earlier, in Twiggs's absence, Lee had been acting commander of the Department of Texas. If the secession crisis had come to a head then, or if Twiggs's return had been delayed past mid-winter, it would have been Lee and not Twiggs on whom the Texas commissioners would have made their demand for the surrender of government property. Without any question, Lee would have given them a flat refusal—in which case it might easily have been Lee, and not Major Robert Anderson, who first received and returned the fire of the secessionists, with San Antonio, rather than Fort Sumter, as the scene of the fight that began a great war. Subsequent history could have been substantially different.

The Coming Fury

THE FAILURE

Most of the figures of the war to come were already known to fame of one sort or another at the outset—except, perhaps, for one. Bad luck dogged the future commander of the Union forces from the moment he entered West Point, when the army got his name wrong. He was born Hiram Ulysses Grant, but the Congressman who wangled his appointment put him down as Ulysses Simpson (his mother's maiden name) Grant, and he could never get it corrected. "U. S." was too good: "Uncle Sam." And Sam Grant he became to his classmates. His record at the academy was unspectacular, and likewise his service in the Mexican War. Nothing seemed to work very well except his supremely happy marriage to Julia Dent. Troubles magnified when the poor young lieutenant was posted to Oregon, and then California where, broke and homesick for his wife, he apparently drank too much, quarreled with his commanding officer, and resigned from the service to avoid the mortification of a trial.

Material success has always seemed the goal, and the American people have won more of it, perhaps, than anyone else on earth. Yet their hearts have never really been in it, and they have not actually had much of a knack for it, and their record is full of ghost towns and lost men and pathetic little paths that go down to nowhere.

The truth is that the enormous drive and energy that won a continent and reshaped world history are always evoked by some undefined goal. The capacity for failure, therefore, is always present, because neither success nor failure in the ordinary meaning of the words is quite what the American really has on his mind.

So we have Ulysses Grant, who was no part of a mystic and who never suspected himself of wanting anything in particular beyond a chance to enjoy life doing congenial work—and who, somehow, was a great man whenever he served a cause and a flat failure whenever he tried to follow the main chance. The soldier who could manage an army as well as any man in American history could never manage his own affairs when those affairs were all he had to worry about. . . .

Grant was supremely fortunate in his marriage. There was in him a great loneliness hidden under a wistful shyness, a groping for understanding, a profound need for genuine communication with another human being. Fulfillment for all of this he found with his wife. The remark that is casually and inaccurately made about many men was literally true, with him: there never was any other woman in his life. So completely did she possess his spirit and his imagination that when she was not with him he seemed to be emotionally crippled. In later years, when some men worried (perhaps more than they really needed to) about whether he might stay on the right track, they knew there was always one remedy for any disturbed state he was in: get Mrs. Grant to him and he would be all right again. . . .

Colonel Dent [his father-in-law] had given Julia sixty acres of unimproved land not far from St. Louis, and on this land Grant resolved to become a farmer. The land must first be cleared of timber, and Grant attended to this himself, making a modest income by hauling the wood to St. Louis in a wagon and peddling it to anyone who would buy. Now and again, on the streets, he would meet army officers he knew. They agreed that Sam Grant looked seedy—a little more stooped, a stubble of beard on his face, wearing a battered hat and a faded army overcoat—and a few perceptive ones, like Longstreet, could see that he was sensitive about poverty. Since the army was a tight little organization in which everybody knew everybody else, it was as gossipy as a ladies' bridge-luncheon club, and exaggerated tales about Grant's troubles on the West Coast had made the rounds. His appearance at St. Louis as, apparently, a down-and-out wood peddler seemed to confirm the worst that had been said. It might be noted, however, that officers who met him in St. Louis reported that he was not drinking now.

There were two years of backbreaking work. The land was cleared and prepared for planting. Grant squared logs and built a house, into which he and his little family moved, and although he was woefully short of capital it looked as if the worst might be over. But just as the first real crop was harvested the panic of '57 hit the country, farm prices dropped almost to zero, and the year's work went for nothing. The next year brought a different kind of bad luck: an unseasonable cold snap in June ruined the crop, and then the old enemy of Grant's childhood, fever and ague, struck him once more, and for six months he was a semi-invalid hardly able to move about the house.

Desperate, he sold the farm, taking a cottage in St. Louis in part payment. There he went into a partnership in a real estate office. The event quickly showed that whatever U. S. Grant might be fitted for, selling real estate and collecting rents did not belong on the list. The venture paid him less than his expenses. An attempt to get an appointment as county engineer fell through. Then the man who had bought his farm could not meet his payments, and that modest source of income dried up. At one time Grant wangled a little job in the St. Louis customhouse, but it was shot out from under him within weeks when a new customs collector took office and fired the entire staff.

Once, during these St. Louis days, Grant met another ex-officer whom he had known slightly at West Point, a man in nearly as bleak a fix as himself—William Tecumseh Sherman, who had left the army to become a banker, had failed, and now considered himself "a dead cock in a pit." Two former army officers, getting on into middle life, loaded with debts, stopping on the street to compare notes, agreeing that West Point offered poor training for nonmilitary pursuits. . . .

In 1860 Grant was driven to unconditional surrender. He had sworn, as a boy, that once he was grown he would do anything on earth except work in his father's tannery. Now he was thirty-eight, he had three children, debts, no income and no prospects; and he went to Jesse Grant and asked for a job.

Jesse gave him a job. (Jesse could have extended more of a helping hand than he did, and he could have extended it much earlier, but Grant left no hint of a complaint on the record.) Actually, it was better than Grant anticipated. He did not have to go to the tannery itself. Jesse had opened a leather store in the mining-boom town of Galena, Illinois, and his two younger sons were running it for him. In this store Ulysses was given a clerkship. The pay was moderate but there seems to have been some sort of profit-sharing arrangement, and any port looked like a good one in the storm that had been breaking over Grant's head. He moved his family to Galena, took a house there, and set out to be a businessman.

The worst of it all was over, although no soothsayer could have guessed how fantastically the road was going to spiral upward. Oddly enough, those hardscrabble years may not have been quite as somber to the man and woman who lived through them as they now seem to have been. Years later, when he was living in the White House, Grant met an old acquaintance from St. Louis, to whose house he used to deliver cord wood—wood which he himself had cut and hauled and which he piled on the buyer's fuel pile, going to the door afterward to get his money. He began to talk about the old days, and unexpectedly he remarked: "Those were happy days. I was doing the best I could to support my family."

Once during those hard days a seamstress was in the Grant home to help with some sewing. Mrs. Grant quietly remarked: "We will not always be in this condition." Her confidence in Grant never wavered, and Grant knew it, and toward the end of his life he told a friend: "I have seen some hard times in my life, but I never saw the moment when I was not sure that I would come out ahead in the end."

People who saw Grant during the last days in St. Louis remembered that he appeared sad and discouraged—and yet this, apparently, was less because of his own troubles than because he saw what other thoughtful men were seeing then: the approaching disruption of the Federal Union. He had voted for James Buchanan, the Democrat, in 1856, fearing that a Republican victory would goad the South into secession. He had followed the Lincoln-Douglas debates attentively, considering himself a Douglas Democrat, and he wrote that when he heard Southern friends discussing a breakup of the Union as casually as if they were talking about a tariff bill, "it made my blood run cold."

Slowly his ideas were changing. He had lived in a slave state, he despised abolitionists, his wife owned slaves given her by her father, he himself had acquired ownership of a field hand from Colonel Dent. Yet in 1859, when he was giving up farming and was desperately pressed for money, and the one slave he owned could have been sold for a thousand dollars, he executed papers of manumission and gave the man his freedom.

Now he was living in Illinois, and the storm clouds were banked up black and ugly on the country's horizon. Whatever the bleak years had really meant to him, they had somehow seasoned him. He was ready to be used, now, and the time was at hand when the country was going to find a use for him.

U. S. Grant and the American Military Tradition

III

The Fateful Thunder

Major Robert Anderson, U. S. A.

When the bow is bent, and the arrow made ready on the string (in Jonathan Edward's phrase about God's wrath), a wonderful clarity descends on the vision of the eyewitness. In excruciating detail he notices every motion, every last word, every final handshake, every step in the ritual dance of men or nations about to start slaughtering each other. The clock ticks noticeably louder. Everyone knows what is about to happen—yet Caesar and the conspirators are still talking, or the telegraph is still clattering with vain messages, or the executioner is fussing with his apparatus. History holds its breath.

Bruce Catton was a master of this genre, the about-to-happen, as the next passage demonstrates. Four months after South Carolina had seceded, the Stars and Stripes still flew from Fort Sumter in Charleston harbor. In January President Buchanan had sent a ship to supply the isolated fort's commander, Major Robert Anderson, with men and provisions; it was driven off with gunfire. By April a kind of armed truce still prevailed, although Lincoln, the new President, had dispatched another (as it would turn out) vain relief expedition. Meanwhile the new Confederate government had placed an elegant West Point graduate, Pierre Gustave Toutant Beauregard, of Louisiana, in command of the ring of fortifications surrounding Sumter. Now the clock began to tick and, with enormous punctilio, the South took its fatal step.

On the morning of April 11 . . . Beauregard set about the composition of the formal demand for Fort Sumter's surrender. He had it finished by noon, and soon after that a boat with a white flag shoved off from a Charleston wharf and headed for the fort. It carried two of Beauregard's aides—Colonel James Chesnut, until December a United States Senator from South Carolina, an aristocrat of aristocrats, whose wife was keeping a diary that would be famous; and Captain Stephen D. Lee, a West Point graduate recently resigned from the United States Army, a man who would win fame and high position as a Confederate officer. With them was Lieutenant Colonel James A. Chisholm, aide-de-camp to Governor Pickens. In due course the boat reached the fort. The officers came on the wharf and were taken inside, and to Major Anderson they gave General Beauregard's message.

During the war that was about to begin, various generals would write demands for surrender. This document, however, had a tone all of its own. It had the dignity and the odd, formal politeness of an age that was ending; it was, furthermore, pure Beauregard from start to finish, as if it had been written partly to make a demand on Major Anderson, partly to satisfy Beauregard's own sense of what was correct, and partly for the appraisal of history. It might have been a restrained argument addressed to a wayward friend rather than a trumpet blast announcing violence. It read:

"Sir: the Government of the Confederate States has hitherto foreborne from any hostile demonstration against Fort Sumter, in the hope that the Government of the United States, with a view to the amicable adjustment of all questions between the two Governments, and to avert the calamities of war, would voluntarily evacuate it.

"There was reason at one time to believe that such would be the course pursued by the Government of the United States, and under that impression my Government has refrained from making any demand for the surrender of the fort. But the Confederate States can no longer delay assuming actual possession of a fortification commanding the entrance of one of their harbors, and necessary to its defense and security.

"I am ordered by the Government of the Confederate States to demand the evacuation of Fort Sumter. My aides, Colonel Chesnut and Captain Lee, are authorized to make such demand of you. All proper facilities will be afforded for the removal of yourself and command, together with company arms and property, and all private property, to any post in the United States which you may select. The flag which you have upheld so long and with so much fortitude, under the most trying circumstances, may be saluted by you on taking it down."

The three Southern officers waited alone for perhaps an hour, while Anderson called his officers together, read the message to them, and asked for their comments. The officers said about what they could have been expected to say, and no one bothered to make a record; they were professional soldiers in a fort which they had been ordered to keep, and to surrender on demand would have been unthinkable. Major Anderson composed a reply to General Beauregard. Like the letter he had just received, what the major wrote had dignity, courtesy, and firmness, and yet there was in his note a flavor faintly odd—as if his voice, had he been saying this instead of writing it, would have quavered just a little.

"General," wrote Major Anderson, "I have the honor to acknowledge the receipt of your communication demanding the evacuation of this fort, and to say, in reply thereto, that it is a demand with which I regret that my sense of honor, and of my obligations to my Government, prevent my compliance. Thanking you for the fair, manly and courteous terms proposed, and for the high compliment paid me, I am, general, very respectfully, your obedient servant, Robert Anderson, Major, First Artillery, Commanding."

This letter was given to the Confederate officers, and they started back to their boat, Major Anderson walking with them. At the edge of the wharf he asked whether Beauregard would open fire at once, without giving further notice. Colonel Chesnut hesitated, then replied: "No, I can say to you that he will not, without giving you further notice." Anderson said he would take no action until he was fired upon; then, moved by the thought that had been preying on his mind for many days—the almost complete exhaustion of the fort's supply of food—he burst out: "If you do not batter us to pieces we will be starved out in a few days."

The remark seems not to have registered, right at first, and the Southern officers got into their boat. Then Colonel Chesnut did a double-take: if the major had said what the colonel thought he had said, there might be no need to open a bombardment. Quickly Colonel Chesnut asked Major Anderson to repeat his last remark. Major Anderson did so, and Colonel Chesnut asked if he might include this in his report to General Beauregard. The major was not enthusiastic about having that casual remark put in a formal report, but he said that he had stated a fact and the colonel could do as he liked.

Like a good subordinate, Beauregard passed the whole business on to the Confederate Secretary of War, telegraphing the text of Anderson's written response and adding the remark to Colonel Chesnut. To show that he wanted Montgomery to say whether the bombardment should be called off, Beauregard ended his telegram with the single word: "Answer."

Jefferson Davis was perfectly willing to call off the shooting, but he wanted something better than Major Anderson's offhand remark on the wharf. Beauregard was informed, in a telegram signed by Secretary Walker but undoubtedly composed by President Davis, that he had better get it in writing.

"Do not desire needlessly to bombard Fort Sumter," said the telegram. "If Anderson will state the time at which, as indicated by him, he will evacuate, and agree that in the mean time he will not use his guns against us, unless ours should be employed against Fort Sumter, you are authorized thus to avoid the effusion of blood. If this or its equivalent be refused, reduce the fort as your judgment decides to be most practicable."

Neither Davis nor Beauregard could overlook the chance that somebody might be trying to pull a fast one. Major Anderson was saying that he would be starved out very soon, but while the major seemed to be a truthful man, Washington of late had been a hotbed of deceit and falsehood. It was known that food was on its way to Fort Sumter. Some sort of Yankee ships—warships, transports, or whatnot—were known to be cruising to and fro off the Charleston bar, and Captain H. J. Hartstene, of the Confederate navy, had just said that in his opinion it was quite possible for these ships to send supplies to Major Anderson at night in small boats. All in all, this was no time for Southerners to be too confiding. To cancel the attack because Major Anderson was about to starve, and then to find that his larder had just been filled and that he could hold out indefinitely, would be a very poor way to begin the Confederacy's struggle for independence.

Beauregard undertook to nail it down. He wrote another letter to Major Anderson, and at eleven o'clock on the night of April 11 the three aides got into their boat once more and started for Fort Sumter, reaching the wharf a little after midnight. Major Anderson took the letter they gave him and once more called his officers into council.

The only real question was the length of time the garrison could hold out, on the food that was available. One week earlier, Lieutenant Hall had made a tabulation. The fort then contained ⅔ of a barrel of flour, 5 barrels of hard bread, just under a barrel of rice, 100 pounds of sugar, 25 pounds of coffee, ⅙ of a barrel of salt, 24 barrels of salt pork, 2 barrels of vinegar, 40 pounds of hominy grits, and ½ a barrel of corn meal. To eat this there were in the fort 10 commissioned officers (including 3 from the Corps of Engineers), 74 enlisted men, and 1 functionary listed as a mail carrier. There were also 43 civilian employees whom Major Anderson had been trying to send ashore but whom he was compelled to keep because the South Carolina authorities would not let him get rid of them—figuring, no doubt, that these men would serve the South by helping to consume the major's food. Most of the stuff Lieutenant Hall had listed was gone by now, and the best judgment Major Anderson could get was that the garrison might possibly hold out for five more days. On the last three of those days there would be no food whatever.

One more letter to General Beauregard, then: Major Anderson would evacuate the fort on April 15, if General Beauregard would furnish him with transportation, and Major Anderson would not before that date open fire—*provided* that the Confederates did not commit, or seem obviously about to commit, some hostile act against Fort Sumter or against the United States flag, and provided also that Major Anderson did not in the meantime receive new instructions or provisions from his government. This was reduced to writing, and the message was given to the Southern officers, who were waiting in one of the casemates of the fort.

Major Anderson's answer was of course no answer at all, as far as the Confederacy was concerned, since it really committed him to nothing, and Beauregard's aides did not even feel that they needed to make the long trip back to Charleston to get Beauregard's verdict. (Consistently with the pattern that had been followed all along, the final activating decisions would be made by remote subordinates, exercising authority that had been delegated down the long chain of command.) With Colonel Chesnut dictating, Captain Lee writing it down, and Lieutenant Colonel Chisholm copying the reply as fast as Captain Lee got it down—they were a busy trio, as Chisholm admitted afterward, for a few candle-lit minutes there in the casemate—Major Anderson got his reply in five minutes: "By authority of Brigadier General Beauregard, commanding the Provisional Forces of the Confederate States, we have the honor to notify you that he will open the fire of his batteries on Fort Sumter in one hour from this time." As the note carefully stated, it was then 3:20 on the morning of April 12.

Since Major Anderson and several of his officers were present when Colonel

Fort Sumter immediately after its evacuation by the Federal garrison

Chesnut dictated all of this, the written reply was no surprise. Major Anderson studied it, and Captain Lee thought he was profoundly moved: "He seemed to realize the import of the consequences, and the great responsibility of his position." Major Anderson walked out on the wharf with the three Southerners and saw them into their boat. Shaking hands with them, he murmured: "If we never meet in this world again, God grant that we may meet in the next." The boat moved off in the darkness, and Major Anderson and his officers went through the fort, arousing the sleeping soldiers, telling them that the battle was about to start, and warning everybody to stay under cover until further notice; Anderson would not try to return the fire until daylight. Most of the officers went to the barbette to take a last look around.

There were bonfires and torches going in all of the Confederate camps and batteries. Sumter was ringed by an almost complete circle of flickering lights, with darkness off to seaward; clouds hid the stars, and there was a hint of rain in the air. From batteries and camps came a jumble of far-off sounds, as soldiers fell in line for roll call, trundled guns into position, made all of the other last-minute preparations. In a Charleston bedroom Colonel Chesnut's wife waited in an agony of suspense. Her husband had told her what was going to happen; she looked out over the dark harbor with the twinkling lights on its rim, listening. . . .

The three aides went ashore at old Fort Johnson, where Major Anderson had once thought he could quarter the families of the married members of his garrison. A Confederate battery was there now, and the officers gave their orders to its commander, Captain George S. James, who had a seacoast mortar tilted at the proper angle; it was to be the signal gun which would tell the encircling troops, the city of Charleston, and the world at large that the most momentous bombardment in American history had begun.

Roger Pryor [a fiery Virginia Congressman who had urged his fellow Southerners to strike a blow, so that Virginia too would join the Confederacy] had gone out to the fort with the military aides, although he had remained in the boat while the others went inside. Now he came in to Captain James's battery, and the captain bowed to him and asked him if he would like to have the honor of firing the first gun. (The blow Pryor had been asking for was about to be struck. It would have the exact result he had predicted, pulling Virginia into the conflict and into the Confederacy, and into a long, tragic bloodletting. . . .)

Pryor seemed as emotionally disturbed as Major Anderson. His voice shook as he told Captain James: "I could not fire the first gun of the war," and Captain James passed the order on to Lieutenant Henry S. Farley. Then Pryor and the three aides got back into the boat and set off for Charleston, to make report to General Beauregard. Before the boat had gone very far, they told the oarsmen to stop rowing, and the boat drifted in utter silence for ten minutes while the men looked toward Fort Johnson. Lieutenant Farley was a little late, but it made no difference. At 4:30 there was a flash of light and a dull explosion as he fired the mortar. Arching high in the night, the shell could be traced by its glowing red fuse. A gunner on Morris Island thought it looked "like the wings of a firefly." It hung in the air, started down, and exploded squarely over Fort Sumter. The boat resumed its journey. In her bedroom, Mary Chesnut went to her knees and prayed as she had never prayed before.

The Coming Fury

Having done what honor required, Major Anderson evacuated Fort Sumter after two days of punishing bombardment, on April 13. Two days later Abraham Lincoln called for 75,000 volunteers. Two days after that, a Virginia convention voted to secede. On the following day, the 18th, Robert E. Lee was offered command of the Federal armies; on the 20th, he politely declined. Then he resigned his commission to serve Virginia. It seemed that most of the best military talent in America would serve the South.

ITEMS IN A BALANCE SHEET

The South did not have the strength in mine, factory, counting house, or field which the Northern states had, nor did it own, far down in reserve, waiting to be accepted and used, the overriding moral force of the anti-slavery cause. Yet it did have, somewhere, in an area beyond easy definition, the power to draw the loyalty of some very remarkable men. . . .

Among them was a handsome six-footer named Albert Sidney Johnston, Kentucky-born, a graduate of West Point, veteran of the Mexican War, former colonel of the 2nd U. S. Cavalry, a man esteemed so highly in Washington that when Lee decided he could not take the job of second-in-command to Winfield Scott, the place was offered to Johnston. Johnston, by now commanding the Department of the Pacific with headquarters at San Francisco, an old soldier getting on for sixty, turned the offer down and resigned his commission. He stayed on for two weeks, so that his successor could take his place, and he was horrified to learn that the War Department (remembering what Twiggs had done in Texas) suspected that he would turn California over to the Rebels unless he was closely watched; and now he was coming east to Richmond, cross-country, hoping that Jefferson Davis somehow would be able to make use of him in the Confederate army. Nothing had been promised to him; he just thought he could be of some service.

There was another Johnston—Joseph Eggleston Johnston, a sprightly and courtly little Virginian in his fifties who, when war came, was quartermaster-general of the United States Army, with the rank of brigadier. He had a trim gray goatee, a knack for winning the adoration of men who worked for him, and an indefinable quality that led soldiers to refer to him as "the gamecock"; he was both kindly and touchy, and although his superiors sometimes found him hard to get along with, his inferiors never did. He would pace his office in the War Department, thinking hard, and when an aide came in to remind him of some unfinished business, he would bite the aide's head off—and then, before the man had left the room, would apologize so pleasantly that the aide would feel no hurt. One morning, a few days after Fort Sumter, he went in to see Secretary Cameron; came out a bit later, head bowed, tears in his eyes, to collect his belongings and go away. Cameron recalled that Johnston had told him he must resign and go south; he owed everything to the United States government, it had educated him and honored him, but he must go with his state. "It was ruin, in every sense of the word," said Cameron, remembering what the gamecock had told him, "but he must go." Johnston went—to Richmond, where Mr. Davis made him a Confederate brigadier and sent him off to command troops in the Shenandoah. An admiring soldier, looking on when Johnston took command, considered him both an intellectual and a fine horseman, and wrote: "He sat his steed like a part of the animal, and there was that about him which impressed us all with the idea that he was at home in the management of an army as well as of a horse." . . .

[Joe Johnston] was well served by his lieutenants. One of them was that singular genius, Brigadier General Thomas J. Jackson, a shy man full of ferocious Presbyterianism, born to fight; and Jackson put over a sly trick on the Baltimore & Ohio Railroad people, confiscating trains that ran through Harpers Ferry and depriving the road at last of forty-two locomotives and 386 freight cars. Most of these were wrecked and thrown into the river, but Jackson was able to haul fourteen locomotives and a few boxcars overland, by road, with horses for motive power, all the way to the town of Strasburg, where they could be put on the Manassas Gap Railroad and added to the Confederacy's stock of railroad equipment. Johnston also had some cavalry, commanded by a bearded young West Pointer named James Ewell Brown Stuart—Jeb Stuart, who would be known to fame a little later, a man who was both an unconscionable show-off and a solid, hard-working, and wholly brilliant commander of light horse. He wore an ostrich plume in his hat, he had a gray cloak lined with scarlet, and he kept a personal banjo player on his staff, riding off to war all jingling with strum-strum music going on ahead, and before he got killed (which came in the final twilight several years later) he gave the Yankees a very bad time of it. . . .

. . . The historian Francis Parkman, considering the state of the war two years later, marveled that an adversary "with means scarcely the tithe of ours" could not only hold the Northern invader at bay but could twice show the ability to take the war into the Northland itself. The reason, he believed, was that the Confederacy—"ill-jointed, starved, attenuated"—had, nevertheless, "a head full of fire." It had claimed the allegiance of some great men, men who had much to lose and much to offer, and the fight between Confederacy and Union came down to "strong head and weak body against strong body and weak head." Parkman named no names, and he did not need to.

The Coming Fury

DEATH ALONG THE POTOMAC

L ong before dawn on the morning of May 24 [1861, eight regiments crossed] the Potomac to seize Alexandria and Arlington Heights and to establish a firm bridgehead on secession soil. The first invasion of the South was under way. It was not much of an invasion and it did not occupy much of the South, but it was a symbol. A great many young men must die before it was finished.

Much would die with them; including a way of looking at life and seeing nothing but its freshness and the fact that it was made to be spent, a special notion of how things might be with the spirit when the ultimate challenge is faced, a feeling for the overtones that can haunt a man's hearing as he goes down the long pathway into the dusk. This also was symbolized, as Federal troops first put their feet on Virginia soil. Among the eight regiments that went across the river (it was two o'clock in the morning and there was a big moon to shimmer on the water and to put mysterious shadows under the dark trees) there was a rowdy, untamed, and not too noteworthy outfit known as the New York Fire Zouaves: a regiment of amateurs led by an amateur, going down to the Alexandria wharves by boat in search of a war that would be all youth and flags and easy valor and rewarding cheers; not destined to be hardened by fire into the company of the elect. The colonel was luckier than the rest. He was named Elmer Ellsworth, and he would die before the illusion had a chance to fade, leaving a name that would live longer than the cold facts required.

Ellsworth was twenty-four; an odd young man, by profession a Chicago patent attorney (it seems the last job on earth for this particular man) and by chosen avocation a drill-master of irregular troops, a wearer of bright uniforms, a dedicated play actor; remembered now because death met him very early, and because there was something in him that had won the affection of Abraham Lincoln. He had trained a patent-leather militia company before the war, winning plaudits, and he had come east on the same train with Lincoln, half bodyguard and half pampered nephew-by-election; when war came, he had helped to recruit a new regiment from among the New York volunteer firemen had seen it clothed in the brilliant uniforms copied from the French Zouaves— baggy red knickers, russet leather gaiters, short blue jacket over a big sash, a red fez for the head, and a go-to-hell grin for the face—and now he was leading the first invasion of the South, taking his men in to occupy Alexandria.

Before the regiment started out, Ellsworth had written a final letter to his parents. (A romantic, off for the wars, would write a "final letter" before any move whatever, casting an innocently calculated shadow for posterity and for himself.) He felt, he said, that "our entrance to the city of Alexandria will be hotly contested," but he was unworried: "thinking over the probabilities of the morrow and the occurences of the past, I am perfectly content to accept whatever my fortune may be." The entrance, as it turned out, was not contested at all. Such Confederate troops as had been in and around Alexandria had decamped, and the invading host got in unopposed; but Ellsworth's own fortune was not diminished thereby. Leading his men down the empty streets, Ellsworth came to a hotel, the Marshall House, and on top of this there was a flagpole flying the Confederate flag. A challenge, obviously; and Ellsworth, followed by soldiers, went inside, hurried to the roof, and with a knife borrowed from a private soldier cut down this emblem of rebellion and started back for the street with the flag tucked under his arm.

In a shadowy hallway he met the proprietor of the inn, a solid Virginian named James T. Jackson, who perhaps had not the clearest conception of what war might mean but who knew that he was not going to be pushed around by any bright young man in red pants; and Jackson produced a shotgun and killed Ellsworth by sending a charge of buckshot through his body, being himself killed a few seconds later by one of Ellsworth's Zouaves, who first shot the man and then, for good measure, ran his bayonet through him. All of these deeds were final; that is, Ellsworth and Jackson stayed dead, and the flag stayed down from the flagpole; and the North suddenly found itself with its first war hero. Ellsworth's body lay in state in the White House, mourned by President Lincoln, and a rash of editorials, poems, sermons, speeches, and quick-steps enshrined him as well as might be.

The war was new. The two deaths were utterly meaningless, although Ellsworth had precisely the end he would have chosen for himself. He died while the day was still bright, a flag under his arm, his name and his uniform still bright. It was a springtime of symbols. Ellsworth meant little alive, much in his coffin, symbolizing a national state of mind, a certain attitude toward the war that would quickly pass and would never return. And so, for that matter, did the innkeeper, Mr. Jackson.

The Coming Fury

THE END OF THE PICNIC

Washington by now [July, 1861] was ringed with camps, very martial-looking, with some of the new three-year volunteer regiments mingling with the ninety-day militia units, and to Northern editors and politicians it seemed that it was high time for a little action. That the generals who would control these formless levies had never handled large bodies of troops before, that the soldiers themselves were mere civilians in arms with very little discipline and no understanding of the need for any, that what was believed to be an army was simply a collection of independent companies and regiments hopelessly unready to maneuver or fight as a coherent mass—of all of these things few people had any comprehension. The pressure for an immediate advance on the new Confederate capital at Richmond became stronger. Horace Greeley, the forceful but eccentric editor of the powerful New York *Tribune*, was sounding off with his "Forward to Richmond!" war-cry; and although General [Irvin] McDowell, commander of the troops around Washington, knew perfectly well that it would be a long time before his men were ready for a battle, there was nothing he could do about it. Ready or not, he was going to have to move. . . .

Early in July, McDowell was directed to organize and launch a thrust at the principal Confederate army, which lay at and around Manassas Junction, some twenty-five miles from Washington, behind a meandering little river known as Bull Run.

The military situation in Virginia was slightly complicated. . . . Up the Potomac River, in the vicinity of Harpers Ferry, there were 16,000 Federal troops commanded by an aged regular, Major General Robert Patterson. Patterson meant well, but he was far past his prime and would very shortly demonstrate that he was much too infirm for field command. Facing him were perhaps 9,000 Confederates under the canny Joe Johnston.

Behind Bull Run there were approximately 20,000 Confederates under Beauregard. Johnston outranked Beauregard, but while Johnston remained in the Shenandoah Valley, Beauregard was virtually independent. Since Beauregard had the biggest force, and since he lay squarely across the line of the Orange and Alexandria Railroad, which looked like the best way for a Federal army to approach Richmond, Beauregard's army was the chosen target.

McDowell, therefore, would march down overland to make his attack. He noted that a railway line ran from Manassas Junction to the Shenandoah Valley, within convenient range of Johnston's men; if Johnston could give Patterson the slip he could quite easily move his troops down to the Bull Run area and reinforce Beauregard. Patterson, accordingly, was instructed to keep pressure on Johnston so that he could not detach any troops. McDowell, whose army would total about 35,000 men, thus would have what ought to be a

Confederate soldiers

decisive numerical advantage when he made his fight. On the afternoon of July 16 his troops started out.

There is nothing in American military history quite like the story of Bull Run. It was the momentous fight of the amateurs, the battle where everything went wrong, the great day of awakening for the whole nation, North and South together. It marked the end of the ninety-day militia, and it also ended the rosy time in which men could dream that the war would be short, glorious, and bloodless. After Bull Run the nation got down to business.

When it set out from Washington, McDowell's army was at least brilliant to look at. The militia regiments wore a variety of uniforms. Many of the contingents were dressed in gray. Others wore gaudy clothing patterned after the French Zouaves—baggy red breeches, short blue coats, yellow or scarlet sashes about the waist, turbans or fezzes for the head. There was a New York regiment which called itself the Highlanders, and it had kilts for dress parade, although on this campaign the men seem to have worn ordinary pants. Regimental flags were of varicolored silk, all new and unstained. Baggage trains, which were somewhat tardy, were immense. A regiment at that time had as many wagons as a brigade would have a little later. From McDowell on down no one knew anything about the mechanics of handling a large army on the march, and logistics were badly fouled up. The fact that most of the soldiers would break ranks as the mood took them—to wander into a field to pick blackberries, to visit a well for drinking water, or simply to take a breather in the shade—did not help matters much. No more informal, individualistic collection of men in uniform ever tried to make a cross-country march. The weather was hot, and great clouds of dust settled over the fancy uniforms.

Beauregard, at Manassas Junction, knew that the Yankees were coming. He had a good intelligence service, with spies in Washington who kept him posted, and in any case there was nothing secret about this move; half of the country knew about it, and Beauregard had ample time to make preparations. He was an able soldier, this Beauregard, but rather on the flashy side, given to the construction of elaborate plans, and he considered that he would smite this invading host by a clever flank attack without waiting for it to assault him. His troops were in line along eight miles of Bull Run, covering the bridges and the fords, and Beauregard planned to swing his right over the stream and strike the Union left before McDowell was ready. Oddly enough, McDowell was planning a somewhat similar move himself—to demonstrate before the Confederate center, cross the bulk of his troops a few miles upstream, and come down hard on the Confederate left.

McDowell's army moved very slowly—which, considering everything, is hardly surprising—and contact with the Confederates was not made until July 18. On this day a Union division prowled forward to Blackburn's Ford, near the center of the line, to make a demonstration; it prowled too far, and was driven back with losses, and the Confederates were mightily encouraged.

Meanwhile, in the Shenandoah Valley, Joe Johnston had given Patterson the slip. He had moved forward and had made menacing gestures, which led Patterson to believe that he was about to be attacked; then, while the old Federal took thought for his defenses, Johnston got most of his men away and took the cars for Manassas. His men would arrive at Bull Run just in time. Johnston himself, ranking Beauregard, would be in command of the united armies, although this was a point that Beauregard never quite seemed to understand.

In any case, the great battle finally took place on July 21, 1861. This was the day on which Beauregard was to make his flank attack, modeled, he proudly remarked, on Napoleon's battle plan at Austerlitz. (Most professional soldiers then had the Napoleon complex, and of all armies that of the French was the most respected.) Beauregard's move, however, was a complete fiasco. Like McDowell, he had no staff worthy of the name, and routine staff work in consequence never got done. Orders went astray, those that did reach their destination were not understood or followed, and the advance of the Confederate right amounted to nothing more than a series of convulsive twitches by a few brigades.

All in all, this was a lucky break for the Confederates. The Rebel army at Bull Run was in no better shape than the Federal army, but when the showdown came it was able to fight on the defensive—which, as numerous battles in this war would show, was infinitely easier for untrained troops. For McDowell's flank move was actually made, and although it was inordinately slow and confused, it did at last put a solid segment of the Union army across Bull Run at a place called Sudley Church, in position to march down and hit the Confederates' left flank. A doughty Confederate brigadier commanding troops at the Stone Bridge, where the main road to Washington crossed Bull Run, saw the Yankees coming and fought a stout delaying action which held them off until Johnston and Beauregard could form a new line, on the wooded plateau near the Henry House, to receive the attack. McDowell sent forward two excellent regular army batteries, and the battle was on.

For men who had never fought before, and who had been given no training of any real consequence, the Northerners and Southerners who collided here did a great deal better than anyone had a right to expect. A good many men ran away, to be sure, but most of them stayed and fought, and the struggle was a hot one. For a time it seemed that the Confederate line would be broken and that the "Forward to Richmond" motif would come to a triumphant crescendo. The two regular batteries that had been doing such good work were advanced to the crest of Henry House Hill, infantry came surging along with them, and a number of the Confederate units weakened and began to drift to the rear.

Then came one of those moments of dramatic inspiration that men remem-

General P. G. T. Beauregard, C. S. A.

ber. Brigadier General Barnard Bee sought to rally some of the wavering Confederate regiments. Not far away he saw a Virginia brigade of Johnston's troops, standing fast and delivering a sharp fire: a brigade led by that former V.M.I. professor, Brigadier General T. J. Jackson.

"There is Jackson standing like a stone wall!" cried Bee, gesturing with his sword. "Rally behind the Virginians!"

So a great name was born. From that moment on the man would be Stonewall Jackson.

Bee's troops rallied. Fresh Confederate troops, just off the train from the Valley, kept coming in on their flank. The two pestiferous Union batteries, placed too far forward to get proper support from their own infantry, were taken by a sudden Confederate counterattack—the Rebels here wore blue uniforms, and the gunners held their fire until too late, supposing the attacking wave to be Unionists coming up to help—and suddenly the Union offensive, which had come so near to success, collapsed, all the heart gone out of it, and the soldiers who had been involved in it turned and headed for the rear.

There was no rout here. The Union attack had failed and the men were withdrawing, but there was no panic. One trouble apparently lay in the fact that the tactical maneuver by which troops fighting in line would form column and go to the rear was very complicated, and most of these green Union troops did not have it down pat; a withdrawal under fire was bound to become disordered and finally uncontrollable, not because the men had lost their courage but simply because they had not had enough drill. McDowell saw that nothing more could be done here and passed the word for a retreat to his advanced base at Centreville, four or five miles nearer Washington.

It was after the beaten army had crossed Bull Run that the real trouble came, and the fault lies less with the soldiers than with the reckless Washington civilians who had supposed that the edge of a battlefield would be an ideal place for a picnic.

For hundreds of Washingtonians had come out to see the show that day. They came in carriages, wagons, buggies, and on horseback, they brought hampers of food and drink with them, and they were spread all over the slanting fields east of Bull Run, listening to the clangor of the guns, watching the smoke clouds billowing up to the July sky, and in general making a holiday out of it. Now, as Union wagon trains, ambulances, reserve artillery, and knots of disorganized stragglers began to take the road back to Washington, all of these civilians decided that it was high time for them to get out of there. They got into their conveyances and went swarming out onto the highway which the army wanted to use, creating the father and mother of all traffic jams; and just as things were at their worst a stray Confederate shell came arching over and upset a wagon on a bridge over a little stream called Cub Run, blocking the road completely.

After this there was unadulterated turmoil, growing worse every moment, with disorganized troops and panicky civilians trying to force their way through a horrible tangle of wheeled vehicles, mounted men riding around and past them, bodies of troops trying in vain to march where they had been told to march; a new surge of fear rising every now and then when someone would shout that Confederate cavalry was coming on the scene. In the weeks before the battle, imaginative newspaper and magazine writers had written extensively about the "black horse cavalry" which the Confederates had developed, and what they said had stuck in men's minds. In the dust and confusion of this disorganized retreat, frightened individuals began to shout that the black horse cavalry was upon them, and outright panic developed, with bewildered thousands dropping their weapons and starting to run, communicating their fears to others by the simple act of running. Before dark there was complete and unregimented chaos spilling all over the landscape, and hardly anyone who could move at all stopped moving until he had reached the Potomac River. For the time being most of McDowell's army had simply fallen apart. The bits and pieces of it might be useful later on, but right now they were nothing more than elements in a universal runaway.

The Confederates might have pursued, but did not. Jefferson Davis had reached the scene, and he conferred extensively with Johnston and Beauregard, almost ordered a pursuit, finally did not; and, as a matter of fact, the Confederate army was almost as disorganized by its victory as the Union army was by its defeat. . . .

It seemed at the time that the casualty lists were fearful, although by the standards of later Civil War battles they would look moderate. The Federals had lost 2,896 men in killed, wounded, and missing, and Confederate losses came to 1,982. For an unmilitary country which had been subconsciously expecting that the war would not really be very costly, these figures were shocking. People began to see that beneath the romance which had been glimpsed in the bright uniforms, the gay flags, and the lilting tunes played by the military bands, there would be a deep and lasting grimness. Holiday time was over. No one was going to play at war any longer. The militia units could go home now; it was time to get ready for the long pull.

For Bull Run was what awakened the North to reality. (It may have had an opposite effect in the South; the victory looked so overwhelming that many Southerners considered the Yankees poor fighters, and expected a speedy final triumph.) Before there could be another campaign, a real army would have to be put together, and expert attention would have to be given to matters of organization, training, and discipline. To attend to this job, President Lincoln plucked victorious George B. McClellan out of the western Virginia mountains and put him in command of the Army of the Potomac.

The American Heritage Picture History of the Civil War

IV

Men at Arms

Union troops in the siege lines outside Petersburg, Virginia

Save for a handful of regulars, the soldiers of the two armies that began the Civil War had joined up because they wanted to, and for reasons as various as the men themselves. They knew nothing of what the life of a soldier would be like, of how it feels to charge into enemy fire. Immersing himself in the letters and memoirs of those who marched and camped and fought, Catton managed somehow to convey to later generations the sights and sounds, the fear and the fury, the reality of that experience. The worst—and the best—of it is the first moment of combat. The scene immediately following takes place before Fort Donelson, Tennessee, in February, 1862, one of General Grant's early victories. There had been some bad moments, the battle was hanging in the balance, and Grant ordered one of his division commanders—a tough, lean regular named C. F. Smith, former commandant of West Point cadets—to move up and take the fort. How do you lead raw recruits? You go first.

In no time the division was ready to advance—2nd Iowa in the lead, four more regiments massed behind it. While Grant rode back to see to the right of his line, Smith rode across the Iowans' front, gestured toward the high ground where lay the Confederate works, and said: "Second Iowa, you must take that fort. Take the caps off your guns, fix bayonets, and I will support you."

The Middle Westerners who made this attack remembered it as long as they lived, for the way was tough—a tangle of fallen timber, a ravine with steep banks, invisible Rebels driving in a hot fire, with double-barreled shotguns charged with buckshot reserved for close range—but even more than the fight itself, they remembered Smith. He was erect on his horse in front of them, his saber held high in the air, and when he had given the command to advance he went on in advance of everybody—turning in the saddle, now and then, to make sure that his men were following him. For faint hearts he had scornful words; seeing some of the soldiers hesitating about getting out into the thick of things, he swung about and made wrathful oration: "Damn you, gentlemen, I see skulkers. I'll have none here. Come on, you volunteers, come on. This is your chance. You volunteered to be killed for love of your country and now you can be. You are only damned volunteers. I am only a soldier and I don't want to be killed, but you came to be killed and now you can be." And so, with a mixture of oaths and sharp words, the old man led them up the wooded slope straight for the Confederate trenches. Men said he was the first man in the works, riding in so close to the Rebels that he could have put his hand on their heads, and one of his soldiers wrote that "by his presence and heroic conduct he led the green men to do things that no other man could have done."

Grant Moves South

"IT SURE BEATS CLERKING"

The volunteer soldier in the American Civil War used a clumsy muzzle-loading rifle, lived chiefly on salt pork and hardtack, and retained to the very end a loose-jointed, informal attitude toward the army with which he had cast his lot. But despite all of the surface differences, he was at bottom blood brother to the G.I. Joe of modern days.

Which is to say that he was basically, and incurably, a civilian in arms. A volunteer, he was still a soldier because he had to be one, and he lived for the day when he could leave the army forever. His attitude toward discipline, toward his officers, and toward the whole spit-and-polish concept of military existence was essentially one of careless tolerance. He refused to hate his enemies—indeed, he often got along with them much better than with some of his own comrades—and his indoctrination was often so imperfect that what was sometimes despairingly said of the American soldier in World War II would apply equally to him: he seemed to be fighting chiefly so that he could some day get back to Mom's cooking.

What really set the Civil War soldier apart was the fact that he came from a less sophisticated society. He was no starry-eyed innocent, to be sure—or, if he was, the army quickly took care of that—but the America of the 1860's was less highly developed than modern America. It lacked the ineffable advantages of radio, television, and moving pictures. It was still essentially a rural nation; it had growing cities, but they were smaller and somehow less urban than today's cities; a much greater percentage of the population lived on farms or in country towns and villages than is the case now, and there was more of a backwoods, hayseed-in-the-hair flavor to the people who came from them. . . .

Because of his unsophistication, the ordinary soldier in the Civil War, North and South alike, usually joined up with very romantic ideas about soldiering. Army life rubbed the romance off just as rapidly then as it does now, but at the start every volunteer went into the army thinking that he was heading off to high adventure. Under everything else, he enlisted because he thought army life was going to be fun, and usually it took quite a few weeks in camp to disabuse him of this strange notion. Right at the start, soldiering had an almost idyllic quality; if this quality faded rapidly, the memory of it remained through all the rest of life.

Early days in camp simply cemented the idea. An Illinois recruit, writing home from training camp, confessed: "It is fun to lie around, face unwashed, hair uncombed, shirt unbuttoned and everything un-everythinged. It sure beats clerking." Another Illinois boy confessed: "I don't see why people will stay at home when they can get to soldiering. A year of it is worth getting shot for to any man." And a Massachusetts boy, recalling the early days of army life, wrote that "Our drill, as I remember it, consisted largely of running around the

Old Westbury town hall, yelling like Devils and firing at an imaginary foe."
One of the commonest discoveries that comes from a reading of Civil War
diaries is that the chief worry, in training camp, was a fear that the war would
be over before the ardent young recruits could get into it. It is only fair to say
that most of the diarists looked back on this innocent worry, a year or so
afterward, with rueful amusement. . . .

Discipline in those early regiments was sketchy. The big catch was that most
regiments were recruited locally—in one town, or one county, or in one part of a
city—and everybody more or less knew everybody else. Particularly, the
privates knew their officers—most of whom were elected to their jobs by the
enlisted men—and they never saw any sense in being formal with them. Within
reasonable limits, the Civil War private was willing to do what his company
commander told him to do, but he saw little point in carrying it to extremes.

So an Indiana soldier wrote: "We had enlisted to put down the Rebellion, and
had no patience with the red-tape tomfoolery of the regular service. The boys
recognized no superiors, except in the line of legitimate duty. Shoulder straps
waived, a private was ready at the drop of a hat to thrash his commander—a
thing that occurred more than once." A New York regiment, drilling on a hot
parade ground, heard a private address his company commander thus: "Say,
Tom, let's quit this darn foolin' around and go over to the sutler's and get a
drink." There was very little of the "Captain, sir" business in those armies. If a
company or regimental officer got anything especial in the way of obedience, he
got it because the enlisted men recognized him as a natural leader and superior
and not just because he had a commission signed by Abraham Lincoln.

Odd rivalries developed between regiments. (It should be noted that the Civil
War soldier's first loyalty went usually to his regiment, just as a navy man's
loyalty goes to his ship; he liked to believe that his regiment was better than all
others, and he would fight for it, any time and anywhere.) The army legends of
those days tell of a Manhattan regiment, camped near Washington, whose
nearest neighbor was a regiment from Brooklyn, with which the Manhattanites
nursed a deep rivalry. Neither regiment had a chaplain; and there came to the
Manhattan colonel one day a minister, who volunteered to hold religious
services for the men in the ranks.

The colonel doubted that this would be a good idea. His men, he said, were
rather irreligious, not to say godless, and he feared they would not give the
reverend gentleman a respectful hearing. But the minister said he would take
his chances; after all, he had just held services with the Brooklyn regiment, and
the men there had been very quiet and devout. That was enough for the colonel.
What the Brooklyn regiment could do, his regiment could do. He ordered the
men paraded for divine worship, announcing that any man who talked, laughed,
or even coughed would be summarily court-martialed.

So the clergyman held services, and everyone was attentive. At the end of the sermon, the minister asked if any of his hearers would care to step forward and make public profession of faith; in the Brooklyn regiment, he said, fourteen men had done this. Instantly the New York colonel was on his feet.

"Adjutant!" he bellowed. "We're not going to let that damn Brooklyn regiment beat us at anything. Detail twenty men and have them baptized at once!"

Each regiment seemed to have its own mythology. Tales which may have been false but which, by their mere existence, reflected faithfully certain aspects of army life. The 48th New York, for instance, was said to have an unusually large number of ministers in its ranks, serving not as chaplains but as combat soldiers. The 48th, fairly early in the war, found itself posted in a swamp along the South Carolina coast, toiling mightily in semitropical heat, amid clouds of mosquitoes, to build fortifications, and it was noted that all hands became excessively profane, including the one-time clergymen. A visiting general, watching the regiment at work one day, recalled the legend and asked the regiment's lieutenant colonel if he himself was a minister in private life.

"Well, no, General," said the officer apologetically. "I can't say that I was a regularly ordained minister. I was just one of these ___ ___ local preachers." ...

Above and beyond everything else, of course, the business of the Civil War soldier was to fight. He fought with weapons that look very crude to modern eyes, and he moved by an outmoded system of tactics, but the price he paid when he got into action was just as high as the price modern soldiers pay despite the almost infinite development of firepower since the 1860's.

Standard infantry weapon in the Civil War was the rifled Springfield—a muzzle-loader firing a conical lead bullet, usually of .54 caliber.

To load was rather laborious, and it took a good man to get off more than two shots a minute. The weapon had a range of nearly a mile, and its "effective range"—that is, the range at which it would hit often enough to make infantry fire truly effective—was figured at about 250 yards. Compared with a modern Garand, the old muzzle-loader is no better than a museum piece; but compared with all previous weapons—the weapons on which infantry tactics in the 1860's were still based—it was a fearfully destructive and efficient piece.

For the infantry of that day still moved and fought in formations dictated in the old days of smoothbore muskets, whose effective range was no more than 100 yards and which were wildly inaccurate at any distance. Armies using those weapons attacked in solid mass formations, the men standing, literally, elbow to elbow. They could get from effective range to hand-to-hand fighting in a very short time, and if they had a proper numerical advantage over the defensive line they could come to grips without losing too many men along the way. But in the Civil War the conditions had changed radically; men would be hit while the rival lines were still half a mile apart, and to advance in mass was simply to invite wholesale destruction. Tactics had not yet been adjusted to the new rifles;

as a result, Civil War attacks could be fearfully costly, and when the defenders dug entrenchments and got some protection—as the men learned to do, very quickly—a direct frontal assault could be little better than a form of mass suicide.

It took the high command a long time to revise tactics to meet this changed situation, and Civil War battles ran up dreadful casualty lists. For an army to lose 25 per cent of its numbers in a major battle was by no means uncommon, and in some fights—the Confederate army at Gettysburg is an outstanding example—the percentage of loss ran close to one-third of the total number engaged. Individual units were sometimes nearly wiped out. Some of the Union and Confederate regiments that fought at Gettysburg lost up to 80 per cent of their numbers; a regiment with such losses was usually wrecked, as an effective fighting force, for the rest of the war.

The point of all of which is that the discipline which took the Civil War soldier into action, while it may have been very sketchy by modern standards, was nevertheless highly effective on the field of battle. Any armies that could go through such battles as Antietam, Stone's River, Franklin or Chickamauga and come back for more had very little to learn about the business of fighting.

Perhaps the Confederate General D. H. Hill said it, once and for all. The Battle of Malvern Hill, fought on the Virginia peninsula early in the summer of 1862, finished the famous Seven Days campaign, in which George B. McClellan's Army of the Potomac was driven back from in front of Richmond by Robert E. Lee's Army of Northern Virginia. At Malvern Hill, McClellan's men fought a rear-guard action—a bitter, confused fight which came at the end of a solid week of wearing, costly battles and forced marches. Federal artillery wrecked the Confederate assault columns, and at the end of the day Hill looked out over the battlefield, strewn with dead and wounded boys. Shaking his head, and reflecting on the valor in attack and in defense which the two armies had displayed, Hill never forgot about this. Looking back on it, long after the war was over, he declared, in substance:

"Give me Confederate infantry and Yankee artillery and I'll whip the world!"

"Hayfoot, Strawfoot!", American Heritage, *April, 1957*

SHERIDAN'S ARMY

The first things [the soldiers of the Army of the Shenandoah] saw were the little things. When the army marched [the new general, Phil] Sheridan was always up near the front, taking personal charge. If traffic jams or road

Infantry drill in camp, the Army of the Potomac

blocks developed, the officer who galloped up to straighten matters out was Sheridan himself. Sometimes he stormed and swore, and sometimes, when others were excited, he was controlled and soft-spoken; either way, he struck sparks and got action. If infantry was ordered to march in the fields and woods so that wagons and guns could have the road, Sheridan got off the road too and went with the foot soldiers. Marches went more smoothly, and camp life ran as if someone was in charge again, and it began to dawn on the men that many of the pesky little annoyances of military existence were disappearing. . . .

It was noticed, too, that army headquarters was managed without fuss and feathers. Headquarters in the Army of the Potomac had been elaborate and formal—many tents, much pomp and show, honor guards in fussy Zouave uniforms, a gaudy headquarters flag bearing a golden eagle in a silver wreath on a solferino background; the whole having caused U. S. Grant, the first time he saw it, to rein in his horse and inquire if Imperial Caesar lived anywhere near. Sheridan made do with two tents and two tent flies, and he had no honor guard. Instead he had a collection of two-gun scouts dressed in Confederate uniforms, who were probably the toughest daredevils in the army.

There were perhaps a hundred of them, the outgrowth of a small detail originally selected for special jobs from the 17th Pennsylvania Cavalry. They were a peculiar combination of intelligence operatives, communications experts, counterespionage men, and sluggers. They spent nearly as much time within the Rebel lines as in their own—they had "learned to talk the Southern language," as one of them put it, and they made themselves familiar with every regiment, brigade, and division in Early's army—and the biggest part of their job was to keep Sheridan at all times up to date on the enemy's strength, movements, and dispositions. If captured, of course, they could expect nothing better than to be hanged to the nearest tree, and they always ran a fair chance of being potted by Yankee outposts, since they did look like Rebels. They tended to be an informal and individualistic lot.

In part, the existence of this group reflected one of Sheridan's pet ideas— that daring and quick reflexes were worth more than muscle. Standing by a campfire with his staff one evening, Sheridan remarked that the ideal cavalry regiment would consist of men between eighteen and twenty-two years of age, none weighing more than 130 pounds and not one of them married. Little, wiry men could stand the pounding better than the big husky ones, Sheridan felt, and a Pennsylvanian who heard him agreed. He had noticed that skinny little chaps from the coal breakers usually outlasted the brawny deer hunters and bear trappers who came down from the mountains. And only young bachelors were properly reckless.

A Stillness at Appomattox

A MODEL MAJOR GENERAL

General Winfield Scott Hancock was a direct actionist, who both looked and acted like a soldier—a burly, handsome man, who somehow managed always to be wearing a clean white shirt even when the army had been in the field for weeks, and who, in an army where the officers were notably profane, was outstanding for the vigor, range, and effectiveness of his cursing. His men liked to tell how, at the Battle of Williamsburg, he had galloped up, outdistancing his staff, to order his troops to the charge—"the air was blue all around him," one of them recalled admiringly. There was a great breezy vigor and bluffness about the man. Earlier in the war, when his brigade was still in training, his men had taken to killing and eating the sheep of farmers near camp, and Hancock had determined to stop it. One afternoon, riding the lines near his camp, he had seen a knot of soldiers in a meadow, bending over the body of a sheep. Putting his horse to the fence, he galloped up, shouting mightily, and the men of course scattered—all except one who tarried too long and whom Hancock, flinging himself from his saddle, seized with strong hands.

"Now, you scoundrel, don't tell me you didn't kill that sheep—I saw you with my own eyes!" roared the general. Just then the sheep, not yet knifed, realized that it was no longer being held and sprang to its feet and scampered nimbly away. Hancock stared at the rocketing sheep, looked blankly at the quaking soldier in his hands—and then threw his head back and made the meadow ring with shouts of laughter.

Mr. Lincoln's Army

"BE PATIENT WITH GENERALS"

Not everyone in shoulder straps was a Grant, a Sheridan or a Hancock. In the Army of the Potomac, particularly, such men often seemed outnumbered by the conceited, the indecisive and the pig-headed, to the endless vexation of people trying to get a job done—like Herman Haupt, struggling to get supply trains through to General John Pope at Manassas in August 1862. While officialdom stumbled, a second defeat at Bull Run was in the offing.

Although he had been trained as a soldier—he had been graduated from West Point in 1835, in the same class with George Gordon Meade—Haupt was essentially a civilian. Resigning his commission shortly after graduation, he had gone into railroad work, had built a good part of the Juniata division of the Pennsylvania Railroad, and had become, successively, division superintendent and chief engineer for that line. He had been brought into the army, somewhat against his will, as a railroad and construction expert, and he was admired in high places. President Lincoln liked to tell about the marvelous bridge Haupt had built "out of beanpoles and cornstalks" down on the Aquia Creek line out of Fredericksburg. Haupt actually belonged in the next century; as it was, in the Civil War most generals failed to appreciate him. He was used to direct action, and generals irritated him. His present job gave them many occasions to do this, and they never seemed to miss a chance. Three days ago, for example, Haupt had bestirred himself to assemble trains to send General Joe Hooker's division forward to Pope. He got the trains lined up, Hooker's troops were at hand ready to go aboard, but Hooker himself had vanished— presumably to seek the fleshpots in Washington. Haupt telegraphed to his good friend and brother railroad man, P. H. Watson, Assistant Secretary of War. Back came Watson's reply:

"General Hooker was in Alexandria last night, but I will send to Willard's and see if he is there. I do not know any other place that he frequents. Be as patient as possible with the generals; some of them will trouble you more than they do the enemy."

That was a judgment with which Haupt was ready to agree. He had no sooner got Hooker out of his hair than General Samuel D. Sturgis got into it. Sturgis showed up with a division of troops, demanding immediate transportation to the front. To make sure that his request for transportation got top priority Sturgis had moved his soldiers out and had seized the railroad—or that part of it which lay within his reach, which was enough to tie up the entire line—swearing that no trains would go anywhere until his division had been moved. Haupt tried to reason with him, but it was no go—Haupt was a colonel and Sturgis was a general, and Sturgis would not listen. Sturgis had the rank and he had the soldiers, and for the moment he had the railroad, too, and no temporary colonel was going to tell him what to do.

Haupt had had to go through that sort of thing before. General Pope had had similar ideas when he first took command in northern Virginia, announcing that his own quartermaster would control the movement of railroad cars just as he ran the wagon trains, and informing Haupt that his function was to do as he was told. Within two weeks the line had got into such a snarl that no trains could move in any direction. Pope came to see that it took a railroad man to run a railroad—he could get a point now and then if it was obvious enough, could John Pope, for all his bluster—and he was glad to hand the road back to Colonel Haupt: particularly so since Haupt by this time had got from the Secretary of War an order giving him complete and unqualified control over the railroad and everything on it, regardless of the orders any army commander might issue. Haupt, therefore, was ready to take Sturgis in his stride; but Sturgis had troops and guns and swore he would use them. Furious, Haupt telegraphed Halleck, getting in return a bristling order which specifically authorized him, in the name of the general-in-chief, to put Sturgis under arrest if there was any more funny business. Haupt summoned Sturgis to his office Sturgis came, rather elevated with liquor, accompanied by his chief of staff.

Haupt showed Halleck's order and explained that he was getting all sorts of troops and supplies forward to General Pope and that Sturgis would simply have to wait his turn. Sturgis was not impressed, and he somehow got the idea that the order Haupt was exhibiting had been issued by General Pope.

"I don't care for John Pope one pinch of owl dung," said Sturgis solemnly—a sentiment which had its points but was hardly germane. Patiently Haupt explained: this order was not from Pope, it was from Halleck, who held the power to bind and to loose. Sturgis shook his head and repeated his judgment of Pope, savoring the sentence as if the thought had been bothering him for a long time. Haupt fluttered the order at him and went over it a third time. Sturgis, his needle stuck in one groove, repeated:

"I don't care for John Pope——"

His chief of staff tugged at his sleeve to stop him, and hastily and earnestly whispered in his ear. Sturgis blinked, finally got the point, and rose to his feet ponderously.

"Well, then," he said—with what, all things considered, might be called owlish dignity, "*take* your damned railroad."

Mr. Lincoln's Army

COLONEL WILDER GETS SOME ADVICE

In August and September of 1862 Generals Braxton Bragg and Edmund Kirby Smith launched a bold but disjointed invasion of Kentucky, hoping to rally the people of that border state to the Southern cause. While Federal general Don Carlos Buell lumbered up in pursuit, panic spread through Ohio, and at Munfordville, Kentucky, a Union colonel would presently find himself in an awkward, unfamiliar situation.

B ragg was driving north, and Buell's men marched hard in a vain effort to overtake him. Bragg came up thirty miles east of Bowling Green, which had marked the center of Albert Sidney Johnston's line just a year earlier, and at Munfordville, where the railroad to Louisville crossed the Green River, he struck a Federal strong point held by 4000 men under Colonel John T. Wilder, who until recently had been an unassuming Indiana business man and who now was about to add a strange little footnote to the story of the Civil War.

Bragg's advance guard attacked the fortifications twice and was repulsed with moderate loss. Then Bragg brought up the rest of his army and sent in a demand for surrender, pointing out that the Federals were surrounded and that their case was hopeless. Through the Confederate lines that night came a flag of truce and a Yankee officer—Colonel Wilder in person, seeking a conference with Major General Buckner, who led a division in Hardee's corps. In Buckner's tent Wilder became disarmingly frank. He was not, he said, a military man at all, but he did want to do the right thing. He had heard that Buckner was not only a professional soldier but an honest gentleman as well; and would Buckner now please tell him if, under the rules of the game, it was Colonel Wilder's duty to surrender or to fight it out?

Somewhat flabbergasted—he said later that he "would not have deceived that man under those circumstances for anything"—Buckner said Wilder would have to make his own decision. (He knew what a weight that was. Seven months earlier he had had to surrender Fort Donelson, his superiors having fled from responsibility, and when he sent a flag through the Yankee lines his old friend Grant had been merciless.) Buckner pointed out that Wilder's men were hemmed in by six times their own numbers and that Bragg had enough artillery in line to destroy the fort in short order; at the same time, if the sacrifice of every man would aid the Federal cause elsewhere, it was Wilder's duty to fight. . . . In the end, Buckner took him to see Bragg, who was curt with him but let him count the cannon in the Confederate works. Wilder counted enough to convince him that the jig was up, and at last he surrendered: a well-meaning but bewildered citizen-soldier who had gone to his enemy for professional advice and, all things considered, had been fairly dealt with.

Terrible Swift Sword

Burnside's army, facing Lee's after Fredericksburg, makes some new friends.

SECRET BROTHERHOOD

This army was doubly deficient—in leadership and in vindictiveness—and the men do not appear even to have tried to hate their enemies. On the contrary, they exercised a good deal of ingenuity in order to open a highly illegal but quite friendly trade with them, with the wide Rappahannock as the bearer of their peaceful cargoes. The classical essentials for a thriving peacetime trade were present; that is, each side had a surplus of goods greatly in demand by the other side, the Federals having plenty of coffee and the Confederates having an excess of tobacco. And as the pickets walked their posts by the river it soon occurred to Northerners and Southerners alike that the war would get on just as well and would be a good deal less onerous to the individual if some of that coffee could be swapped for some of that tobacco.

It is probable that every regiment which was stationed on the river took part in this trade at one time or another, and the routine was always much the same. The following appears to have been typical:

Sunny winter day: 17th Mississippi on picket on the Rebel side of the stream, 24th New Jersey guarding the shore just opposite. Shouted conversation over the water reveals a mutual desire to trade. Jersey men presently get a small board, whittle it into something resembling the shape of a boat, put in a mast, use an old letter for a sail, put a load of coffee aboard, point it for the Confederate shore, and let it go. The intention is good, but the performance is poor: the homemade craft capsizes in a mid-river gust of wind and floats off downstream, bottom up, its cargo a total loss.

Among the Mississippians there seem to have been men who knew a bit more about the design and construction of sailing vessels, and they presently brought a much more practical craft down to the water—a little boat two feet long or thereabouts and five or six inches wide, carefully hollowed out to provide cargo space and equipped with rudder and sails that would actually work. This boat made a successful passage. The Jersey soldiers who received it took from its hold a note reading:

"Gents U. S. Army: We send you some tobacco by our packet. Send us some coffee in return. Also a deck of cards, if you have them, and we will send you more tobacco. Send us any late papers if you have them." The letter was signed by "Jas. O. Parker, Co. H., 17th Mississippi Vols."

The vessel's lading was as stated in the manifest, and in addition there was a small book, *Questions on the Gospels*, by the Reverend R. Bethell Claxton, D.D., which one of the Federals kept with him through the rest of the war. And the Jersey men sent coffee and hardtack over on the little boat's return trip, with a note promising that there would be a deck of cards the next time the outfit came on picket. The boat made a number of round trips and became quite famous—so much so that the better part of each regiment would come down to the shore to greet it.

This tendency on the part of the soldiers to forget that there was a war on worried the high command, and stern orders were issued, to which the soldiers paid no more attention than they had to. Now and then the thing went farther than toy boats loaded with coffee and playing cards. Men crossed the river at times to get together personally with their enemies, and a Confederate general left a half-scandalized, half-amused account of how he nabbed a few Yankee soldiers visiting his own men and prepared to send them off to Richmond as prisoners of war, only to have his men plead almost tearfully that he just couldn't do it—they had given the Yankees their word of honor that if they came over to visit they would be allowed to go back again. In the end the general relented on a stern don't-let-it-happen-again basis. The elements in this war were mixed and contradictory. If one side robbed corpses and the other side robbed housewives, there was on both sides, deep in the bones and the spirit, this strange absence of rancor, which may, in the end, explain why it was that the two sections were finally able to reunite after a war which would seem to have left scars too deep for any healing.

Glory Road

A CHEER FOR THE ENEMY

The Federals [went] flocking into [captured] Vicksburg. It was an odd sort of occupation. There was no cheering, and nobody turned any handsprings. Grant noted that "the men of the two armies fraternized as if they had been fighting for the same cause," and an officer who guided a wagon train of rations into the city wrote that the sight of the first Confederate brigade he passed, "every man of which looked so gaunt and hungry," moved him so deeply that he simply stopped and broke open his barrels and boxes of hardtack, sugar and coffee and dealt out a liberal allowance to everybody within sight. He was rewarded, he said, by "the heartfelt thanks and cheers" of the Confederates, and that night when his own men complained that their rations were deficient "I swore by all the saints in the calendar that the wagons had broken down and the Johnnie Rebs had stolen all of the grub." One Confederate staff officer who rode a white pony, on which he had daily made the circuit of the Confederate lines, was brightly accosted by a Unionist, who sang out: "See here, Mister— you man on the little white horse. Danged if you ain't the hardest feller to hit I ever saw; I've shot at you more'n a hundred times!" He remembered, too, that the only cheer he heard on the day of Federal occupation was a cheer which one Federal outfit raised for "the gallant defenders of Vicksburg."

Grant Moves South

OVER-AGE

The 37th Iowa Volunteer Infantry, numbering 914 rank and file [was] a regiment like all others except for one thing—everyone from colonel to drummer boy was safely past the upper military age limit of forty-five years. (Many of them were over sixty, some were in their seventies, and one sprightly private confessed to the age of eighty.)

This was Iowa's famous "Graybeard Regiment," recruited by special arrangement with the War Department as a means of showing that there were plenty of draft-proof citizens who were perfectly willing to go to war. There was a tacit understanding that the regiment would be given guard and garrison duty as much as possible, but there was nothing binding about this. The 37th was in no sense a home-guard outfit; it had enlisted for the full three years and eventually it was to campaign in Missouri, Tennessee, and Mississippi, hiking in the rain and sleeping in the mud like anybody else. During its three years only scattered detachments got into actual fighting—the total casualty list was only seven—but 145 men died of disease, and 364 had to be mustered out of service for physical disability, and when the regiment at last was paid off, in May of 1865, it was revealed that more than thirteen hundred sons and grandsons of members of the regiment were in Federal military service. So old were these men, and so young their state, that not a man in the regiment could claim Iowa as his birthplace. There had been no Iowa when these Iowans were born.

This Hallowed Ground

SYNTHESIS

Lee's army was immobilized, if still dangerous, behind entrenchments at Petersburg, the end not far away. But the great army slowly wearing him away was very different from the one that back in '61 had answered Lincoln's call for volunteers. In it Catton perceived glimpses of the future.

Underneath the grousing and the bills of complaint the army was trying to maintain a sense of the continuity of its own experiences and traditions. It had to do this, because actually this simply was not the army it used to be. Something like 100,000 combat men had come down across the Rapidan early in May (the flags were all flying and everything was bright and blowing and the dogwood blossoms lit the shadows in the woods) and 60,000 of them had been shot while many other thousands had been sent home as time-expired veterans, and so much the greater part of the men who had started out were not with the army any more. There were 86,000 men in the ranks at the end of June, and most of them were new men. What those who were gone had left behind them was the confusing raw material out of which a new morale would have to be made.

Always the army reflected the nation, and the nation itself was changing. Like the army, it contained many new people these days. The war had speeded everything up. The immigrant ships were coming faster, there were more factories and slums and farms and towns, and the magical hazy light that came down from the country's past was beginning to cast some unfamiliar shadows. The old unities were gone: unities of blood, of race, of language, of shared ideals and common memories and experiences, the very things which had always seemed essential beneath the word "American." In some mysterious way that nobody quite understood, the army not only mirrored the change but represented the effort to find a new synthesis.

What was going on in front of Petersburg was not the development of a stalemate, or the aimless groping of frozen men stumbling down to the last dead end of a cold trail. What was beginning meant more than what was ending, even though it might be many years before anyone knew just what the beginnings and the endings were. Now and then there was a hint, casually dropped, as the country changed the guard here south of the Appomattox River, and the choking dust hung in dead air under a hot copper sun. The men who followed a misty dream had died of it, but the dream still lived, even though it was taking another form.

There was in the 67th New York Infantry a young German named Sebastian Muller, who got off an immigrant ship in 1860 and walked the streets unable to find work because he could speak no English and because times in this land of promise were harder than he had supposed they would be. The war came and in 1861 a recruiting agent got him, and to his people back in the fatherland Muller wrote: "I am a volunteer soldier in the Army of the United States, to fight the rebels of South America for a sacred thing. All of America has to become free and united and the starry banner has to fly again over the new world. Then we also want to have the slaves freed, the trading of human beings must have an end and every slave should be set free and on his own in time. . . . Evil of all kinds, thievery, whoring, lying and deception have to be punished here."

Muller served in the 67th and on June 20, 1864, the regiment's time expired and it was sent back for muster-out. But he had enlisted a couple of months late, and he and a few others were held in service and were transferred to the 65th New York to serve out their time, and two days after the 67th went back home Muller was a picket in an advanced gun pit on the VI Corps front, and a Rebel sniper drew a bead on him and killed him. A German comrade wrote a letter of consolation to Muller's parents: "If a person is meant to die on land, he will not drown. If death on the battlefield is to be his lot, he will not die in the cradle. God's dispositions are wise and his ways are inscrutable." The chaplain added a note saying that Muller had died without pain and had been given "a decent Christian burial." That was that.

In the 19th Massachusetts there was an Irish sergeant named Mike Scannell—[who had] won his chevrons by carrying the flag at Cold Harbor—and in the II Corps debacle over by the Jerusalem Plank Road Mike and his flag were out in front and were taken by the Confederates, one of whom came at Mike with leveled bayonet, ordering: "You damned Yankee, give me that flag!" Mike looked at the Southerner and he looked at the bayonet, and he replied:

"Well, it is twenty years since I came to this country, and you are the first man who ever called me a Yankee. You can take the flag, for that compliment."

Nothing much had happened. A German who could not tell Virginia from South America had seen a sacred thing in the war and had died for it, and an Irishman after twenty years of rejection had been accepted, at the point of a bayonet but in the language of his time and place, as a full-fledged American.

The synthesis was taking place.

A Stillness at Appomattox

VETERAN BRIGADE, NEW RECRUITS

The [Iron Brigade] had been whittled thin these last few months. In mid-August [1862] it had mustered in its four regiments close to twenty-four hundred men. Three battles and five weeks later it stood at less than a thousand, and just before Antietam, General Gibbon had appealed to the high command to give him a new regiment—a Western regiment, if possible, since the Iron Brigade men came from Wisconsin and Indiana and would get on better with men from their own part of the country. A few weeks after Antietam his request was granted, and on October 9 the brigade was drawn up on the parade ground to give formal welcome to its new comrades, the brand-new soldiers of the 24th Michigan Volunteer Infantry.

The welcome was of the coldest, and the ceremony seems to have pleased no one. On one side of the parade stood the four regiments of veterans—19th Indiana and 2nd, 6th, and 7th Wisconsin: rangy, sun-tanned men in worn and dusty uniforms, who lounged in the ranks with that indefinable easy looseness which only veterans possess and who wore the black slouch hats which were the distinguishing headgear of this brigade as if they were badges of great honor—which, as a matter of fact, they were. The veterans looked across the open ground at the newcomers with complete and unconcealed skepticism and hostility. In every line of their bearing—in the set of their jaws, the tilt of their heads, the look about their eyes peering out from under those valued hatbrims—they expressed for all to see the age-old, impersonal, unformulated feeling of the veteran for the recruit: We have had it and you have not, and until you have been where we have been and have done what we have done we do not admit you to any kind of fellowship.

The boys from Michigan got the message perfectly. They came up to line nervously that morning, thoroughly aware that the newness and neatness of their uniforms proclaimed them rookies with the test of manhood still ahead of them. Their very numbers were a count against them. Here they were, one regiment, with nearly as many men present for duty, armed and equipped, as were present in all four of the regiments across the parade. With their arrival the brigade had nearly doubled in size. And with the inexorable illogic of the soldier, it was somehow just then the fault of these boys from Michigan, and a just ground for shame to them, that they brought 900 to the field instead of the veterans' 250.

In addition to which they wore the regulation forage caps instead of the black hats which the brigade had made famous.

Yet this mere matter of being new and green and clumsy would not, of itself, have caused real estrangement between the four veteran regiments and the one new one. The veterans would have been wary, of course, reserving judgment until they had seen these newcomers under fire, treating them with a lofty but not really malicious contempt until after their first battle, and then either outlawing them entirely or receiving them to full brotherhood without reservation. But they would not have given them a cold and savage hostility, which was what even the least sensitive mental antennae were picking up on this field today. For a damning word had come to camp ahead of this new regiment. Here, said camp rumor—unsubstantiated, but accepted as gospel—here were *bounty men.*

The bounty man was comparatively a new addition to the Army of the Potomac. For the most part, the army was still made up of what even then were beginning to be called "the old 1861 regiments": volunteers in the purest sense of the word, men who had enlisted for no earthly reason except that they wanted to go to war, moved by that strange and deceiving light which can lie upon the world very briefly when one is young and innocent. That light was leaving the landscape rapidly in 1862, and volunteering was much slower. To stimulate it, various states, cities, and counties were offering cash bounties to recruits: solid rolls of greenbacks, adding up, in some cases, to as much as a thousand dollars, and in all cases to several hundreds.

Now this business of the bounty somehow summed up all of the contrasting truths about the war—boom times, noble ideals becoming sullied, great opportunities for the calculating; plus the fact, beginning to be visible to private soldiers, that the man who was moved by pure patriotism and by nothing else was quite likely to get the worst of it. For while the bounties were enabling local units of government to fill their quotas, they were also bringing into the army a great many men whose primary concern in enlisting had been neither the saving of the Union nor the satisfaction of some sacred and indefinable inner instinct, but solely the acquisition of sudden wealth. Some of these men, having taken the money, might earn their wages by becoming good and faithful soldiers. Others would slack and skulk and beyond any question would desert the first time occasion offered—going off to some other state to enlist for another bounty, as likely as not. All of the confusion and contradiction of war were mixed up in this bounty system, in the way it worked and in the fact that it had been adopted at all.

The old volunteer regiments of the army were, conceivably, the last reservoir of the original hope, enthusiasm, and incredible lightness of spirit with which the war had begun. Beyond the scheming and the driving and the solid achieving of the governors and the generals and all the others, the war finally would come down to this spirit that lived in the breasts of the enlisted men. It was what the war was ultimately about, and if the war was finally going to be won it was what would win it, the men who had carried the spirit being killed, the spirit somehow surviving. The veteran inevitably drew a sharp distinction between the man who volunteered because this spirit moved him and the bounty boy who joined up for what there was in it; and here, in the Iron Brigade itself, proudest and hardest of the army's warriors, there was a bounty regiment!

Actually, there was nothing of the kind. Camp rumor once again had outrun the truth. Like every one of the thousands of regiments in the Civil War armies, this 24th Michigan had its own history, different from all of the others, just as each soldier had his individual biography, unwritten but unique. In plain fact, instead of being one of the first of the bounty regiments, this outfit was one of the last of the old rally-round-the-flag groups of simon-pure volunteers.

In July 1862 the mayor of Detroit had called an open-air mass meeting of patriotic citizens to consider how Detroit would provide recruits under the most recent call for 300,000 volunteers. The meeting had been a failure—had, indeed, broken up in an actual row. There had been hissings, catcalls, fisticuffs, until finally the speech-making dissolved in a free-for-all fight, with Southern sympathizers tearing down the speaker's rostrum and manhandling the speakers, and the sheriff and his deputies coming on the scene with drawn revolvers to restore order and send everybody home. Good citizens felt this as a shame and a disgrace. The rowdies who broke up the meeting, they declared, were not native Copperheads but secessionists-in-exile from Canadian Windsor, across the river. Detroit must redeem its good name; it did so, finally, by holding a new, better-policed citizens' meeting at which it was agreed that Wayne County should raise an extra regiment in addition to the six called for by the new quota.

A rousing campaign for recruits was put on. Judge Henry A. Morrow, who had seen some service in the war with Mexico, was made colonel of this extra regiment, and Sheriff Mark Flanigan—he who had led the flying wedge of deputies to subdue secession at the lamentable first mass meeting—was announced as lieutenant colonel; and by the end of August the regiment had been fully recruited. Many of the recruits were wage earners with families, and it would be some time before the army paymaster would make his rounds. To avert hardships, Detroit businessmen raised a relief fund and some of the men drew money from it—whence came the report that the 24th was a bounty regiment.

The 24th took off for the East just before the Army of the Potomac fought at Antietam, and it left Detroit in a fine glow of patriotic sentiment. Nearly all of its officers carried presentation swords—Colonel Morrow's the gift of the

Dead of the 24th Michigan Infantry, Gettysburg, 1863

Detroit bar, Lieutenant Colonel Flanigan's the gift of the deputy sheriffs of Wayne County, while one of the company officers carried one given by the printers of the Detroit *Free Press*, of whose composing room he had been foreman. The regiment was feted along the road en route east: there is mention of an elaborate banquet at Pittsburgh, where every man was presented with a bouquet by a pretty girl and where, as a veteran wrote later, "a portion of the regiment was in a fair way of being captured." The regiment got to Maryland just in time to see the dusty files of the Army of the Potomac marching up to the shattering fight at Antietam. After that battle was over the 24th was moved up to join the army, and it camped on the battlefield in dismaying closeness to a huge pile of amputated arms and legs.

Then came the ceremony by which the 24th joined the Iron Brigade. Colonel Morrow unfortunately felt that the occasion called for a speech and made one, pulling out all the stops to let the brigade know how glad the 24th was to be here. He drew for his pains a dead silence, not a cheer or a ripple to show that anybody had heard him. A diarist in the 24th wrote glumly: "A pretty cool reception, we thought. We had come out to reinforce them, and supposed they would be glad to see us."

The camp comradeship which these recruits had heard so much about would apparently have to be earned. It could be earned only in battle. Meanwhile, the regiment might as well get ready. It was drilled prodigiously; Colonel Morrow gave the boys battalion drill for six hours every day, with an additional four and one half hours of "other evolutions of the school of the soldier." When General Gibbon left the brigade for divisional command early in November, he told Morrow and the other field officers they had the best-drilled regiment he had ever seen for a rookie regiment.

This was heartening as word trickled down through the ranks. But it was not enough. There were those four veteran regiments which refused to warm up. The brigade broke camp and began a long march from the upper Potomac to the Rappahannock as the Army of the Potomac moved glacially southeast in a well-meant effort to get around Robert E. Lee's flank. As it moved it outmarched the wagon trains and the men went hungry. The 24th, which was living those days under an almost unendurable tension anyway, waiting for the chance to fight its way into the brigade's fellowship, set up a chant one rationless morning of "Bread! Bread! Bread!" The veteran regiments, equally unfed and for that matter equally capable of kicking up a noisy row over it, looked at them coldly and refused to join in the clamor. Once more the 24th had been put in its place.

December came, and the Iron Brigade, along with most of the rest of the army, went into camp near a little town called Falmouth, a mile or so upstream from the charming colonial city of Fredericksburg. There were flurries of snow and there was a good deal of cold rain, with abominable mud underfoot, and for the 24th Michigan there began that endless process of attrition which, for some regiments, was even more deadly than battle itself. Boys began to get sick, and many of the sick ones died. Like all new regiments, the 24th held formal military funerals in such cases, until one day a rookie soldier on the firing squad mistakenly loaded his musket with ball cartridge and shot a comrade through the body. This might have caused the veterans to jeer—clumsy soldiers who shot each other at a military funeral!—but it did not happen. The veterans were not even admitting the 24th to the implied comradeship of derision. They were simply cold and aloof.

This new regiment would have only one chance at salvation. Before long, by signs which even the private soldiers could read, the army would go across the Rappahannock to fight. When that day came, the 24th would have to prove itself. Its salvation, like so many other values in this strange and terrible war, would in the end have to be bought by the stand-up valor of the private soldier.

Glory Road

The 24th bought their way into the fraternity of the Iron Brigade by desperate courage on the field of Fredericksburg, even pausing during an attack to run through the manual of arms in highly professional style—parade-ground bravado under a hail of bullets. At Gettysburg, the Iron Brigade lost two-thirds of its men, and little of it remained thereafter except a great reputation. But in that fearful struggle, the 24th Michigan lost eight out of ten men, a final payment on what was almost a ghostly acceptance.

V

The Valley of the Shadow

Unknown dead, Gettysburg National Cemetery, near where Lincoln spoke

June, 1863, found Robert E. Lee and his Army of Northern Virginia again crossing the Potomac and heading north into Pennsylvania, striking the enemy's country. Trudging in pursuit came the long-suffering Army of the Potomac, up from the river, over many hot and muddy roads, with a new commander, General George Gordon Meade, at its head. Pennsylvania had taken alarm and called out its unblooded militia; Washington worried about a Confederate blow at the Capital; and the two armies groped toward a fateful meeting in the little town of Gettysburg.

The order was out for forced marches—Meade disagreed with Hooker's strategy, feeling that his cue was to follow Lee north and force him to turn and fight—and for a day or so the fate of the Union was going to rest on the sinewy legs of the men who had to do the marching.

The army came up from the Potomac, and some of the men were taken up a narrow strip of land between the river and the Chesapeake and Ohio Canal, the march continuing long after dark, rain coming down and mud underfoot and Cimmerian darkness all around. [General Andrew] Humphreys was in command—Humphreys, grandson of the naval constructor who had designed the U.S.S. *Constitution*, a slim dapper driver who had taken over Berry's old division in the III Corps. Humphreys was a grim courtly man who just before he took his troops up to the stone wall at Fredericksburg had bowed to his staff and had said pleasantly: "Gentlemen, I shall lead this charge; I presume, of course, you will wish to ride with me?" Since it was put like that, staff had so wished, and five of the seven officers got knocked off their horses. He was a stickler for the regulations, and the United States Army has possessed few better soldiers, and he was driving his men north now without regard for human frailty.

The march went on and on, and men fell out and lay down in the mud and went to sleep. When the rain stopped, men who kept going lighted candles and stuck them in the muzzle of their rifles, and the straggling column lurched on, will-o'-the-wisp fires flickering in the night, and the riverbank was lined for ten or fifteen miles with officers and men who could not keep up. One survivor wrote that "it was impossible to say whether colonels and brigadier generals had lost their commands, or regiments and brigades had lost their commanders." When day came, after a sketchy bivouac, the column pulled itself together—Humphreys was the man to see to that—and by noon all hands were accounted for and the march was going on compactly again.

Up past Frederick they went, pulling for the Pennsylvania line, and the men's spirits rose with the green fields and blue mountains about them, citizens cheering them on when they passed through towns, girls standing by farmhouse doors to wave flags and offer drinks of cold water. The army had its own method of greeting these girls. The wolf-call whistle was unknown to soldiers of that era, but they had an equivalent—an abrupt, significant clearing of the throat, or cough, which burst out spontaneously whenever a line of march went by a nice-looking young woman, so that at such a time, as one veteran said, "the men seemed terribly and suddenly afflicted with some bronchial affection." Coughing and grunting, and vastly pleased with themselves, the men followed the dusty roads, and while they had no idea where they were going, it seemed to them that at last they were marching to victory.

Glory Road

A FIVE-DOLLAR FINE

As it reached Pennsylvania the army began to encounter militia regiments—regiments dressed in fancy uniforms, carrying the full complement of equipment, with muskets polished until the barrels shone like mirrors. The veterans looked at these militiamen with dour curiosity and uttered wisecracks designed to put the holiday soldiers in their places. North of Frederick the XII Corps encountered the New York 7th, a dandy regiment wearing, among other things, nice white gloves. There was a rain coming down and the roadside was muddy, and the militiamen were not looking their best as [General Henry W.] Slocum's veterans cast critical eyes on them. The XII Corps advised the militiamen to come in out of the rain before the dress-parade uniforms got spoiled, asked them where their umbrellas were, and suggested that the boys join the army someday and see what soldiering was like. On another road the VI Corps met a Brooklyn home-guard regiment dressed in uniforms of natty gray, and the veterans coldly advised the militia to dye those uniforms blue: if they ever got into a fight the Army of the Potomac was apt to shoot anybody it saw who came to the field in a gray uniform. Now and then a veteran would ask the home guards where they buried their dead.

As it moved the army covered a very wide front, thirty-five or forty miles from tip to tip. Orders were vague because plans were vague. Lee's army was somewhere between York, on the east, and Chambersburg on the west, and as June ended it became apparent that the Confederates were beginning to pull their far-flung detachments together, heading toward some sort of concentration east of the long barrier of South Mountain. Meade considered that when it came to a fight the line of Pipe Creek, a meandering little stream along the Pennsylvania border, would be a good place for the Army of the Potomac to make its stand. He was uneasy about it—Halleck was warning him that he was pretty far west and that Lee might be able to make a dash around his right and strike at Baltimore or Washington—and he kept his men pushing on, tentacles of cavalry reaching forward, looking for a contact. In York an agent of the

Sanitary Commission got inside the Rebel lines and took a look at one of Ewell's camps, finding the Rebels "well stripped for action and capable of fast movement."

"Physically, the men looked about equal to the generality of our own troops, and there were fewer boys among them," this man wrote. "Their dress was a wretched mixture of all cuts and colors. There was not the slightest attempt at uniformity in this respect. Every man seemed to have put on whatever he could get hold of, without regard to shape or color. . . . Their shoes, as a general thing, were poor; some of the men were entirely barefooted. Their equipments were light as compared with those of our men. They consisted of a thin woolen blanket, coiled up and slung from the shoulder in the form of a sash, a haversack swung from the opposite shoulder, and a cartridge box. The whole cannot weigh more than twelve or fourteen pounds." He asked one of these lanky Rebels if they had no shelter tents, and the soldier was scornful of such comforts, saying, "I just wouldn't tote one."

John Buford was leading his cavalry division north from Frederick and Emmitsburg, prowling close to the slope of South Mountain, trying to find the enemy. On the last day of June, after narrowly missing a collision at the little town of Fairfield, he drew a bit farther to the east and late in the afternoon brought his men into the town of Gettysburg, a pleasant place in the open hilly country where many roads converged, with the long blue mass of the mountain chain lying on the horizon off to the west. Confederate patrols had been in the town, and they went west on the Cashtown pike as Buford's troopers came in. Somewhere not far beyond them, clearly, there must be a solid body of Rebel infantry. Buford strung a heavy picket line along a north-and-south ridge west of town, threw more pickets out to cover the roads to the north (army intelligence warned that Ewell's corps was apt to be coming down those roads from Carlisle before long), and snugged down for the night with headquarters in a theological seminary. . . .

There was a bright moon that night, and most of the army kept to the road long after the sun had gone down. Nothing had actually happened yet, but there was a stir in the air, and the first faint tug had been felt from the line that had been thrown into Gettysburg, a quiet hint that something was apt to pull the whole army together on those long ridges and wooded hills. . . .

Colonel Strong Vincent, leading a brigade in the V Corps, took his men through a little town, where the moonlight lay bright on the street, and in every doorway there were girls waving flags and cheering. The battle flags were broken out of their casings and the men went through the town in step with music playing, and Gettysburg lay a few miles ahead. Vincent reined in his horse and let the head of the column pass him, and as the colors went by he took off his hat, and he sat there quietly, watching the flags moving on in the silver light, the white dresses of the girls bright in the doorways, shimmering faintly in the cloudy luminous dusk under the shade trees on the lawns. To an aide who sat beside him the colonel mused aloud: There could be worse fates than to die fighting here in Pennyslvania, with that flag waving overhead. . . .

There was the long white road in the moonlight, with the small-town girls laughing and crying in the shadows, and the swaying ranks of young men waving to them and moving on past them. To these girls who had been nowhere and who had all of their lives before them this was the first of all the roads of the earth, and to many of the young men who marched off under the moon it was the last of all the roads. For all of them, boys and girls alike, it led to unutterable mystery. The column passed on through the town and the music stopped and the flags were put back in their casings, and the men went marching on and on.

In the Gettysburg cemetery, quiet on a hilltop just south of the town, there was a wooden sign by the gatepost—just legible, no doubt, in the last of the June moonlight, if anyone had bothered to go up there and read it—announcing that the town would impose a five-dollar fine on anyone who discharged a firearm within the cemetery limits.

Glory Road

"DO YOU SEE THOSE COLORS?"

On July 1st, 2nd, and 3rd, 1863, the town of Gettysburg might—very theoretically—have grown rich on fines. On those three days a battle of ever increasing intensity gripped the two armies. Toward the end of the seesaw fighting of the second day came the great moment of the 1st Minnesota Regiment, part of the corps led by General Winfield Scott Hancock.

It was getting dark and the air was streaky and blurred with smoke, and the advancing Confederate masses were almost indistinguishable in the twilight. Reinforcements were coming up from the Union right and rear at last, and officers were casting forward looking for the spots where these new troops were needed the most.

Among these officers was Hancock, and he saw a Confederate brigade advancing toward him, its uneven line coming up out of a little hollow a hundred yards off. He trotted back, saw a Union regiment coming up in column of fours, and galloped over to it, It was the 1st Minnesota out of his own corps. Hancock pointed to the Rebel line, whose flags were just visible in the murk.

"Do you see those colors?" he demanded. The regiment's Colonel Colville had just been released from arrest, which he had incurred by refusing to make his men wade a creek on the march north. He looked forward and nodded laconically.

General George E. Pickett, C. S. A.

"Well, capture them!" barked Hancock.

Down the ridge came the 1st Minnesota, still in column of fours, and it hit the slightly disordered Rebel column and knocked it back. The Rebels quickly rallied from the shock—they greatly outnumbered this lone Minnesota regiment—and they formed a firing line in the underbrush and woods on the edge of the ravine, and the Minnesota men swung into a line of their own, and the fire lit the dusk like great flashes of irregular sheet lightning. The Confederates worked their way around on each flank and got the 1st Minnesota into a pocket, sending their fire in from three sides, and the whole war had suddenly come to a focus in this smoky hollow, with a few score Westerners trading their lives for the time the army needed. Off to the left, [Lieutenant Colonel Freeman] McGilvery saw what was up, and while the Confederate batteries by the Emmitsburg road concentrated their fire on him he swung his guns around and pounded the underbrush with canister, and on the other side Hancock found some more troops and sent them in. After a time the Confederates began to draw back, and when they came out into the open the guns hit them hard, and finally they went into full retreat.

What was left of the Minnesota regiment came back to reorganize. It had taken 262 men into action and it had 47 men left, and the survivors boasted that while the casualties amounted to 82 per cent (which seems to have been a record for the Union Army for the entire war) there was not a straggler or a prisoner of war on the entire list. They had not captured the flag that Hancock had asked them to capture, but they still had their own flag and a great name, plus those 47 exhausted survivors, and as they came back it might have been as John Bunyan wrote: "So he passed over, and all the trumpets sounded for him on the other side."

Glory Road

THERE COMES THE INFANTRY!

The climax at Gettysburg came on the afternoon of the third day. After the greatest cannonade in all previous American history, General Lee threw his final blow at the long Federal line along Cemetery Ridge.

The smoke lifted like a rising curtain, and all of the great amphitheater lay open at last, and the Yankee soldiers could look west all the way to the belt of trees on Seminary Ridge. They were old soldiers and had been in many battles, but what they saw then took their breath away, and whether they had ten minutes or seventy-five years yet to live, they remembered it until they died. There it was, for the last time in this war, perhaps for the last time anywhere, the grand pageantry and color of war in the old style, beautiful and majestic and terrible: fighting men lined up for a mile and a half from flank to flank, slashed red flags overhead, soldiers marching forward elbow to elbow, officers with drawn swords, sunlight gleaming from thousands of musket barrels, lines dressed as if for parade. Up and down the Federal firing line ran a low murmur: "There they are. . . . There comes the infantry!"

Lee was putting fifteen thousand men into this column—George Pickett riding into storybook immortality with his division of Virginians, Heth's division led today by General Pettigrew, two brigades of Pender's division under General Trimble, coming out of the woods to march across a mile-wide valley to the heights where the Yankees were waiting with shotted guns. Rank after rank came out of the shadows, and the Rebel cannon were all silent now, gunners standing aside to let the infantry come through, and for the moment the Federal guns were silent too, as if both armies were briefly dazzled by the war's most dramatic moment. In the Confederate line there were officers on horseback, and if the Federals looked closely they might have seen one who held his sword high over his head, his black felt hat on the point of it as a guide for his brigade—General Lewis Armistead, who was coming over the valley to meet death and an old friend.

Back in the spring of 1861, when the country was just breaking apart and officers of the regular army were choosing their sides, there was a farewell party one evening in the officers' quarters of the army post at the little California town of Los Angeles. The host was Captain Winfield Scott Hancock, and he was giving the party to say good-by to certain Southern officers who were going east to Richmond, where they would take commissions with the new Confederacy. The departing guests were sad—it was not easy for those regulars to cut loose from the army they had given their lives to—and a tragic shadow lay across the little gathering, and just before the party broke up Mrs. Albert Sidney Johnston sat at the piano and sang "Kathleen Mavourneen." Good-by and good-by, the gray dawn will be breaking soon and our old comradeship in this intimate little army world is fading, it may be for years and it may be forever. When the song was ended Major Armistead came over and put his hands on Hancock's shoulders, tears streaming down his cheeks, and said: "Hancock, good-by—you can never know what this has cost me." Then the guests left, and next morning Armistead and the others started east, and a little later Hancock himself came east to fight on the Northern side, and he and Armistead had not seen each other since. Now Hancock was on his horse on Cemetery Ridge, waiting with the guns all around him, and Armistead was coming up the slope with his black felt hat on the end of his sword, and the strange roads of war the two old friends had followed were coming together at last. . . .

Long and bright and perfectly aligned, the lines came down the far slope and began crossing the valley, and the open space in front was dotted by little bursts of smoke as the rival skirmishers began to shoot at each other. This was the moment General Hunt had been waiting for, and all along the left of the Union line the guns opened fire and began to hit those neat ranks, tearing ragged holes in them. On Little Round Top the rifled guns that had been lugged up over the rocks the afternoon before were finding the range, and McGilvery's long line was flaming and crashing, and the Rebels were closing the gaps as they moved forward—no Rebel yell now, the men were coming on silently, they were still out of musket range. The yelling and the firing and the stabbing would come later.

Pickett's division was at the southern end of the advancing line, and Pickett's objective was the clump of trees under which General Webb had been smoking his pipe. Pickett wanted to mass his troops for greater impact, and he had his brigades to do a half left wheel to bring them closer to the center. The maneuver was done smartly, and the waiting Yankee infantry praised it, but as the brigades swung around they offered their flanks to McGilvery, and his gunners took cruel advantage. Pickett's men were in the open and the range now was hardly half a mile, and shell ripped down the ranks from end to end, one shell sometimes striking down ten men before it burst. Along Hancock's line the guns were silent, for they had nothing left but canister and they would have to wait for point-blank range. Gibbon was riding along the line—an aide had found a horse for him at last—cautioning his men to take it easy and not to fire until the enemy got in close, and the gray lines came swinging up the rise, nearer and nearer.

Webb's brigade would get it first, and the Confederates continued to crowd in toward the center, building up the strength that would overwhelm the little rectangle of torn, littered ground which the brigade was holding. Webb had two Pennsylvania regiments in line behind a low stone wall that ran just in front of the little clump of trees and extended a few rods toward the north, and the rest of his brigade was on the crest of the ridge, perhaps a hundred yards in the rear. Hancock had put three batteries in here, and they had been almost completely destroyed. Beside the trees and down close to the wall were the two guns that remained of Battery A, 4th U. S., commanded by a girlish-looking young lieutenant named Alonzo Cushing. The ground around these guns was hell's half acre. Four guns had been dismounted, caissons and limbers had been exploded, nearly all of the horses had been killed, and there were just enough men left to work the two guns that remained. It had been impossible to remove the wounded, and they lay there amid smashed wheels, fragments of wood and indescribable mutilated remains of men and animals. One gunner, dreadfully cut by a shell fragment, had been seen to draw a revolver and put himself out of his pain by shooting himself through the head.

Cushing had been wounded three times, and he was there by his two guns, a sergeant standing beside him to hold him erect and to pass his orders on to the gunners. (He was calling for triple charges of canister.) The Rebel artillery had renewed its fire, and this part of the line was being hit again, and the advancing Rebel infantry was up to the post-and-rail fences by the Emmitsburg road now, barely two hundred yards away. One of Cushing's two guns was knocked out, and he was almost entirely out of ammunition. The Federal infantry opened fire and the smoke cloud settled down again, thick and stifling. Dimly the men behind the wall could see the Confederates coming in over the fences, brigade lines disordered, the spearhead of the charge a great mass of men sweeping over the fences and up the last of the slope like an irresistible stream flowing uphill.

Farther south the nine-month Vermonters got their chance. . . . Hancock was down there with them, pointing to the exposed flank of Pickett's line, and the Vermont regiments swung out, wheeled toward the right, and opened up a blistering flanking fire at close range. Some Pennsylvanians and a New York regiment went in with them, and the Confederate lines here gave way and began to fall back, and as the men wavered McGilvery's cannoneers pounded them afresh, three dozen guns hitting them all at once.

Just south of the clump of trees the stone wall ended and the men had raised a little breastwork of earth. Behind this barrier were the regiments commanded by Colonel Norman J. Hall. . . . The advancing Confederates here went down into a little hollow, seeming to vanish from sight. Then they came up out of it, appearing suddenly, as if they had popped up out of the earth, so close that Hall's men could see the expressions on their faces. The breastwork blazed from end to end as the men from Massachusetts and New York and Michigan opened fire. The Rebel line staggered visibly, came to a halt, and opened its own fire in reply, and then it began to drift slowly to its left, toward the dense crowd by the clump of trees.

In front of Ziegler's Grove, to the north, Pettigrew's division was coming up to the Emmitsburg road. It had lagged slightly behind the rest of the Confederate attack, but it still kept its formation, and Hays's men looked in admiration at the trimness of its lines and, as they admired those lines, made ready to destroy them. The 8th Ohio had been posted west of the road in skirmish formation, and this regiment drew back and got into a little country lane on the Rebel flank and opened fire. Along the ridge and in the grove the Federals waited, and the foremost Federal brigade stood up to level its muskets, and the Rebel line came very near. Then at last every musket and every cannon in this part of the Yankee line opened at once, and the whole Confederate division disappeared in an immense cloud of smoke and dust. Above this boiling cloud the Union men could see a ghastly debris of guns, knapsacks, blanket rolls, severed human heads, and arms and legs and parts of bodies, tossed into the air by the impact of the shot. One observer wrote: "A moan went up from the field, distinctly to be heard amid the roar of battle, but on they went, too much enveloped in smoke and dust now to permit us to distinguish their lines of

General Lewis A. Armistead, C. S. A.

movement, for the mass appeared more like a cloud of moving smoke and dust than a column of troops."

The mass rolled in closer, the Federals firing into the center of the storm cloud. The men with the improvised buckshot cartridges in smoothbore guns had a target they could not miss, and the XI Corps artillery on Cemetery Hill was sending shell in through the gaps in the Yankee line. Suddenly Pettigrew's men passed the limit of human endurance and the lines broke apart and the hillside was covered with men running for cover, and the Federal gunners burned the ground with shell and canister. On the littered field, amid all the dead and wounded, prostrate men could be seen holding up handkerchiefs in sign of surrender.

But if the right and left of the charging Confederate line had been smashed, the center was still coming on. Cushing fired his last remaining charge, and a bullet hit him in the mouth and killed him. Most of the Pennsylvanians behind the wall sprang up and ran back to the crest, and the few who remained were overwhelmed as the Rebel line rolled in and beat the life out of them. Most of the Rebels stayed behind the wall or crowded in amid the clump of trees and opened fire on the Yankees on the crest, their red battle flags clustering thick, men in front lying prone or kneeling, men in the rear standing and firing over their heads. A handful leaped over the wall, Armistead in the lead, and ran in among the wreckage of Cushing's battery. Armistead's horse had been killed and his hat was down on the hilt of his sword now, but the sword was still held high, and through the curling smoke the Union soldiers got a final glimpse of him, one triumphant hand resting on a silent cannon.

This was the climax . . . the next few minutes would tell the story, and what that story would be would all depend on whether these blue-coated soldiers really meant it. There were more Federals than Confederates on the field, but right here where the fighting was going on there were more Confederates than Federals, and every man was firing in a wild, feverish haste, with the smoke settling down thicker and thicker. From the peach orchard Confederate guns were shooting straight into the Union line, disregarding the danger that some of their own men would be hit, and the winging missiles tore ugly lanes through the disorganized mass of Yankees.

A fresh Union regiment was moving up through Ziegler's Grove, and as the men came out into the open they heard the uproar of battle different from any they had ever heard before—"strange and terrible, a sound that came from thousands of human throats, yet was not a commingling of shouts and yells but rather like a vast mournful roar." There was no cheering, but thousands of men were growling and cursing without realizing it as they fought to the utmost limits of primal savagery. The 19th Massachusetts was squarely before the clump of trees, and the Confederate mass kept crowding forward, and for a time the file closers in the rear of the Massachusetts regiment joined hands and held the thin line in place by sheer strength.

Gibbon was down with a bullet through his shoulder, Webb had been wounded, and Hancock was knocked off his horse by a bullet that went through his saddle and drove a tenpenny nail and bits of wood deep into his thigh. Except for one valiant staff officer, there was not a mounted man to be seen. Hunt was in the middle of the infantry, firing his revolver. On the open crest of the ridge men were volleying at the Confederates behind the wall and among the trees. From the left, regiments were running over to help, coming in through the smoke like a mob gone out of control.

These were Halls's men, and men from Harrow's brigade on the left—famous old regiments, 20th Massachusetts and 7th Michigan and "that shattered thunderbolt" (as an officer on Gibbon's staff called it), the remnant of the 1st Minnesota. They were not "moving by the right flank" or "changing front forward" or executing any other recognized tactical maneuver, and they were not obeying the commands of any officers, although their officers were in their midst, yelling hoarsely and gesturing madly with their swords. No formal tactical move was possible in that jammed smoky confusion, and no shouted command could be heard in the everlasting din. One soldier wrote afterward that the only order he remembered hearing, from first to last, was "Up, boys—they're coming!" right at the start. This was not a controlled movement at all. It was simply a crowd of armed men running over spontaneously to get into the middle of an enormous fight, Yankee soldiers swarming in to get at their enemies, all regimental formations lost, every man going in on his own.

Some of the men stopped and fired over the low earthen barricade toward the front where there were still Rebels in the open. Others jammed in toward the clump of trees, firing through gaps in the crowd ahead, sometimes hitting their own comrades. Off to the left the Vermonters were still out in front, facing north, tearing the Confederate flank to tatters, and from the right Hays's men and the guns in the grove were firing in obliquely. The heavy smoke went up toward the sky, so heavy that Lee over on Seminary Ridge could get nothing but an occasional glimpse of red battle flags adrift in the murk.

Back on the crest, facing the clump of trees, the line swayed as men worked up their nerve. The mounted staff officer was shouting, men were yelling to each other, and a color-bearer jumped up and ran forward, waving his flag. The staff was broken by a shot, and he grabbed the stump and held the ragged colors above his head, and by ones and twos and then all along the crest men sprang to their feet and followed him, firing as they ran. Armistead was stretched out on the ground now with a bullet in him, and the other gray-coats who had got in among the guns were down too, and the Federals came in on the Rebel mass among the little trees, and the smoke hid the hot afternoon sun.

Pickett's men were in a box now. On their left Pettigrew's division had evaporated, on the right they were dissolving under an unceasing flank fire, in front they were getting a head-on assault that was too heavy to take, and there was no support in sight. Longstreet had sent a brigade up to cover their right, but in the blinding fog the brigade had lost its direction and was heading straight for McGilvery's ranked cannon, which blasted it with deadly aim, and the Vermont regiments wheeled completely around and got the brigade in flank. It fell apart and its bits and pieces went tumbling back to Seminary Ridge. And suddenly the tension was gone and the firing was dying down, and the Confederates by the clump of trees were going back to their own lines or dropping their muskets and raising their hands in surrender. Meade came riding up to the crest just now, and an officer met him and told him that Lee's charge had been crushed, and Meade raised his hand and cried "Thank God!" The last of the fugitives went back toward their starting point, Federal gunners following them with shell, and Gibbon's weary soldiers were sending a great mass of Rebel prisoners back to the rear. The fighting was over.

Hancock was on a stretcher, dictating a note to Meade. He believed that a quick counterattack now would take the Rebel army off balance and finish it, and he urged that the men be sent forward without delay. He added proudly: "I did not leave the field so long as a Rebel was to be seen upright." An aide came up to him and handed him a watch, a pair of spurs, and other trinkets. They came from Lewis Armistead, whom the aide had found dying there beside Cushing's last gun. Armistead had asked that these mementos of an old friendship be sent to Hancock, and he had gasped out some sort of farewell message. "Tell Hancock I have done him and my country a great injustice which I shall never cease to regret" was the way the aide had it; he may have dressed it up a good deal or, for that matter, he may have dreamed it all, and it does not matter much either way. Armistead had died, going beyond regrets forever, and as if he had been waiting for this last message, Hancock had the stretcher-bearers carry him off to the field hospital.

The smoke drifted away and the noise died down, and a soldier who looked out over the ground where the men had fought said that he looked upon "a square mile of Tophet." . . .

One day they would make a park there, with neat lawns and smooth black roadways, and there would be marble statues and bronze plaques to tell the story in bloodless prose. Silent cannon would rest behind grassy embankments, their wheels bolted down to concrete foundations, their malevolence wholly gone, and here and there birds would nest in the muzzles. In the museums and tourist-bait trinket shops old bullets and broken buckles and twisted bayonets would repose under glass, with a rusty musket or so on the wall and little illustrated booklets lying on top of the counter. There would be neat brick and timber cabins on the hillsides, and people would sleep soundly in houses built where the armies had stormed and cried at each other, as if to prove that men killed in battle send forth no restless ghosts to plague comfortable civilians at night. The town and the woods and the ridges and hills would become a national shrine, filled with romantic memories which are in themselves a kind of forgetting, and visitors would stand by the clump of trees and look off to the west and see nothing but the rolling fields and the quiet groves and the great blue bank of the mountains.

But first there would have to be a great deal of tidying up. . . .

An officer . . . wrote that on no other field had he seen such appalling numbers of dead. In places where the infantry fire had been especially intense the dead men lay in great rows, and in the twilight it seemed as if whole brigades had made their bivouac there and had gone to sleep. On the ground covered by Pickett's charge one officer wrote that "I saw men, horses, and material in some places piled up together, which is something seldom seen unless in pictures of battles, and the appearance of the field with these mounds of dead men and horses, and very many bodies lying in every position singly, was terrible, especially as the night lent a somber hue to everything the eye rested on."

A fearful odor of decay lay over the field. A cavalry patrol went through Gettysburg to scout the Cashtown road to the west, and as it came out by the fields where dead bodies had been lying in the heat for four days the cavalrymen sickened and vomited as they rode. The country here was the ultimate abomination of desolation: "As far as the eye could reach on both sides of the Cashtown road you see blue-coated boys, swollen up to look as giants, quite black in the face, but nearly all on their backs, looking into the clear blue with open eyes, with their clothes torn open. It is strange that dying men tear their clothes in this manner. You see them lying in platoons of infantry with officers and arms exactly as they stood or ran—artillery men with caisson blown up and four horses, each in position, dead. You meet also limbs and fragments of men. The road is strewn with dead, whom the rebels have half buried and whom the heavy rain has uncovered. . . .

Details were at work all over the field, collecting the last of the helpless wounded and burying the dead. This last was an almost impossible job, since more than five thousand men had been killed in action. Federals who were buried by men of their own regiments were given little wooden markers, with the name and regimental identification carved with a jackknife or scrawled with pencil, but in hundreds and hundreds of cases no identification was possible and the men went into the ground as "unknown." Long wide trenches were dug and the men were laid in them side by side, and sometimes there was nothing more in the way of a gravestone than a little headboard at one end of the trench stating the number of bodies that were buried in it. In places the burial details just gave up and did not try to make graves, but simply shoveled earth over the bodies as they lay on the ground.

Glory Road

General Winfield Scott Hancock (seated)
with generals of his command

VALLEY OF DRY BONES

As the summer and fall wore on, the battlefield was policed up and the tidy modern cemetery began to take shape. November 19, 1863, was set for its dedication because it would fit well into the busy schedule of the famous orator, Edward Everett.

The great day came at last, and there were troops in Gettysburg again, and bands, and special trains bringing distinguished guests, and there was a big parade through the town and up to the hill, with parade marshals in their sashes, horses shying and curvetting affectedly, much pomp and circumstance, and a famous orator with an hour-long speech in his hand. There was also Abraham Lincoln, who had been invited more or less as an afterthought—the invitation went to him on November 2, suggesting that he might honor the occasion by his presence—and Mr. Lincoln was to say a few words after Mr. Everett had made the speech. After the usual fuss and confusion the procession climbed the hill and the honored guests got up on the flag-draped speakers' stand, and eventually a certain degree of quiet was restored. A chaplain offered a prayer, and a glee club sang an ode composed especially for the occasion, and at last the orator got up to make his speech.

An oration was an oration in those days, and it had to have a certain style to it—classical allusions, a leisurely approach to the subject matter, a carefully phrased recital of the background and history of the occasion, the whole working up to a peroration which would sum everything up in memorable sentences. Mr. Everett was a master of this art form and had been hard at work for many weeks, and he stood up now in the center of the field where five thousand men had died and began his polished cadenced sentences. He recalled how the ancient Greeks commemorated their heroic dead in the days of Pericles. . . .

There were many thousands of people at this ceremony, and among them were certain wounded veterans who had come back to see all of this, and a knot of these wandered away from the crowd around the speakers' stand and strolled down along Cemetery Ridge, pausing when they reached a little clump of trees, and there they looked off toward the west and talked quietly about what they had seen and done there.

In front of them was the wide gentle valley of the shadow of death, brimming now with soft autumn sunlight, and behind them the flags waved lazily about the speakers' stand and the voice droned on, building up toward a literary climax. The valley was a mile wide, and there was the rolling ground where the Rebel guns had been ranked, and on the crest of this ridge was the space where a girlish artillery lieutenant had had a sergeant hold him up while he called for the last round of canister, the ground where file closers had gripped hands and dug in their heels to hold a wavering line together, the place where the noise of men desperately fighting had been heard as a great mournful roar; and the voice went on, and the governors looked dignified, and the veterans by the trees looked about them and saw again the fury and the smoke and the killing.

This was the valley of dry bones, waiting for the word, which might or might not come in rhythmic prose that began by describing the customs of ancient Athens. The bones had lain there in the sun and rain, and now they were carefully arranged state by state under the new sod. They were the bones of men who had exulted in their youth, and some of them had been unstained heroes while others had been scamps who pillaged and robbed and ran away when they could, and they had died here, and that was the end of them. They had come here because of angry words and hot passions in which they had not shared. They had come, too, because the drums had rolled and the bands had blared the swinging deceitful tunes that piped men off to battle . . . three cheers for the red white and blue, here's a long look back at the girl I left behind me, John Brown's body lies a-moldering in the grave but we go marching on, and Yankee Doodle on his spotted pony rides off into the eternal smoky mist of war.

Back of these men were innumerable long dusty roads reaching to the main streets of a thousand youthful towns and villages where there had been bright flags overhead and people on the board sidewalks cheering and crying and waving a last good-by. It had seemed once that there was some compelling reason to bring these men here—something so broad that it would encompass all of the terrible contradictory manifestations of the country's pain and bewilderment, the riots and the lynchings, the hysterical conspiracies with their oaths written in blood, the hard hand that had been laid upon the countryside, the scramble for riches and the scheming for high place, and the burdens carried by quiet folk who wanted only to live at peace by the faith they used to have.

Perhaps there was a meaning to all of it somewhere. Perhaps everything that the nation was and meant to be had come to a focus here, beyond the graves and the remembered echoes of the guns and the wreckage of lives that were gone forever. Perhaps the whole of it somehow was greater than the sum of its tragic parts, and perhaps here on this wind-swept hill the thing could be said at last, so that the dry bones of the country's dreams could take on flesh.

The orator finished, and after the applause had died away the tall man in the black frock coat got to his feet, with two little sheets of paper in his hand, and he looked out over the valley and began to speak.

Glory Road

VI

Missionary Ridge

General Grant (left) and his staff visiting Lookout Mountain after the battle, 1863

The twin victories of mid-1863—Gettysburg and the capture of Vicksburg— damaged the Confederacy, but by no means destroyed its capacity to fight. Just a month before Lincoln delivered his Gettysburg Address, the Army of the Cumberland was defeated at the Battle of Chickamauga in northern Georgia and forced back to Chattanooga, Tennessee. There Braxton Bragg's Confederate army brought the Union armies under siege. Things looked black when Washington gave Grant supreme command of the Federal forces in the west, which is to say from the Alleghenies to the Mississippi. Grant replaced the defeated General William S. Rosecrans as head of the Army of the Cumberland, with tough General George H. Thomas, called "The Rock of Chickamauga" from his valiant rear-guard stand in that debacle. Despite an injured leg, Grant himself rode to Chattanooga by a back road, opened supply lines, and called in General William Tecumseh Sherman with part of his Army of the Tennessee. For further support he obtained several corps from the Army of the Potomac, led by General Joseph ("Fighting Joe") Hooker. Then Grant prepared to strike Bragg, whose positions looked impregnable.

As Catton makes clear, the elements of these three Union armies disliked each other almost as much as they did the Rebels. The easterners of the Army of the Potomac, sneered at as "kid-glove and paper-collar" soldiers, thought the Westerners unkempt, undisciplined backwoodsmen; and both the Potomac and Tennessee men looked on the Cumberlands as losers. Fires of resentment and a fierce desire to prove themselves burned within Thomas's men as this spectacular three-day battle opened on November 23, 1863.

Maybe the real trouble was that the battle was too theatrical. People could see too much; most particularly, the Confederates could see too much. They were up in the balconies and all of the Federals were down in the orchestra pit, and when the fighting began, every move down on the plain was clearly visible to the Southerners on the heights. Perhaps just watching it did something to them.

Or it might have been the eclipse of the moon, which took place a night or two before the battle. There had been a great silver light over mountain and plain and rival battle lines, and it died and gave way to a creepy rising shadow as the moon was blotted out, so that the armored ridge was a silent, campfire-spangled mass outlined against a pale sky, with darkness coming up out of the hollows. Both armies looked on in awed silence, and the sight seems to have been taken as an incomprehensible omen of ill fortune. (Ill fortune, but specifically for whom? The Army of the Cumberland decided finally that it must mean bad luck for the Rebs: up on the mountain crest the Johnnies were a lot closer to the dying moon than the Federals on the plain . . .)

Or, finally, it may be that everybody had been waiting too long. The armies had been in position for two months, or nearly that, with nothing much to do but look at each other. Day after day and week after week the Confederates had lounged in their trenches, looking down on men who could not conceivably do them any harm, and during all of that time the Federals had lounged in their own trenches, looking up at foes who seemed to be beyond all reach. What would happen when the men finally went into action might be strangely and powerfully affected, in a quite unpredictable way, by those long weeks of waiting and watching.

If justice existed on earth and under the heavens, Braxton Bragg would have been right; his position was impregnable. Missionary Ridge rose five hundred feet above the plain, sparse trees and underbrush littering its steep rocky slope; it ran for more than five miles, from southwest to northeast, and the Confederates had all of it. At its base, fronting the plain, they had a stout line of trenches, and on the crest they had another line, studded with cannon. Halfway up, at the proper places, there were other trenches and rifle pits manned by soldiers who knew what to do with their rifles when they got a Yankee in the sights. To the west, a detachment held Lookout Mountain—not the crest, which rose in a straight palisade no army could scale, but the steep sides which ran down from the foot of the palisade to the edges of the Tennessee. The detachment was not large, but the mountainside was steep and the Yankees were not up to anything menacing, and it was believed that this detachment ought to be able to hold its ground. Across the flat country between Lookout and the southwestern end of Missionary Ridge, there was a good line of fieldworks held by infantry and artillery. And at the upper end of Missionary Ridge, where the high country came down to the river a few miles upstream from Chattanooga, there was broken hilly ground held by some of the best men in all the Confederacy—the division of Irish-born Pat Cleburne, a tremendous soldier who had trained his men to the precise pattern which had been glimpsed by his pugnacious Irish eyes.

Bragg was right, by any standard anyone could use. His main position could not be taken by assault, not even if nearly a third of the Confederate army had been sent up toward Knoxville to squelch General Burnside.

The Army of the Cumberland held the low ground south of Chattanooga. Lookout Mountain looked down from one side and Missionary Ridge looked down on it from the other, and men who had heard about Fredericksburg and Gettysburg, with their doomed charges on high ground, could look up at these heights and have disturbing thoughts. On November 23 Thomas moved his army forward. It drove Confederate skirmishers and advance guards off the plain and seized a little detached hill, named Orchard Knob, which came up out of the flat ground a little outside Chattanooga. If Thomas wanted to order an assault on Bragg's position he had an excellent place to take off from, but there was little reason to think that this would help very much. Missionary Ridge was still five hundred feet high, and it was studded with Rebels from top to bottom.

This was the nut that U. S. Grant was expected to crack, and as he made his plans he did just what Thomas's grumpy men had thought he would do. He gave the big assignments to Sherman and to Hooker, and to the outlanders these officers had brought in with them. The Army of the Cumberland would have the inglorious job of looking menacing and helping to pick up the pieces, while the men from the Army of the Tennessee and the Army of the Potomac had the starring parts.

Grant proposed to hit the two ends of the Confederate line at once. Hooker would strike at Lookout Mountain, and Sherman—moving his army upstream, across the river from Chattanooga, and crossing over by pontoons—would hit the upper end of Missionary Ridge. While they were breaking into the Confederate flanks, Thomas's men could attack the center. The latter attack would not accomplish anything in particular, for it would be suicide to expect troops to take that tremendous height, but if they could apply enough pressure to keep Bragg from reinforcing his flanks their job would be done. Sherman and Hooker would win the battle.

It was ordered so, and the men of the Army of the Cumberland got the full implication of it. They were veterans, and in any ordinary circumstances they would have been happy enough to let somebody else's army do all of the heavy fighting. But these circumstances were not ordinary. Their pride had been bruised badly enough in recent weeks, and now it was being hit harder than ever. In the eyes of the commanding general, obviously, they were second-class troops. They waited in helpless, smoldering anticipation for the battle to begin.

It began on November 24, after a good many delays, when Hooker sent his Easterners forward from Lookout Valley to seize the mountain that looked down on the road and the river and the city of Chattanooga. At the same moment Sherman got his army across the Tennessee, above Chattanooga, and sent it driving in on the northern end of Missionary Ridge.

Hooker's men found their job unexpectedly easy. They outnumbered the Confederates on Lookout Mountain by a fantastic margin—five or six to one, as far as a good estimate is possible—and they clambered up the rocks and steep meadows and drove the defenders out of there with a minimum of effort and a maximum of spectacular effect. The Cumberlands (and the newspaper correspondents) were all down in the valley, watching. They saw the high ground sparkling with musket fire and wreathed in smoke, and a mist came in and veiled the top of the mountain from sight; and then at last the mist lifted, and the Union flag was flying from the crest of the mountain, the Confederates had all retreated, and Joe Hooker was a fine handsome dashing soldier whose men had scaled a mountain and licked the Rebels in front of everybody. The newspapers blossomed out with great stories about "the battle above the clouds." The left end of Bragg's line had been knocked loose from its moorings, although actually the achievement was not as solid as it seemed. Hooker's men still had to come down the eastern slope and crack the battle line in the plain, and that would take a little more doing.

While Hooker was at it, Sherman's rowdies from the Army of the Tennessee attacked Pat Cleburne's men and found that they had taken on more than they could handle.

Missionary Ridge did not run in a straight line to the edge of the Tennessee River, as Grant and everyone else on the Federal side supposed. It broke up, before it reached the river, into a complex of separated hills with very steep sides, and Sherman's men no sooner took one hill than they found themselves obliged to go down into a valley and climb another one, with cold-eyed Rebel marksmen shooting at them every step of the way—and occasionally rolling huge rocks down on them. By the end of the day the Army of the Tennessee had had some very hard fighting and had not yet gained a foothold on the end of the ridge. Sherman believed (apparently mistakenly) that Bragg was drawing men from his center to reinforce Cleburne, and he called for help.

When the battle was resumed the next morning, nothing went right. Sherman's men hammered at the northern end of Missionary Ridge and got nowhere. Hooker took his troops down from the slope of Lookout Mountain and headed south, to strike the other end of the Confederate line, but he went astray somewhere in the wooded plain; there was a stream that needed bridging, the pontoons were missing, and this blow at the Confederate left missed fire completely.

On Orchard Knob, Grant and Thomas watched the imperfect progress of the unsatisfactory battle. Sherman continued to believe that the Confederates in his front were being strengthened, and he was calling for more reinforcements. Some of Thomas's troops were sent to him, but he still could not push Pat Cleburne's men off the heights. By midafternoon his attack had definitely stalled, with severe losses, and Hooker's push had not materialized. If anything was to be done the Army of the Cumberland would have to do it.

What was planned and what finally happened were two different things. Grant told Thomas to have his men attack the Confederate line at the base of Missionary Ridge, occupy it, and await further orders; the move seems to have been regarded as a diversion that might lead Bragg to strengthen his center by withdrawing some of the men who were confronting Sherman. No one had any notion that the Army of the Cumberland could take the ridge itself. Thomas apparently was dubious about the prospect of taking even the first line of trenches; he was slow about ordering the men forward, and Grant had to prod him before they finally began to move.

The men were impatient, for a powerful excitement had been rising in them all day. They had heard the unending crash of Sherman's battle off to their left, and they sensed that things were not going right. Straight ahead of them was the great ridge, and they looked at it with an irrational, desperate sort of

General Braxton Bragg, C. S. A.

longing. One of them remarked afterward that they were keyed up to such a
pitch that "if General Grant had said the word Missionary Ridge would have
been taken in thirty minutes time."

The word came—not to take the ridge, just to take the trenches at its
base—and the men surged forward in one of the most dramatic moves of all the
war. The battle line was two miles wide, eighteen thousand men in four solid
infantry divisions, moving toward an impregnable mountain wall that blotted
out half the sky. Flags snapped in the wind, and Thomas's carefully drilled men
kept a parade-ground alignment. The Confederate guns high above them
opened with salvos that covered the crest with a ragged dirty-white cloud; from
some atmospheric quirk, each shot they fired could be seen from the moment it
left the gun's muzzle. The Cumberlands kept on going and, from Orchard
Knob, Federal artillery opened in support. General Gordon Granger, who had
done so much to save the day at Chickamauga, was on Orchard Knob, and he
was so excited that he forgot he was commander of an army corps and went
down into the gun pits to help the cannoneers. Thomas stood on the hill,
majestic as ever, running his fingers through his whiskers. Beside him, Grant
chewed a cigar and looked on unemotionally.

The plain was an open stage which everybody watched—the generals back on
Orchard Knob and the Confederates on Missionary Ridge. Crest and sides of
the ridge were all ablaze with fire now, and the Army of the Cumberland took
some losses, but it kept on moving. Up to the first line of trenches at the base of
the mountain it went, the men swarmed over the parapet, and in a moment the
Confederate defenders were scampering back up the hillside to their second and
third lines. The Cumberlands moved into the vacated trenches, paused for
breath, and kept looking up at the crest, five hundred feet above them.

The rising slope was an obvious deathtrap, but these men had a score to
settle—with the Rebels who had whipped them at Chickamauga, with the other
Federal armies who had derided them, with Grant, who had treated them as
second-class troops—and now was the time to settle it. From the crest of the
ridge the Confederates were sending down a sharp plunging fire against which
the captured trenches offered little protection. The Federals had seized the first
line, but they could not stay where they were. It seemed out of the question to
go forward, but the only other course was to go back, and for these soldiers who
had been suffering a slow burn for weeks, to go back was unthinkable.

The officers felt exactly as the men felt. Phil Sheridan was there, conspicuous
in dress uniform—he was field officer of the day, togged out in his best—and he
sat on his horse, looked up the forbidding slope, and drew a silver flask from his
pocket to take a drink. Far above him a Confederate artillery commander
standing amid his guns looked down at him, and Sheridan airily waved the flask
to offer a toast as he drank. The Confederate signaled to his gun crews, and his
battery fired a salvo in reply; it was a near miss, the missiles kicking up dirt and

gravel and spattering Sheridan's gay uniform. Sheridan's face darkened; he growled, "I'll take those guns for that!" and he moved his horse forward, calling out to the men near him: "All right, boys—as soon as you catch your breath you can go on again." All up and down the line other men were getting the same idea. Brigadier General Carlin turned to his men and shouted: "Boys, I don't want you to stop until we reach the top of that hill. Forward!" The colonel of the 104th Illinois was heard crying: "I want the 104th to be the first regiment on that hill!" And then, as if it moved in response to one command, the whole army surged forward, scrambled up out of the captured trenches, and began to move up the slope of Missionary Ridge.

Back on Orchard Knob the generals watched in stunned disbelief. Grant turned to Thomas and asked sharply who had told these men to go on to the top of the ridge. Thomas replied that he did not know; he himself had certainly given no such order. Grant then swung on Granger: was he responsible? Granger replied that he was not, but the battle excitement was on him and he added that when the men of the Army of the Cumberland once got started it was very hard to stop them. Grant clenched his teeth on his cigar and muttered something to the effect that somebody was going to sweat for it if this charge ended in disaster; then he faced to the front again to watch the incredible thing that was happening.

Up the side of the ridge went the great line of battle. It was a parade-ground line no longer. The regimental flags led, men trailing out behind each flag in a V-shaped mass, struggling over rocks and logs as they kept on climbing. Confederate pockets of resistance on the slope were wiped out. Now and then the groups of attackers would stop for breath—the slope was steep, and it was easy to get winded—but after a moment or so they would go on again.

Looking down from the crest, the Confederates kept on firing, but the foreknowledge of defeat was beginning to grip them. The crest was uneven, and no defender could see more than a small part of his own line; but each defender could see all of the charging Federal army, and it suddenly looked irresistible. The defensive fire slackened here and there; men began to fade back from the firing line, irresolute; and finally the Federals were covering the final yards in a frantic competitive run, each regiment trying to outdo the others, each man trying to beat his fellows. A company commander, running ahead of his colors, grabbed the coattails of one of his men, to hold him back so that he might reach the crest first.

No one could ever determine afterward what unit or what men won the race, and the business was argued at old soldiers' reunions for half a century. Apparently the crest was reached at half a dozen places simultaneously, and when it was reached, Bragg's line—the center of his whole army, the hard core of his entire defensive position—suddenly and inexplicably went to pieces. By ones and twos and then by companies and battalions, gray-clad soldiers who had proved their valor in a great many desperate fights turned and took to their heels. Something about that incredible scaling of the mountainside had been just too much for them. Perfectly typical was the case of a Confederate officer who, scorning to run, stood with drawn sword, waiting to fight it out with the first Yankee who approached him. An Indiana private, bayoneted rifle in his grip, started toward him—and then, amazingly, laid down his weapon and came on in a crouch, bare hands extended. There was a primeval menace in him, more terrifying than bayonet or musket, and the officer blinked at him for a moment and then fled.

As resistance dissolved, the victorious Federals were too breathless to cheer. They tossed their caps in the air, and some of them crossed the narrow ridge to peer down the far side, where they saw what they had not previously seen—whole brigades of Confederates running downhill in wild panicky rout. The Federals turned and beckoned their comrades with swinging arms and, regaining their wind, with jubilant shouts: "My God! Come and see them run!"

General officers began to reach the crest. Sheridan was there, laying proudly possessive hands on the guns that had fired at him. General [Thomas J.] Wood . . . was riding back and forth laughing, telling his men that because they had attacked without orders they would be court-martialed, each and every one. He found the private who had charged the Confederate officer bare-handed and asked him why he had done such a thing; the man replied simply that he had thought it would be nice to take the officer prisoner.

The Battle of Chattanooga was over now, no matter what Sherman or Hooker did. With a two-mile hole punched in the center of his line, Bragg could do nothing but retreat, and as his army began to reassemble on the low ground beyond the mountain, it took off for Georgia, with Cleburne's men putting up a stout rear-guard resistance. Phil Sheridan got his division into shape and took off in pursuit, figuring that it might be possible to cut in behind Cleburne and capture his whole outfit, but his pursuit was little more than a token. The Army of the Cumberland was temporarily immobilized by the sheer surprise of its incredible victory. Nobody wanted to do anything but ramble around, yell, and let his chest expand with unrestrained pride.

Oddly enough, it was a long time before the soldiers realized that they themselves were responsible for the victory. They tended to ascribe it to Grant and to his good management, and they told one another that all they had ever needed was a good leader. One officer who had shared in all of this army's battles wrote that during the uproar of this conflict "I thought I detected in the management what I had never discovered before on the battlefield—a little common sense." When Grant and Thomas came to the top of the ridge the men crowded about them, capering and yelling. Sherman himself was thoroughly convinced that the battle had gone exactly as Grant had planned it; to him the whole victory was simply one more testimonial to the general's genius.

Washington felt much the same way; but Washington also remembered that Burnside was still beleaguered in Knoxville, and when Lincoln sent a wire of congratulations to Grant he added the words: "Remember Burnside." Grant started Granger off to the rescue with an army corps; then, figuring that Sherman would make a faster march—and feeling apparently a little disillusioned about Granger after noticing the man's unrestrained excitement during the battle—he canceled the order and sent the Army of the Tennessee. . . .

Sherman's men relieved the Knoxville situation without difficulty, except that the pace at which Sherman drove them marched them practically out of their shoes. They found the Federals in Knoxville ragged and hungry—the food allowance had been reduced to a daily issue of salt pork and bran bread, so unappetizing that it took a half-starved man to eat it. . . . Before too long, full railroad connections with Chattanooga were restored, which meant that plenty of food and clothing could come in. Half of the army came gaily down to the station to greet the first train—a ten-car freight train which, when the doors were opened, turned out by some triumph of military miscalculation to be loaded with nothing but horseshoes. . . .

The shadows were rising that winter, tragically lit by a pale light of Southern valor and endurance which were not enough to win and which the victorious Federals glimpsed as they looked back on the immediate past. A man in the 46th Ohio recalled strolling along the fighting line at the northern end of Missionary Ridge, the day after the Battle of Chattanooga had ended, and looking down at the unburied body of a dead Confederate, and he wrote:

"He was not over 15 years of age, and very slender in size. He was clothed in a cotton suit, and was barefooted—barefooted, on that cold and wet 24th of November. I examined his haversack. For a day's ration there was a handful of black beans, a few pieces of sorghum and a half dozen roasted acorns. That was an infinitely poor outfit for marching and fighting, but that Tennessee Confederate had made it answer his purpose."

This Hallowed Ground

That evening a worker for the Christian Commission, visiting a field hospital, asked a wounded Federal where he had been hurt. "Almost up," replied the soldier. The Commission man explained that he meant "in what part are you injured?" The soldier, still gripped by the transcendent excitement of the charge, insisted: "Almost up to the top." Then the civilian drew back the wounded man's blanket and saw a frightful, shattering wound. The soldier glanced at it and said: "Yes, that's what did it. I was almost up. But for that I would have reached the top." He looked up at the civilian, repeated faintly, "Almost up," and died.

Grant Takes Command

VII

Mr. Lincoln's General

General Grant at City Point, Virginia, 1865

It had taken Abraham Lincoln over three years to find a commander worthy of the job. He had inherited the shrewd but infirm Winfield Scott, who had been general-in-chief since 1841; then there had been vain, Napoleonic George B. McClellan, professional and popular but riven with doubts and slow to move; and there were Halleck, Hooker, Burnside and Pope, none of them a match for Lee. But now, suddenly, after all his successes in the West, there was this fighter, Grant. Lincoln was drawn to him, and Congress set about reviving the old rank of lieutenant general—once held by George Washington—with this stubby, unimpressive-looking fellow in mind.

He might very nearly never have gotten into the war at all, if only because of his constitutional inability to put himself forward. In 1861, Catton notes, Grant "had written to the War Department, citing his record and suggesting that he might be qualified to command a regiment. Nothing had come of it. (Years later his letter was found in a forgotten file. Apparently no one had ever read it.) He had tried to offer his services to an old army acquaintance named George B. McClellan, who was a glittering major general of volunteers in Ohio, but McClellan had been too busy to talk to him. . . ." Fortunately the Governor of Illinois, Richard Yates, spotted Grant, and gave him a volunteer regiment and a colonelcy. Soon he became a brigadier general, in command at Cairo, Illinois, seized Paducah, Kentucky, and in November, 1861, at Belmont, Missouri, fought his first battle as a commanding general. It was a victory that turned into a tactical defeat and a rather close call personally for Grant.

There was hard fighting that afternoon, and Federal losses were severe. In the end, the scorched column made its way to the landing, all units in hand except for the 27th Illinois, which got temporarily isolated, had to move farther up the river, and was taken off by the boats later in the evening. Earlier in the day, some Federal wounded had been put in farmhouses near the place where the transports had tied up; and, as the infantry went aboard the steamers, Grant rode out to see if these men could not be evacuated. While details carried some of them to the boats, Grant rode back to the regiment he had posted to guard the landing, fearing that the Confederates might come to close quarters and make a final attack while the embarkation was in process—but the guard had left. Returning to the boats, Grant found that the guard had already gone aboard; he prepared to bring the men back to their post, then concluded that this would take more time then he had to spare, and himself rode out again to satisfy himself that all stragglers and detached units had reached the landing.

He found nobody, except for a column of advancing Confederates who came within fifty yards of him without especially noticing him; he was riding through a cornfield where the dry stalks were still more than head high, and this apparently made him hard to see. He got back to the riverbank just as a whole line of Rebel infantry reached the fringe of the woods on the far side of the cornfield and began to open fire.

As far as personal peril goes, this was about as bad a spot as Grant got into in all the war; and as the bullets whined about his ears he gave way, suddenly, to a desperate thought of home: what would become of Julia and the children, if he should be killed here? For a moment the thought possessed him with power, and far away in their home in Galena, Julia Grant, going to her bedroom to rest after some household task or other, suddenly saw a distinct but mysterious vision: Grant mounted and in the field, gazing at her with a peculiar intensity. When they met a few days later, they found that this odd experience had come to her at the moment when Grant, all alone on his horse, was the target for concentrated rifle fire, and was thinking of his wife and children; and they both felt that it was the depth of his feeling that projected this strange vision into the house in Galena.

. . . All of the Federal steamers but one had cast off their moorings and were moving upstream. At the foot of the steep, muddy bank where this last vessel was tied up, a little knot of Union soldiers waited disconsolately, not knowing what they were supposed to do next.

One of these men remembered that, as they stood there, a man on horseback appeared at the top of the bank and called to them sharply: "Get aboard the boat—they are coming." They looked up, saw that the rider was Grant, and hastened to obey. They heard Grant shout to the boat's captain: "Chop your lines and back out"; then, after the lines had been cut, members of the boat's crew laid a plank from the deck to the shore, Grant's horse settled down on its haunches and slid down the bank, and then Grant calmly rode aboard on the swaying plank, the last Federal soldier to leave Belmont.

Grant dismounted, went to the texas deck, and entered the captain's stateroom just behind the pilot house, lying down on a sofa to catch his breath. After a moment he arose, to go out on deck and see what was going on; Rebel musketry fire was getting heavy, by now, and Grant had no more than stood up when a bullet ripped through the bulkhead and struck the head of the sofa where he had been lying.

Grant Moves South

"UNCONDITIONAL SURRENDER"

By the following February, 1862, Grant was conducting amphibious warfare on the Western rivers, taking Fort Henry on the Tennessee and Fort Donelson on the Cumberland. The latter was a tougher nut to crack, but the end came not long after General C. F. Smith's attack, described at the beginning of Chapter IV.

At about three in the morning, a Confederate flag of truce came through Smith's lines, with a message for the commanding general.

Smith and his staff had made a bivouac in the trodden snow, and an officer from the 2nd Iowa came to this bivouac to report that the Rebel officer who came in with the flag was asking if there was a Federal officer present who could negotiate terms for a Confederate surrender. Smith mounted and rode forward, and Major Thomas J. Newsham, of his staff, reported that Smith bluntly told the Confederate: "I make no terms with Rebels with arms in their hands—my terms are unconditional and immediate surrender!" Then, bearing a letter which the Confederate gave him, Smith set off to Grant's headquarters.

Grant was in the kitchen of the little farmhouse, stretched out on a mattress on the floor. Smith stalked in, stood by the open fire to get the chill out of his long legs, and as Grant drew on some clothing the onetime commandant of cadets handed the letter to him, saying: "There's something for you to read, General." While Grant was reading it, Smith inquired if anyone had a drink. Dr. Brinton owned a flask, and he handed it to Smith, who took a long pull at it, returned the flask, and then raised one foot and gazed at it ruefully.

"See how the soles of my boots burned," he said. "I slept last night with my head in the saddle and with my feet too near the fire; I've scorched my boots."

Grant finished reading the letter. It was signed by his friend from the Old Army, General Simon Bolivar Buckner, who, by an odd turn of events, was now the commanding officer in Fort Donelson, and—as the flag-of-truce officer had told Smith—it asked for an armistice and the appointment of commissioners to settle terms of surrender. Grant gave the letter to Smith, asking: "What answer shall I send to this, General?"

"No terms to the damned Rebels!" barked Smith. Grant chuckled, then sat at the kitchen table, drew up a tablet, and began to write. Presently he read aloud, to Smith and the other officers, what he had written. It would become one of the most famous dispatches in American military history. Addressed to General Buckner, it went as follows:

> Sir: Yours of this date proposing Armistice and appointment of Commissioners to settle terms of Capitulation is just received. No terms except unconditional and immediate surrender can be accepted. I propose to move immediately upon your works. I am sir, very respectfully
> Your obt. svt.
> U. S. GRANT
> *Brig. Gen.*

Smith gave a brief grunt, and remarked, "It's the same thing in smoother words." Then, taking the letter, he stalked out of the room to deliver it to the waiting Confederate.

Grant Moves South

ON THE BATTLEFIELD: FORT DONELSON

Riding back to headquarters in the twilight, Grant passed many dead and wounded men from both armies. One scene particularly struck him: a Federal lieutenant and a Confederate private, both desperately wounded, lay side by side, and the lieutenant was trying without much success to give the Confederate a drink from his canteen. Grant reined in and looked at the two, then asked his staff officers if anyone had a flask. One officer finally produced one; Grant took it, dismounted, and walked to the two wounded men, giving each man a swallow of brandy. The Confederate murmured, "Thank you, General," and the Federal, too weak to speak, managed to flutter one hand in an attempt at a salute. Grant called to Rawlins: "Send for stretchers; send for stretchers at once for these men." As the stretcher party came up Grant got on his horse; then he noticed that the stretcher bearers, picking up the Union officer, seemed inclined to ignore the Confederate.

"Take this Confederate, too," he ordered. "Take them both together; the war is over between them."

The men were borne away, and Grant and his party rode off. There were so many dead and wounded men that the horses were constantly shying nervously, and Grant at last turned to Colonel Webster with the remark: "Let's get away from this dreadful place. I suppose this work is part of the devil that is left in us all." They got out to more open ground, and as the general watched the wounded men limping, hobbling and crawling toward the rear he was obviously depressed. One officer remembered hearing Grant—who rarely recited poetry—intoning the verse:

> Man's inhumanity to man
> Makes countless thousands mourn

Grant Moves South

BETWEEN THE LINES: CHATTANOOGA

Before the Battle of Missionary Ridge, Grant went riding out along the picket lines, where he had several strange encounters. To understand one of them it is necessary to know that at times the ill-clad Confederates sometimes wore captured Federal uniforms.

While Grant waited for Sherman, he began to find that the situation at Chattanooga was in some respects unusual. The Confederates had been holding their dominant position for so long that they seemed to look on all of the Yankees in Chattanooga as their ultimate prisoners; regarding them so, they found little reason to make a tough war out of it. Grant went out one day to inspect the Federal lines, and he reached a point where Federal and Confederate picket posts were not far apart. As he approached the Federal post the sentry turned out the guard; Grant dismissed it and rode on—only to hear, before he had gone fifty yards, another cry: "Turn out the guard for the commanding general!" Immediately a snappy set of Confederates came swarming out, formed a neat military rank, came to attention, and presented arms. Grant returned the salute and rode away. . . . A little later he reached a spring which soldiers of both armies sometimes used. On a log by the spring was a soldier in blue, his musket at his side. Grant asked him what corps he belonged to, and the man, getting up and saluting respectfully, replied that he was one of Longstreet's men. Before they went their separate ways, Union commander and Confederate private had quite a chat.

This Hallowed Ground

So Lincoln described his new general, remarking that Grant might be in a room with you for a minute or so before you noticed him. It had happened several times to him, Lincoln said. Indeed Grant was unobtrusive almost to the point of invisibility, even in his moment of triumph in 1864.

"QUIETEST LITTLE FELLOW YOU EVER SAW"

Grant never could make an entrance, and he came to Washington like an unsung job-hunter from the far places. The White House had designated proper persons to meet the train and escort him to his hotel, but somehow the arrangements fell through and Grant was met by nobody. He arrived late in the afternoon of March 8, accompanied by his son Fred (going on fourteen . . .), and Grant got to Willard's Hotel unattended, travel-stained and rumpled, a plain linen duster hiding most of his uniform. A bored registration clerk looked at him, saw nobody in particular, and said that there might be a room on the top floor. Grant said this would be all right, and signed the register, and the clerk swung the book around, to write down a room number after the name, and saw the entry: "U. S. Grant and son, Galena, Ill." The clerk suddenly came alive, remembered that there was a fine reservation on the second floor—bridal suite, or some such, apparently—and came bustling out from behind the desk to carry the general's bag upstairs personally. Grant and his son freshened up, and then came down to the dining room for dinner.

For a few minutes all was quiet. But Fred Grant remembered all his life how the people at the nearby tables looked, looked again, and began to whisper excitedly to one another. There was a general buzz of "There's Grant!" and presently some officious citizen stood up, hammered on a table with his knife until he had everyone's attention, and called out that he had the honor to

announce that Lieutenant General Grant was present in the dining room
People scrambled to their feet, there was a rhythmic shout of "Grant! Grant
Grant!" and someone called for three cheers, which were promptly given. Gran
stood up, fumbled with his napkin, bowed impersonally to all points of the
compass, and then sat down and tried to go on with his dinner. He did not ge
much to eat, because too many people were swarming about him, and before
long the general and the boy left the dining room and went up to their living
quarters.

Not long after this a political person came to Grant's door—forme
Secretary of War Simon Cameron, as Fred remembered it; Congressman James
K. Moorhead of Pennsylvania, by reporter [Noah] Brooks's account—and he
bustled Grant off to the White House. There was a presidential reception this
evening, it had been reported that Grant might make an appearance, and al
though the March night was wet and raw an oversized crowd was present. . .

When Grant came inside the White House the crowd parted like the Red Sea
waves, leaving an open lane for him, everybody telling his neighbor that this
really was General Grant; and at the far end of the lane there was Abraham
Lincoln, all lanky six feet four of him, wearing (as a sympathetic friend
confessed) a collar one size too large and a necktie "rather broad and
awkwardly tied." Lincoln stepped forward, his hand outstretched, a smile on his
face, and Grant walked toward him; a White House secretary considered it "a
long walk for a bashful man, the eyes of the world upon him," and when the
walk ended and the two men shook hands President Lincoln's three-year search
for a general had ended. The President pumped Grant's hand vigorously, saying
"Why, here is General Grant! Well, this is a great pleasure, I assure you!" The
handshaking over, the two stood together for a moment, Lincoln beaming down
in vast good humor (he was the taller of the two men by a good eight inches
and Grant looking up at him, his right hand grasping the lapel of his uniform
coat. Then the President beckoned to Secretary of State William H. Seward
who took Grant off to present him to Mrs. Lincoln; and a few minutes late
Seward led him into the East Room, where most of the crowd was waiting.

When Grant came in enthusiasm boiled over, and people began to cheer and
press forward, and Grant had to stand up on a sofa, partly so that he could
shake the hands that were thrust at him and partly to avoid being trampled
underfoot. Gideon Welles, Secretary of the Navy, looked on uneasily, considering
the scene "rowdy and unseemly," and Brooks said of the cheering crowd that
"it was the only real mob I ever saw in the White House." Incredibly enough
Grant had to stand on the sofa for the better part of an hour, and Brooks wrote
"For once at least the President of the United States was not the chief figure in
the picture. The little, scared-looking man who stood on a crimson-covered sofa
was the idol of the hour."

Grant Takes Command

Grant made it clear he would not be a Washington general, and was soon back in the Western theater of war to confer with his subordinates and lay plans for the future.

A NIGHT OUT

A t Nashville Grant talked with the man he most wanted to see, Sherman, and with a few others especially trusted—McPherson, Grenville Dodge, John A. Logan, [John] Rawlins, and the hardheaded young general who had won Grant's heart at Chattanooga, Phil Sheridan. With these men for a few days Grant had a conference in which casual informality was blended with attention to business; Grant could relax here, with these men, even while attending to important affairs, as he never could relax at headquarters in the East. As a matter of protocol he took his officers to the State House to call on Governor Andrew Johnson. Looking back afterward, Dodge remembered that "we were a hard-looking crowd" in service uniforms that showed much wear, and he said that a quizzical look in the governor's eye indicated that Andy Johnson had taken note of this fact. Grant came to the rescue by telling the governor that he had not given his men time to change to dress uniforms, and Dodge reflected that "Grant knew we had no others" than the stained clothes they were wearing.

After they got away from the State House the generals went to the theater to see *Hamlet* . . . and Sherman, who liked going to the theater above all other pleasures, felt that the unskillful actors were murdering the play, and said so repeatedly, out loud, until Dodge managed to quiet him by pointing out that the audience was full of soldiers and that if their attention were drawn to Grant's party they would probably create a scene. When the play at last reached the graveyard sequence, and Hamlet picked up Yorick's skull to soliloquize over it, some soldier in the audience, who had seen enough skulls and open graves for a dozen dramatists, sang out: "Say, pard, what is it—Yank, or Reb?" In the uproar that followed Grant's party left the theater, and then they went all over Nashville looking for a restaurant where they could buy some oysters. They found one at last, sat around a table talking brightly over bowls of stew, and dawdled so much that the proprietress (recognizing neither her customers nor the fact that they constituted enough top brass to suspend any military regulation) ejected them, somewhat wrathfully, with the remark that General Grant's curfew regulations compelled her to close at midnight.

Grant Takes Command

"GRANT MEANS BUSINESS"

What Grant really was would appear when the battles came. Meanwhile, although everyone in and out of the army was trying to appraise him all anyone could be sure of was that he was the last chance. He himself had told his intimates at Nashville that the coming campaign had to be the last one, and implicit in his promotion had been the belief that he was the man who would win the war; implicit, also, was the notion that he would win it quickly, and this built up added pressure. Men looked for more than they could see; wanting to see greatness, and seeing instead the very essence of the ordinary, they felt that there must be unfathomable depths here, a quality no one could understand because nobody could see it. Even Sherman once cried out: "To me he is a mystery, and I believe he is a mystery to himself." An officer who served with him in the West agreed: "There is no great character in history . . . whose sources of power have seemed so difficult to discover as General Grant's." A woman who saw something of him in Washington wrote that although he was the most democratic of men he seemed to keep everyone at arm's length, and said that "he walked through a crowd as though solitary." Lieutenant Morris Schaff of Meade's staff saw "a fascinating mystery in his greatness," and said that at headquarters Grant somehow was "the center of a pervasive quiet."

The mystery perhaps came because Grant did not look the part. Incurably, he remained the man who could walk into a room without being noticed; there must be more here than met the eye, because what met the eye usually seemed to be nothing at all. Men who talked with him felt that there was an air of reserve about him; yet this was largely because Grant found it hard to relax with strangers. General Jacob Cox felt this reserve when he met Grant in east Tennessee, but he concluded that Grant simply had no knack for small talk except when he was with men he knew well. Grant would smoke, listen, look pleasant and say nothing—and yet with people he knew he enjoyed light conversation and was very much at his ease. Sherman agreed that "Grant is really social and likes to see people and hear them talk of old times and old things." Sherman warned that on duty Grant did not like to hear much talk: "The best way to deal with Grant is 'on paper,' giving dates, facts and figures." A man who visited Grant at Chattanooga believed that Grant's success was due mostly "to his fine common sense and the faculty he possesses in a wonderful degree of making himself understood." A mail clerk at Grant's headquarters said that an officer warned him when he came to work: "All you have to do to get along with the general is to take straight orders and go straight at them. He will tell you what to do but not how or where or why to do it. He will turn his back and expect it to be done. Look him straight in the eye and don't say 'Sir' too much." This same clerk told Hamlin Garland after the war that he never knew Grant to hesitate about anything, and never saw him flurried or excited:

"He was a man who always knew just exactly what he wanted to do."

Some men looked at Grant and to their dismay saw in him no trace of breeding or gentility. They felt that the nation's principal general ought to have these qualities, but Grant evidently did not; like the President who had appointed him, he was just an outlander. The distinguished Richard Henry Dana, Jr., expressed it after he met Grant in Willard's Hotel one day late in April. Dana concluded sadly that the man was no gentleman; he "had no gait, no station, no manner"; he was smoking a cigar, he had "rather the look of a man who did, or once did, take a little too much to drink," and altogether he seemed to be an "ordinary, scrubby looking man with a slightly seedy look, as if he was out of office on half pay." A week or so later Dana visited the White House, saw Lincoln, found him no better, and wrote to his father: "Such a shapeless mass of writhing ugliness as slouched about in the President's chair you never saw or imagined." In a letter to his wife, Dana admitted that it was hard to keep from feeling an interest in the President—"a sympathy and a kind of pity"—and it seemed clear that Lincoln had "qualities of great value"; yet Dana could not avoid the belief that "his weak points may wreck him, or wreck something."

The war had got into the wrong hands. There was no help for it, and Back Bay and Beacon Street were suffering along with tidewater Virginia. The country was finding its leaders, to say nothing of its stoutest followers, among the men who had no ancestors as Massachusetts and Virginia understood such matters; the salient fact of the war this spring was that Lincoln and Grant had at last gone into partnership, and a well-bred observer was bound to shudder at the thought.

Grant himself seems to have understood that the army would judge him by what he did rather than by what he looked like; and here, as the man in Chattanooga had said, he had no trouble making himself understood. One day not long before the opening of the campaign Brigadier General Rufus Ingalls, chief quartermaster of the Army of the Potomac, needed to confer with him. In this army a meeting with the commanding general was always a formal occasion, with everybody turned out just so, and Ingalls put on his best uniform and boots of a dazzling polish and rode over in a covered wagon drawn by four dapple-gray horses which had been groomed as carefully as if the fate of the nation depended on it. Four orderlies, all in their best and riding horses equally well cared-for, rode in attendance, and altogether it was as showy and impressive as anything one would care to see.

On a road near Culpeper, Ingalls saw Grant riding toward him, coming back from a review. Ingalls had his driver pull to a halt; Grant saw him, and rode over beside the wagon to shake hands—after all, he and Ingalls had been classmates at West Point. Ingalls remarked that he had business to talk about, and Grant said: "Very well—we can talk it over here as well as any place."

Grant dismounted, and Ingalls got down from his comfortable seat, and the two men started walking up and down the road together, Ingalls explaining what he had on his mind, Grant nodding his head, now and then asking a question.

The road was extremely muddy. There was a slow drizzle. There was a good deal of traffic, and every time a horse or wagon went by the generals were spattered. They kept on walking back and forth for an hour, and at last Grant said: "That's all—goodbye, General." Grant mounted and rode away, Ingalls got in his wagon and went back to the Army of the Potomac, and the meeting was over; and Ingalls was muddy and bedraggled, the shine on his boots all gone. He was heard to mutter that this was the last time he would dress up to call on any general, and when he saw Meade, Ingalls said: "I tell you, Meade, Grant means business." And the orderlies wagged their heads and remarked that the general-in-chief did not care much about spit and polish.

Grant Takes Command

"WE HAD BETTER LEAVE HIM ALONE"

While he was in Washington, Grant told the generals, he had grappled with one of the most vexing problems of army administration—the fact that the various army staff departments, quartermaster, commissary, ordnance and so on, were by tradition and established practice out from under the control of army commanders. These agencies considered themselves independent, and they were quite likely to ignore orders from a field commander unless the orders were confirmed by their own chiefs in Washington. Grant insisted that the general-in-chief must have control, and when a certain commissary officer refused to carry out one of his orders Grant told him (as Dodge recalled it) that "while he could not force him to obey the order he could relieve him and put in his place one of the line officers, who would obey all the orders." The matter finally went to President Lincoln, and Grant said the President told him that although he could not legally give him command of the staff departments, "there is no one but myself that can interfere with your orders, and you can rest assured that I will not."

It appeared that the White House would support Grant all the way. Somewhat similar to this anecdote is a tale Rawlins told to William Conant Church, editor of the *Army and Navy Journal*. As Church remembered it, Grant a little later this spring ran afoul of Secretary Stanton, who complained that Grant was withdrawing too many men from the Washington fortifications and demanded an explanation.

"I think I rank you in this matter, Mr. Secretary," said Grant.

"We shall have to see Mr. Lincoln about that," Stanton replied.

So off to the White House they went, secretary of war and general-in-chief, where the secretary explained the point at issue. To him President Lincoln replied:

"You and I, Mr. Stanton, have been trying to boss this job, and we have not succeeded very well with it. We have sent across the mountains for Mr. Grant, as Mrs. Grant calls him, to relieve us, and I think we had better leave him alone to do as he pleases." . . .

[A] unique relationship . . . quickly developed between the President and his general-in-chief. It was quite unlike anything any other general had with Abraham Lincoln; the President trusted Grant as he had trusted none of his predecessors, trusted him so completely that he did not even ask him how he intended to use the immense power that had been given him. The first thing Grant did on his return from Nashville was to go to the White House, where for the first time he and Lincoln talked with no third party present; and Grant seems to have felt that he had better be somewhat reticent, because both Stanton and Halleck had warned him not to tell the President his plans—the President found it almost impossible to keep a secret. But this interview had hardly begun when Lincoln gave Grant the same warning. People were always asking him, he said, what was going to happen next, "and there was always a temptation to leak," so he did not want to know what Grant was going to do. . . .

A few days after this interview Grant gave an account of the conversation to the newest member of his staff, Horace Porter. . . . President Lincoln, said Grant (as Porter wrote it down afterward), "told me that he did not pretend to know anything about the handling of troops, and it was with the greatest reluctance that he ever interfered with the movements of army commanders; but he had common sense enough to know that celerity was absolutely necessary. . . .

Somewhat diffidently, Lincoln told Grant of a campaign plan of his own, "which he wanted me to hear and then do as I pleased about." Lincoln brought out a map of Virginia, marked to show all the positions the Union and Confederate armies had occupied thus far, and pointed to two streams which empty into the Potomac: might not an army land between the mouths of those streams and then advance safely with the two rivers protecting its flanks? Grant did not describe this proposal to Porter, telling him only that the President made a suggestion which was quite impracticable "and it was not again referred to in our conversations." In his *Memoirs*, Grant said simply: "I listened respectfully but did not suggest that the same streams would protect Lee's flanks while he was shutting us up."

Grant Takes Command

VIII

War as Hell

General William Tecumseh Sherman, U. S. A.

General Sherman could not remember ever having said "War is hell." This is what he did say, in a speech to a G.A.R. convention in Ohio in 1880: "There is many a boy here today that looks on war as all glory, but boys, it is all hell. You can hear this warning voice to generations yet to come. I look upon war with horror." But what matters mainly is that he spoke truth from terrible experience. And the horror of the slaughter-pens of the Civil War is not hidden from or romanticized for Bruce Catton's readers. At Spotsylvania, in May, 1864, for example, in a Confederate-held salient shaped like a mule shoe, Union infantry had seized some forward trenches—only to receive a fierce counterattack.

There were wild flurries of hand-to-hand fighting. Here and there the Confederates came all the way up to the line of trenches, and there were places where Federals crouched on one side of a log breastwork while Confederates crouched on the other side, not five feet away. Men shot through the chinks between the logs, or jabbed through them with bayonets, or held their muskets overhead at arm's length, muzzles pointed downward, to shoot blindly over the parapet. Now and then soldiers on either side would clamber on top of the logs, firing at point-blank range until they were killed. There were times when soldiers leaned over the parapet, seized their opponents, and hauled them over bodily, making prisoners of them.

The fighting was worst of all at a place a few hundred yards west of the actual tip of the salient, a place where the trench made a sudden turn, and this spot was known forever after, with excellent reason, as the Bloody Angle. The trenches were knee-deep in mud and rainwater, wounded men drowning there, dead men falling on top of them. For a final touch, the soldiers occasionally had to stop fighting and lift the broken bodies out of the trench so that they themselves could stand there.

Where the fighting was not actually hand-to-hand opposing troops in most places were not more than a few dozen yards apart, and the men on both sides fired without a letup; and as a matter of fact the fighting in such cases was probably deadlier than it was at the angle itself, because if the battle lines were a little farther apart they were unprotected. One Confederate officer said afterward that "there was one continuous roll of musketry from dawn until midnight," and the storm of bullets splintered the log breastworks, whipped trees and bushes into fragments, killed and wounded men and then cut up their bodies until they were unrecognizable, and made it impossible for the Federals to do anything with the guns they had captured. The guns simply stood there in the mud, no one firing them, no one hauling them away, dead bodies lying across the trails and under the wheels.

Lee kept sending in more troops, and a Federal headquarters staff officer asserted that the Confederates made five separate assaults during the day. Far to the rear, Lee had men building a new entrenchment across the base of the mule shoe, and to save his army he had to hold the disputed ground until this line of works was finished. Building it was an all-day job, so the Confederates up in front had to stay there and slug it out. Hancock's men stayed there too . . . and the rifle fire rose to a pitch never heard in any battle before. Along the line of the disputed trench there were occasional lulls, as exhausted men tried to catch their breath and nerve themselves for a new effort; then, as often as not, a whole regiment would suddenly stand erect, fire a hasty volley, and duck down immediately afterward to escape the volley that would come in reply. The rain kept on falling, and the battleground was all soft mud in which dead and wounded men sank half out of sight. The wounded men who lay in the mud were in a bad plight, because it was hard for stretcher bearers to work here. Federal doctors said afterward that in ordinary battles most of the wounded were able to walk, or to drag themselves, back to the dressing stations; but at Spotsylvania on May 12 not one-quarter of the wounded could get to the rear without being carried. Meade's medical director wrote that "the amount of shock and depression of vital power was noticed to be comparatively much greater in the wounded of this battle than in any preceding one of the campaign." This was especially true, he said, among the wounded from Hancock's corps, which went into action without breakfast or a morning cup of coffee. . . .

Wright's Corps . . . sent a division (with [General] Emory Upton's brigade in front) up to the western face . . . of the salient at about six in the morning. These men helped Hancock's soldiers hold on to the ragged position in and near the captured earthworks—it appears that they were the ones engaged at the Bloody Angle—but although they maintained a steady fire they were unable to blast the Confederates out of the way. Once Upton ordered a battery right up to the front, in a move that was as fantastic as it was horrible. The gun crews were under fire all the way, horses were killed in full gallop and were dragged along by the frantic teams, the wheels of the guns ran over dead and wounded men and rammed them deeper into the mud, and although the effect of the guns' fire, when at last they got into battery, was devastating—they were firing canister at foes only a few yards away—the fire did not last long because most of the gunners were quickly shot. The guns stayed there, silent and useless as the ones that had been captured earlier, black and ugly on a desolate, rain-swept landscape, gun carriages and caissons reduced almost to kindling wood by the incessant storm of rifle fire.

Grant was up at dawn, and he sat in a canvas chair by a campfire in front of the headquarters tents, getting progress reports and sending staff officers about with orders. Once Meade came over for a brief conference, returning before long to his own headquarters to order Warren to make an attack along the right of the Union line. The campfire was more smoke than flame, by now, and the gusty wind alternately hid Grant behind clouds of smoke and flipped the cape of his overcoat over his face, so now and then he got up to pace back and forth in the unrelenting rain. The first reports he got showed that things were going well, and when he learned that Hancock had captured almost all of a division of Confederate troops he displayed what was, for him, outright enthusiasm, remarking that this was the kind of news he wanted to get. Not long afterward Meade came back, bringing with him a prisoner—Major General Edward Johnson, commander of the captured division. Johnson had known both Grant and Meade before the war, and Grant gave him a chair by the . . . fire and chatted with him in friendly fashion before having him escorted to the rear. . . .

Men who looked at the captured works that day saw things worse than any the war had yet shown them. A brigadier in Wright's corps said that in the Bloody Angle trench, between traverses in a space measuring no more than fifteen by twelve feet, he counted 150 bodies. A Pennsylvania officer reported that in places the dead men were sprawled eight or ten bodies deep, filling the rifle pits, and a man in the 5th Maine who went to look for a company officer who had been killed said that the man's body had been so dreadfully mangled by rifle fire that "there was not four inches of space about his person that had not been struck by bullets." Confederate testimony was much the same, edged sometimes by awe at the determination of the Federal attacks. A North Carolina man wrote to his mother that "there has never been such fighting I reckon in the history of war," adding that "Old Grant is certainly a very stubborn fighter."

Grant Takes Command

The battle just before that at Spotsylvania, in a forested tract called the Wilderness, had another kind of horror.

IN THE WILDERNESS

Darkness brought a pause, but in this battle even a lull was not a time of quiet. As the firing died down, the front was alive with the sound of axes and falling trees, as soldiers worked desperately to improvise wooden breastworks. Any movement at all—details going into the forest to collect wounded men, patrols trying to explore the front, displaced soldiers wandering about trying to find their regiments—could set off a new wave of firing, with everybody grabbing his musket and letting off a few rounds until it sounded, in the rear, as if the battle had started up all over again. Here and there it had been possible to put field artillery in position, and when the infantry began firing the guns would join in, flogging the thick woods with shell, stabbing the night with flame, here and there causing an accidental casualty.

Malignant little fires worked through the underbrush and the matted dead leaves all across the front, and along with all of the other sounds of battle there was a steady calling by wounded men who wanted to be rescued before they were burned to death. In front of the 5th Maine a disabled Federal screamed for help when the flames reached him. Two men ran forward to help, and each was shot down, skirmish-line shooting being heavy just now. At last a sergeant who dared not go forward took careful aim with his musket and shot the wounded man to death to put him out of his agony. In front of Wadsworth's division, where lay many dead and wounded of both armies, a dying Confederate kept calling: "My God, why hast Thou forsaken me!" After the war General Humphreys estimated that at least 200 Federals died in the forest fire that night.

Grant Takes Command

"YOU DON'T KNOW HOW TO HATE"

If Lee's army had not suffered much, the town of Fredericksburg had suffered dreadfully. In plain English, the town had been sacked, and the destruction which General Hunt's guns had caused had been the least of its woes. Both before, during, and after the actual fighting, the Army of the Potomac had unleashed upon this historic town the spirit of unrestrained rowdyism. The very divisions which had mustered the incredible heroism to make the repeated attacks on the stone wall had also put on display the very essence of jackbooted vandalism. A veteran of the 118th Pennsylvania left a description:

"The city had been rudely sacked; household furniture lined the streets. Books and battered pictures, bureaus, lounges, feather beds, clocks, and every conceivable article of goods, chattels, and apparel had been savagely torn from the houses and lay about in wanton confusion in all directions. Fires were made, both for warmth and cooking, with fragments of broken furniture. Pianos, their harmonious strings displaced, were utilized as horse troughs, and amid all the dangers animals quietly ate from them." A soldier in another Pennsylvania regiment noted "great scenes of vandalism and useless destruction of books, furniture, carpets, pianos, pictures, etc.," and reported a grotesque carnival aspect in streets still swept by Confederate shell as Union soldiers cavorted about in women's dresses and underwear. "Some of these characters," he added, "might be seen with musical instruments, with big horns, violins, accordions, and banjos"; and he noted that his own regiment took several hundred bottles of wine out of someone's cellar, a part of this wine appearing later on the colonel's own mess table. One illiterate private rifled an express

Hard ground, winter graves: City Point, Virginia, during the siege of Petersburg

office and carried off a huge bundle of receipts and canceled checks under the impression that he was robbing a bank and getting money.

Brigadier General Alfred Sully, from Howard's division, took over a handsome house for his headquarters and told members of the 1st Minnesota, of which he had previously been colonel, to go through it and take anything they wanted. It belonged to his brother-in-law, who, he said, was a damned Rebel. Perversely, the Minnesota boys took nothing whatever from it and even established a guard there so that nobody else could loot it either. The regimental historian, maintaining that the sack of Fredericksburg was justified by the laws of war, added regretfully that "it would be pleasanter to remember Fredericksburg had there been no looting."

Some of the higher officers, indeed, looking back on it, did argue that by the ancient rules of warfare Fredericksburg was properly open to pillage. An inhabited town, it had been called on to surrender before the battle and it had refused, and the troops had then taken it by storm. Since time immemorial, a town taken under such conditions was fair prey for the men who had captured it. But the men who looted Fredericksburg were not going by the books. The Army of the Potomac behaved there as it had never behaved before, and none of the explanations commonly advanced for lawless behavior by Union troops in this war holds good in this case.

Looting, pillaging, and illegal foraging by Federal soldiers are usually blamed on loosely disciplined Western troops, or on the riffraff bounty men, or on the German regiments brought up in the European tradition, or on the excesses natural to an army which is supplying itself from the enemy's country, or on the studied policy of commanders like Sherman and Sheridan who were frankly out to make Southern civilians tired of the war. But not one of these reasons is any good here. Fredericksburg was ransacked, not by free-and-easy Westerners but chiefly by Easterners of the II Corps and the V Corps, crack outfits with excellent discipline. The army contained no bounty men to speak of, and the German regiments were not in Fredericksburg. The army was not living off the enemy's country but was solidly planted on its own supply lines, and it was under the direction of a general who, however breath-taking some of his deficiencies may have been, was at least a good, amiable man who tried not to make war on civilians. If the usual explanations are good, Fredericksburg should have survived the occupation with minor damage. Actually, the army all but took it apart. . . .

This was the country of the boisterous forty-niner, the hell-roaring lumberjack, and the riverman who was half horse and half alligator. Without rancor (and also without the slightest hesitation) it annihilated Indian tribes so that it could people a wilderness, asserting that the only good Indian was a dead Indian and remarking casually of its own pioneers that the cowards never started and the weak died along the road. As it faced the cathedral aisles of endless virgin forests it shouted for immediate daylight in the swamp, even if whole generations must be brutalized for it. It was the country that invented the bucko mate and the Shanghai passage, and if the skysails of its incredible clippers gleamed on the farthest magic horizon they were taken there by men under the daily rule of clubs and brass knuckles. This nation accepted boiler explosions as the price of steamboat travel and it would boast presently of a dead gandy-dancer for every crosstie on the transcontinental railroad. It wore seven-league boots and scorned to look where it planted them, and each of its immense strides was made at immense human cost. And the army of this country, buckling down to it at last in a fight which had to go to a finish, was going to be very rough on enemy civilians, not because it had anything against them but simply because they were there.

Of genuine hatred this army had practically none. The wild young men who ruined ancestral portraits and pranced in the smoky streets wearing the embroidered undergarments of gentlewomen were expressing nothing but plain hooliganism, which somehow was the obverse side of the medal that had laid nine hundred corpses in front of the stone wall west of town. Both sides of the medal bespoke raw youth which cheered and guffawed by turns, whose noble best forever went arm in arm with its ugly worst.

Before Burnside pulled his men back across the river there was a truce, and details from both armies went out to relieve such wounded as still lived and to bury the dead. In front of that stone wall, where all the dead men were Yankees, the lifeless bodies were nearly all naked. During the cold night needy Rebels had come out to help themselves to the warm coats and pants and the good Yankee shoes which the dead men would no longer need. An officer from the 48th Pennsylvania, supervising the work on one detail, fell into conversation with a Confederate officer, and the Confederate told him: "You Yankees don't know how to hate—you don't hate us near as much as we hate you." The Confederate gestured toward the pitiful naked rows of despoiled corpses and asked in effect: Do you think we could treat your dead that way if we didn't hate you?

Glory Road

It was spring, 1863. Desertion was a problem,
and the army met it in the old, hard way.

HARD WAR

Desertion was no longer being treated as a minor fault. The V Army Corps was drawn up in an open field one day, solid masses of bronzed veterans grouped around three sides of an open square, tattered flags motionless above them. One of the soldiers remembered afterward:

"The impressive silence was not broken by a single sound. Each line of soldiers looked more like the section of a vast machine than a line composed of

Union wounded

living men. The silence was suddenly and sadly broken by the sounds of approaching music—not the quick, inspiring strains with which we were so familiar, but a measured, slow and solemn dirge, whose weird, sorrowful notes were poured forth like the moanings of lost spirits. Not a soldier spoke, but every eye was turned in the direction from which came the sad and mournful cadences, and we saw the procession."

First came a band playing the "Funeral March." Then came sixty men from the provost guard, spick-and-span in dress uniforms, rifles at the shoulder. After them were four soldiers carrying a black coffin, followed by a condemned deserter in blue pants and white shirt, a guard on either side of him; then four more men with another coffin, followed by another prisoner, and another detachment with another coffin, and so on—five condemned deserters in all, each preceded by his coffin, with a final detachment from the provost guard bringing up the rear. The procession came to the open side of the square, where five graves had been dug. A coffin was put on the ground before each grave, and each prisoner sat on the end of his coffin. Black blindfolds were put on the prisoners, thousands of men looking on in utter silence, and then the chaplains came up beside the condemned men for a final word and a prayer. The chaplains retired, and a firing squad of twelve men took post facing each prisoner, one blank charge in every twelve rifles, so that any member of a firing squad might later, if it comforted him, think that perhaps he himself had not actually killed anyone. An officer stepped out, brisk and businesslike, sword hooked up at his side, and the great silence was broken by his thin cry: "Ready—aim—*fire!*" And the thing was done, five bleeding bodies lay across the coffins, and the band piped up a quickstep while the soldiers marched off the field.

Glory Road

GUERILLA WARFARE IN THE SHENANDOAH VALLEY

Guerilla warfare was putting an edge on the fighting that had been seen nowhere else in Virginia. In modern terms, the Confederacy had organized a resistance movement in territory occupied by the hated Yankees; had organized it, and then had seen it get badly out of hand.

The Valley was full of men who were Confederate soldiers by fits and starts—loosely organized and loosely controlled, most of them, innocent civilians six days a week and hell-roaring raiders the seventh day. They owned horses, weapons, and sometimes uniforms, which they carefully hid when they were not actually using them. Called together at intervals by their leaders, they would swoop down on outposts and picket lines, knock off wagon trains or supply depots, burn culverts and bridges behind the Federal front, and waylay any couriers, scouts, or other detached persons they could find. They compelled Union commanders to make heavy detachments to guard supply lines and depots, thus reducing the number of soldiers available for service in battle. To a certain extent they unintentionally compensated for this by reducing straggling in the Federal ranks, for the Northern soldier was firmly convinced that guerillas took no prisoners and that to be caught by them was to get a slit throat.

So the guerillas gave the Federal commanders a continuing headache—and, in the long run, probably did the Confederacy much more harm than good.

The quality of these guerilla bands varied greatly. At the top was John S. Mosby's: courageous soldiers led by a minor genius, highly effective in partisan warfare. Most of the groups, however, were about one degree better than plain outlaws, living for loot and excitement, doing no actual fighting if they could help it, and offering a secure refuge to any number of Confederate deserters and draft evaders. The Confederate cavalry leader, General Thomas L. Rosser, called them "a nuisance and an evil to the service," declaring:

"Without discipline, order or organization, they roam broadcast over the country, a band of thieves, stealing, pillaging, plundering and doing every manner of mischief and crime. They are a terror to the citizens and an injury to the cause. They never fight; can't be made to fight. Their leaders are generally brave, but few of the men are good soldiers."

Jeb Stuart, not long before his death, endorsed this sentiment, saying that Mosby's was the only ranger band he knew of that was halfway efficient and that even Mosby usually operated with only a fourth of his supposed strength, while Lee wrote to the Confederate Secretary of War strongly urging that all such groups be abolished, asserting: "I regard the whole system as an unmixed evil."

The worst damage which this system did to the Confederacy, however, was that it put Yankee soldiers in a mood to be vengeful.

By this time the Union authorities had had a good deal of experience with guerillas and they were getting very grim about it. Much of this conditioning had been gained in states like Tennessee and Missouri, where neighbor was bitter against neighbor and barn burnings and the murderous settlement of old grudges went hand in hand with attempts to discomfit the Yankee invader, and most Federal generals considered guerillas as mere bushwhackers, candidates for the noose or the firing squad. An exception was generally (though by no means always) made in the case of Mosby's men, who were recognized as being more or less regular soldiers, but the attitude toward the rest was summed up by a Union general along the upper Potomac, who said: "I have instructed my command not to bring any of them to my headquarters except for interment." . . .

A Michigan cavalryman remembered riding past a little home and seeing, in he gate of the fence by the road, an old woman, crying bitterly, blood flowing from a deep cut in one arm. He rode up to her and she told him that some soldier had struck her with his saber and then had taken her two cows. He wheeled and spurred after his regiment, found the officer in charge of the herd of confiscated cattle, recovered the two cows—or, at any rate, two cows which might have been the ones—and with the officer he tried in vain to find the man who had used the saber. Then he took the cows back to the woman, who thanked him in tearful surprise and told him that if he was ever captured by Mosby's men he should have them bring him to her home, and she would give testimony that would save him from being hanged.

So the army made its way back down the Valley, leaving desolation behind it, and the war came slowly nearer its end in the black smoke that drifted over the Blue Ridge. The war had begun with waving unstained flags and dreams of a picture-book fight which would concern no one but soldiers, who would die picturesquely and without bloodshed amid dress-parade firing lines, and it had come down now to burning barns, weeping children, and old women who had been hit with sabers. In the only way that was left to it, the war was coming toward its close. Phil Sheridan passed the word, and his scouts laughed and went trotting off to spy on the Rebels and play a clever game with the threat of a greased noose; and the guerillas met in dark copses on the edge of the army and rode out with smoking revolvers to kill the cripples, and now and then one of them was caught.

It happened so with a group of Sheridan's scouts, who captured a Captain Stump, famous as a Rebel raider, a man they had long been seeking. He had been wounded, and when he was caught they took his weapons away and brought him to Major Young, who commanded the scouts, and Major Young had a certain respect for this daring guerilla, so he told him:

"I suppose you know we will kill you. But we will not serve you as you have served our men—cut your throat or hang you. We will give you ten rods' start on your own horse, with your spurs on. If you get away, all right. . . . But remember, my men are dead shots."

Captain Stump was bloody and he had been hurt, but he was all man. He smiled, and nodded, and rode a few feet out in front of the rank of his captors—skinny young men, 130 pounds or less, unmarried, the pick of the Yankee cavalry. Major Young looked down the rank, and called out: "*Go!*"

A cavalryman wrote about it afterward:

"We allowed him about ten rods' start, then our pistols cracked and he fell forward, dead."

A Stillness at Appomattox

"THAT BRIGHT PARTICULAR STAR"

This was a war in which the top generals often came under fire, and in which a great number were killed. One of the most promising of such men, from whom the country might have expected much in years to come, was Major General James B. McPherson, whose life was snuffed out at the Battle of Atlanta.

McPherson was one of the attractive men in the Union army. He was young and brilliant; had been an honor man at West Point, was loved by Sherman as that grim soldier might have loved a gifted younger brother, and he wore a trim curly beard and had dancing lights of laughter in the corners of his eyes. He was thought to be somewhat Puritanical—he had said once that if to be a soldier a man had to forget the claims of humanity, "then I do not want to be a soldier"—yet he was full of life and bounce, and in captured Vicksburg he and brother officers had strolled through the streets in the evening, serenading Southern belles with sentimental vocalizing after the camps were still. . . . What had they sung? "Juanita," perhaps?

> Far o'er the mountain
> Breaks the day too soon. . . .

It does not matter much. McPherson was engaged to Miss Emily Hoffman of Baltimore, and he had planned to take leave in the winter of 1864 and go north and marry her. But the winter became very busy, and after Grant was summoned east and there were promotions all along the line Sherman had called McPherson in and had told him he could not have leave just now; McPherson was an army commander, the army had to be made ready for hard fighting, and his leave would have to wait until fall, or until next winter, or until some other time. McPherson had acquiesced, and he was still a bachelor; and now, late in July, he was bringing his army in on Atlanta from the east while Thomas's men buried the dead in front of Peachtree Creek, and Hood caught his formations off guard and was threatening to inflict a ruinous defeat.

McPherson was at lunch when the news reached him. He got his horse and galloped off to the scene of action, and along the way advancing Confederate skirmishers had found a gap in the Union lines and were pushing through for the rear. McPherson ran into some of them, wheeled to retreat, and was shot dead from the saddle; and farther on his leading division repulsed a frontal attack just in time to turn around and meet an attack that was coming in from the rear. General John A. Logan succeeded to McPherson's command and rode down the fighting lines, his felt hat clutched in one hand, his black hair and mustachios streaming in the wind, crying out to his men: "Will you hold this line for me? Will you hold this line?" The men liked Logan, and as they plied ramrods in hot musket barrels they began to chant his nickname—"Black Jack! Black Jack!" They held the line, beating off assaults that seemed to come

Major General James B. McPherson, U. S. A.

bewilderingly from all directions; and as the hot day wore away, the Army of the Tennessee at last managed to hold its position, Hood's counterblow was broken, and by evening the Union army was safe again.

Grim General Sherman wept unashamedly when McPherson's body was brought to headquarters. After the battle he wrote to Emily Hoffman in Baltimore, the girl who by now would have been Mrs. McPherson if Sherman had not intervened; a girl from a strongly Southern family which had not approved of her engagement to this Union general. When the telegram that announced McPherson's death came the girl heard a member of her family say: "I have the most wonderful news—McPherson is dead." Emily Hoffman went to her bedroom and did not come out of it for a solid year, living there with curtains drawn, trays of food brought to her door three times every day, speaking no word to anyone. To her, Sherman poured out his heart in a long letter:

"I yield to no one on earth but yourself the right to exceed me in lamentations for our dead hero. Rather the bride of McPherson dead than the wife of the richest merchant of Baltimore. . . . I see him now, so handsome, so smiling, on his fine black horse, booted and spurred, with his easy seat, the impersonation of the gallant knight."

Lamenting thus, Sherman thought of the fire-eaters who had helped bring on the war, and he lashed out at them: "The loss of a thousand men such as Davis and Yancey and Toombs and Floyd and Beechers and Greeleys and Lovejoys, would not atone for that of McPherson." Then, looking darkly into the mist of war that still lay ahead of him, this uncontrollable fighter tried to put a personal grief into words:

"Though the cannon booms now, and the angry rattle of musketry tells me that I also will likely pay the same penalty, yet while life lasts I will delight in the memory of that bright particular star which has gone before to prepare the way for us more hardened sinners who must struggle to the end."

The bright particular star was gone forever, and something that could never be regained went out of the war when McPherson died, just as had happened with the deaths of thousands of other young men who might have swung a golden light across the dark infinite sky; and meanwhile there was Hood's army in Atlanta, still defiant and still dangerous, and the war could not stop because something irreplaceable had been lost, even though many women had to retreat to darkened rooms to live in the muted dusk of grief. The war had to be won. . . .

This Hallowed Ground

*Sherman's army twisting and destroying railroad iron
over burning crossties, Georgia, 1864*

MARCHING THROUGH GEORGIA

Every morning each brigade would send out a detail of foragers—from twenty to fifty men, led by an officer and followed by a wagon to bring back what was seized—and this detail, whose members knew the route the army was following, was not expected to return to camp until evening. The foragers were ordered to stay out of inhabited dwellings and to seize no more food than was actually needed, but they were under the loosest sort of control and in any case they were joined, followed, and aided by a steadily growing riffraff of armed stragglers, who were known contemptuously as "bummers" and who knew very little restraint of any kind. Between the regular foraging parties and the lawless bummers, plantations that lay in this army's path were bound to have a very rough time.

There were some large and imposing plantations in the territory the army was crossing; Georgia was fat and fertile, the barns and smokehouses were crammed, and the men felt that they were in a land of surpassing richness. Earlier, on the way from Chattanooga down to Atlanta, they had felt that Georgia was a pretty poor state and remarked that they never saw any residences to compare with the regular farm buildings north of the Ohio. But the army had not gone two days on its move east from Atlanta before an Illinois soldier was writing that he "could begin to see where the 'rich planters' come in," and he added: "This is probably the most gigantic pleasure excursion ever planned. It already beats everything I ever saw soldiering and promises to prove much richer yet."

The whole Army of the Tennessee was making the same discovery, and it was responding with joyous whoops; and as it moved, the great march to the sea began to resemble nothing so much as one gigantic midwestern Halloween saturnalia, a whole month deep and two hundred and fifty miles long. A captain looked back on it all as "a kind of half-forgotten dream, now gay and lightsome, now troubled and gruesome." He recalled that there was "no fighting worthy of the name" and said that he and his mates "occupied ourselves chiefly in marching from one fertile valley to another, removing the substance of the land." Typical was one veteran's comment: "Our men are clear discouraged with foraging; they can't carry half the hogs and potatoes they find right along the road." . . .

Near Milledgeville the army had a brush with a few thousand Georgia militia, stiffened by a little regular cavalry. A brigade from the XV Corps routed the militia with practiced ease, and when the men crossed the field after their enemies had fled they saw with horror that they had been fighting against old men and young boys. One Federal wrote feelingly that "I was never so affected at the sight of dead and wounded before," and asserted: "I hope we will never have to shoot at such men again. They knew nothing at all about fighting and I think their officers knew as little."

Plantations were looted outright; men who had set out to take no more than hams and chickens began carrying away heirlooms, silver, watches—anything that struck their fancy. Here and there Southern patriots felled trees to obstruct roads, or burned bridges; there was never enough of this to delay the army seriously, but there was just enough to provoke reprisals, and barns and houses went up in smoke as a result. A general remarked that "as the habit of measuring right by might goes on, pillage becomes wanton and arson is committed to cover the pillage." An Illinois soldier confessed that "it could not be expected that among so many tens of thousands there would be no rogues," and another man from the same state burst out: "There is no God in war. It is merciless, cruel, vindictive, un-Christian, savage, relentless. It is all that devils could wish for."

This Hallowed Ground

The bloody little Battle of Wilson's Creek, Missouri, on August 10, 1861, happened to be a Confederate victory, but strategies and outcomes are often matters of mildest interest to plain people. The farmer's wife of this episode might have spoken for millions.

... BUT 'TWAS A FAMOUS VICTORY

Near the place where one of the Confederate batteries had been posted there was a farmhouse, and during the battle the farmer's wife had taken refuge in the cellar. She came out after the battle ended and found a party of soldiers helping themselves to apples from her trees. An officer rode up and told the men to stop it, but the woman assured him that she did not mind; there were plenty of apples, everybody had had a pretty bad morning, let them take all they wanted. Then, looking at the boys fresh from the battle that had been raging at her own doorstep, she asked, as an afterthought, a question which might have been asked by the harassed Missouri majority, the farm people on whose homesteads the fighting and the marauding were taking place and who stood to be plundered and fought over no matter which army was present. "Are you Lincoln's folk, or Jeff Davis's folk?" she inquired. Jeff Davis's folk, the boys said.

Terrible Swift Sword

IX

Year of Jubilo

Men of the 107th Colored Infantry

Slavery, either its abolition or its preservation, was not the cause of the war; such at least was the official position of the two sides at the outset. Many Southerners deplored it, and in the North the abolitionists were regarded as a minority of noisy extremists. That the anachronistic institution was in fact the underlying problem, a social and racial issue of the deepest emotional character for both sides, was perceived only slowly—and acted upon by the Lincoln administration mostly as a means of winning the war. The President had said he meant to preserve the Union; and if that required freeing all the slaves, or none, or simply some of them, he would do whatever was necessary.

It was the slaves themselves, knowing little of states' rights or Constitutional questions, who understood very clearly and simply where history was tending. And they voted with their feet. Freedom was coming at last with the Yankee armies, and the blacks flocked after them. And it came to pass that the problem of dealing with them was first dumped into the hands of one of the wiliest political generals in American history, the celebrated (and much-despised) Benjamin F. Butler of Massachusetts.

Ben Butler [was the] man seemingly appointed now, in the infinite Providence of God, to cast his own strange ray of revealing light on the way the war must go. To the relief of everyone, Butler had been lifted out [of the military control] of Maryland and had been set down, by the Federal War Department, at Fort Monroe, at the tip of the Virginia peninsula. Here, trying to be an administrator and a warrior, succeeding imperfectly in each, he would bring up for definition the one thing both sides did not want mentioned just now—the deep underlying wrong of human slavery. Meaning nothing more than a good lawyer's shrewdness, he helped to define the war.

Into Butler's lines, late in May, came three fugitive Negro slaves, men whose master had had them using pick and shovel to erect a battery for Confederate guns. Their arrival was unwelcome. The fugitive slave law remained on the books; legally, General Butler was required to deliver these chattels up to their lawful owner, and nobody in Washington had so much as hinted that he might do something different. The lawful owner turned out to be a Colonel Charles Mallory, in the Confederate service, and Colonel Mallory wanted his possessions returned to him. Butler, wholly devoid of feeling, had a lawyer's cunning; had also, apparently, an instinct for the inner meaning of things. Property of men in rebellion against the United States, he held—spades, wagons, farms, whatnot—could be taken over by the national authority as contraband of war; these three colored men were indisputably property, owned by a man in a condition of unrelieved rebellion, and they were, accordingly, *contrabands.* General Butler would hold them and use them. He had given a word to the national language and an idea to the national administration, and the word and the idea would go on working.

Other Negroes came, in the days that followed, and Butler presently told the War Department that he would keep these people and use them, letting the strong men build wharves, dig trenches, build roads, and do similar things, having the women cook meals and launder clothes, suffering the children to exist: "As a matter of property to the insurgents it will be of very great moment, the number I now have amounting, as I am informed, to what in good times would be of the value of $60,000." At least a dozen of the fugitives, he learned, had been building batteries on Sewell's Point, commanding the approaches to Norfolk; and so Butler argued that "as a military question it would seem to be a measure of necessity to deprive their masters of their services."

Unquestionably; and when Major J. B. Cary, of the Confederate army, came to see General Butler, and suggested that the Constitution required the general to deliver up errant slaves under the fugitive slave act, Butler had a ready answer. "I replied that the fugitive slave act did not affect a foreign country, which Virginia claimed to be, and that she must reckon it as one of the infelicities of her position that in so far at least she was taken at her word." . . .

The news got about the plantation grapevine, and before long the general found himself harboring dozens, scores, and hundreds of fugitive slaves. He put all who were able-bodied to work, and in spite of himself he found himself, within weeks, controlling a "contraband camp" with 900 inhabitants. He advanced, at one time this spring, into the Virginia village of Hampton, from which point, before long, he was obliged to withdraw; when he withdrew, huge numbers of Negroes (who had been working for him, in Hampton) followed him, pursued, as Butler believed, by gray-clad soldiers who threatened to shoot the men "and to carry off the women who had served us to a worse than Egyptian bondage."

Butler wrote to the War Department for guidance. (His tongue may have been in his cheek at the time, but nevertheless he wrote.) He had, he said, treated able-bodied Negroes "as property liable to be used in aid of rebellion" and so as contraband of war. Now he had many of these people on his hands. Were they in fact property? If so, whose property were they? Their owners had abandoned them, or had been legally bereft of them. He, who now possessed them, did not own them and did not want to own them; were they now, therefore, property at all? "Have they not become, thereupon," he asked, as plaintively as if he had deep convictions on the matter, "men, women and children? . . . I confess that my own mind is compelled by this reason to look upon them as men and women. If not free born, yet free, manumitted, sent forth from the hand that held them never to be reclaimed."

Secretary Cameron agreed. He wrote a reply which went all the way around Robin Hood's barn to insist that the war was being fought to preserve the

Union and protect the Constitutional rights of all citizens, one of these rights being the right to repossess slaves who had fled from servitude; but at the same time, "in states wholly or partly under insurrectionary control," things were a bit different. Congress, very significantly, had recently held that slaves employed in hostility to the United States were no longer slaves. To be sure, in a state like Virginia (where there were slave owners who still professed loyalty to the Union) the case might be difficult. Still, the War Department felt that "the substantial rights of loyal masters are still best protected by receiving such fugitives, as well as fugitives from disloyal masters, into the Service of the United States, and employing them under such organizations and in such occupations as circumstances may suggest or require." At the same time, the General must be careful to do no proselytizing. His troops must not encourage "the servants of peaceable citizens in a house or field" to run away and join up with Uncle Sam. He must be passive; and, in his passivity, he must be firm.

The Coming Fury

I KNOW STAR-RISE

The use of colored troops was an experiment to which the Administration had been driven partly by the demands of the abolitionists and partly by sheer desperation, the supply of white manpower having slackened. The implications of this experiment were faced by few people, and there probably would be time enough to worry about them after the war had been won. At the moment the great riddle was whether it was possible to turn colored men into good soldiers.

Most of these ex-slaves were illiterate, used to servile obedience, and living (presumably) in deep awe of Southern white men. They were husky enough, and yet they somehow lacked physical sturdiness and endurance, and they had been held at the bottom of the heap for so long that they seemed to be excessively long-suffering by nature. Somewhere, far back in dim tribal memories, there may have been traditions of war parties and fighting and desperate combat, but these had been overlaid by generations of slavery, and most colored folk saw themselves as pilgrims toiling up the endless slopes of heartbreak hill—pilgrims whose survival depended on the patient, uncomplaining acceptance of evil rather than on a bold struggle to overthrow evil.

That was the sticking point. The average Northern white man of that era might refuse to associate with the Negro and hold himself to be immeasurably the Negro's superior—the superiority, of course, grew out of the natural order of things, and need not actually be proved—but there was a war on and the country needed soldiers, and if Federal corpses were the price of victory, it hardly paid to be finicky about the original color of the corpses' skins. The real trouble lay in the assumption that while it was all right to let the Negro get shot it was foolish to expect him to do any serious fighting first.

A young officer who left his place in a white regiment to become colonel of a colored regiment was frankly told by a staff officer that "we do not want any nigger soldiers in the Army of the Potomac," and his general took him aside to say: "I am sorry to have you leave my command, and still more sorry that you are going to serve with Negroes. I think it is a disgrace to the army to make soldiers of them." The general added that he felt this way because he was sure that colored soldiers just would not fight.

Most men felt the same way. In support of the belief it was pointed out that in many years of American bondage there had never been a really serious slave revolt. Even John Brown himself, carrying fire and sword below the Potomac, had been able to recruit no more than a dazed corporal's guard of colored followers. Surely this proved that even though slaves might not be happy with their lot they had no real combativeness in them?

There might be flaws in the argument. It quite overlooked the fact that for many years the fabulous underground railroad had been relieving the explosive pressures the slave system had been building up, and had been in fact a great deterrent to slave revolt, for it took out of slavery precisely the daring, energetic, intelligent slaves who might have planned and led an uprising if they had been unable to escape. The argument also overlooked the fact that if American slaves rarely made any trouble the people who owned them were always mortally afraid that they would do so some day. The gloomy island of Haiti was not far enough away to let anyone forget that black men there had risen in one of the most bloody, desperate revolts in human history, winning their own freedom and practically annihilating the master race in the process. Oddly enough, the general belief that colored men would not fight ran parallel with a conviction that they would fight with primitive viciousness if they ever got a chance.

Yet whatever prejudice might say, the hard fact now was that colored men were being enlisted as soldiers in large numbers and that there were times when it was impossible to avoid using them in combat. The use of Hinks's division was an example. They had stormed rifle pits and captured guns, and although Hancock's veterans saw in that fact nothing more than evidence that the Confederacy had only second-rate troops in line, Baldy Smith—who was far from being prejudiced in their favor—said afterward that Negro soldiers under certain circumstances might be as good as any.

No matter how it might use them, however, the army certainly had not assimilated them. It had not tried to and if it had tried it would have failed, and it did not matter much anyway for it was no longer possible for this army to be homogeneous. It had become a representative cross section of an extremely mixed population; and now, as a final step, it contained long columns of colored men whose memories, as one of their officers said, were "a vast, bewildered chaos of Jewish history and biography," the residue of chanted spirituals and the preaching of untaught plantation clergymen, men who in their innocence attributed every historic event to the doings of the great Moses.

When . . . dark battalions came up to . . . the front, they added a new dimension to army life and gave it a strange new flavor. Always there had been groups of soldiers to sit around campfires in the evening, singing about their homesickness and the girls they wanted to get back to, about their comradeship, and, occasionally, about their patriotism, but when these black soldiers sang there was a haunting and a mystery in the air. For if the white soldier looked back with profound longing to something precious that had been left far behind, the colored soldier's homesickness seemed to be for a place where he had never been at all. He had nothing to look back to. Everything he could dream of lay ahead of him, and his dreams were apocalyptic, not to be expressed in ordinary words.

So when the colored troops met by the campfire to sing—and it was their favorite way to spend the evening—they sang made-up, spur-of-the-moment songs, which had never existed before either in words or in music, songs which grew out of the fire and the night and the dreams and hopes which hovered between fire and night forever.

All of the colored troops were officered by white men, and these white officers listened, fascinated, to the campfire singing, and when they wrote about it they tried to tell why it moved them so deeply. There would be a hundred men sprawled in a fire-lit circle, dark faces touched with fire; and one voice would go up, rich and soft and soaring:

> I know moon-rise,
> I know star-rise . . .

and half a dozen men would come in with a refrain:

> . . . Lay dis body down.

The singer would grope his way two lines nearer to the thought that was drawing him on:

> I walk in de moonlight,
> I walk in de starlight . . .

and now more voices would sound the refrain:

> . . . Lay dis body down.

Finally the song would be finished, and a white officer who listened said that the changed refrain would sound like "a grand creation chorus":

> I'll walk in de graveyard,
> I'll walk troo de graveyard
>   To lay dis body down.
> I go to de judgment in de evening of de day
>   When I lay dis body down.
> And my soul and your soul will meet in de day
>   When I lay dis body down.

They were men coming up out of Egypt, trailing the shreds of a long night from their shoulders, and sometimes they sang in the wild imagery of a despairing journey through parted waters to a land of promise:

> My army cross over,
> My army cross over . . .
> O Pharoah's army drownded . . .
> My army cross over.
>
> We'll cross de mighty river,
> We'll cross de River Jordan,
> We'll cross de danger water . . .
>   My army cross over.

Most of the men were straight from the plantation. On many matters their ignorance was absolute. Yet they were men without doubts, and always their faith reached out to the future. A man in the VI Corps, talking to one of them, learned that men who could not read one word of Scripture could cite Biblical authority for their belief that the North would win the war. There was a prophecy, they said, which foretold that while the South would prevail for a time, in the end it would be overthrown. The VI Corps soldier searched his own Bible and at last concluded that the reference was to words in the eleventh chapter of the Book of Daniel:

"And in those times there shall many stand up against the King of the South: also the robbers of thy people shall exalt themselves to escape the vision; but they shall fall. So the King of the North shall come, and cast up a mount, take the most fenced cities; and the arms of the South shall not withstand, neither his chosen people, neither shall there be any strength to withstand."

A Rhode Island soldier who had served along the Carolina coast remembered how a group of fugitive slaves had come within the Union lines after a harrowing nine-day flight through swamps. One man explained his perseverance: "I seed de lamp of life ahead and de lamp of death behind," and another said that, on coming up to the Federal outposts, "When I seed dat flag, it lif me right up."

A Stillness at Appomattox

As 1864 came on, the foreknowledge of defeat begin to grip the South. In February Sherman took the Army of the Tennessee on a destructive raid into the rail junction and Confederate arsenal town of Meridian, Mississippi. It had a startling effect on blacks for miles around, with portents for all to see.

DRUMBEAT OF REVOLUTION

Black smoke lay on the land as the troops marched away, and a scar that would be a long time fading; and as the column swung back toward home territory it was followed, as Sherman recalled, by "about ten miles of Negroes."

No other Yankee raid into Southern territory brought back such an array of contrabands—five thousand of them by soldiers' count, at least eight thousand by the estimate of angry Mississippians. These fugitives had swarmed in from long distances, some of them carrying small children, none of them equipped for a long journey. Soldiers said some had come three hundred miles to join the column. Many died along the way. All were hungry and weary, yet they seemed to be cheerful, and while they had no real notion where the Army of the Tennessee was going they knew that its road was the road away from slavery, and they followed it with pathetic eagerness.

A Wisconsin soldier who watched them suspected that the average colored refugee had, deep within him, some very sober thoughts, for all his surface gaiety. "He was not only breaking up old associations, but was rushing out into a wholly new and untried world. . . . He was not certain of a full meal three times a day, or even once a day, and he must have sadly wondered what was to become of him." Reflecting on all of this, the soldier remembered that a number of people in the North and in the South were arguing that the Negro slave was in reality quite satisfied with his lot, and he wrote angrily: "Such talk is mere twaddle."

Grant and Sherman were right; slavery was doomed, and the war was passing sentence upon it, no matter what doubts might assail the President. Of all societies, that of the South was least fitted to stand the shock of revolution, and the war was revolutionary. The destruction of Meridian and the ten-mile column of hopeless, hopeful colored folk who trailed out behind the triumphant Northern army simply underlined the Confederacy's inescapable problem.

For secession had been an attempt to perpetuate the past: to enable a society based on slavery to live on, as an out-of-date survival in the modern world. Slavery was above all else a primitive mechanism, and the society that relied on it could survive, in the long run, only if the outside world propped it up. But the Southern society was not itself primitive at all. It needed all of the things the rest of the world needed—railroad iron, rolling mills, machine tools, textile machinery, chemicals, industrial knowledge, and an industrial labor force—yet it clung to the peculiar institution that prevented it from producing these things itself, and it relied on the rest of the world to make its deficiencies good. Now the rest of the world had ceased to contribute, except for the trickle that came in through the blockade. Instead, that part of the outside world that lay nearest—the North—was doing everything it could to destroy such industrial strength as the South possessed, and what it destroyed could not be replaced. The valor that sent Southern youth out to fight barefooted in cotton uniforms with a handful of acorns in the haversack was not enough. Federal soldiers would be destructive because destruction pointed to victory, and as cotton gins and clothing factories went up in smoke the peculiar institution itself would crumble, dim human aspirations seeping down into a submerged layer and undermining all of the foundations.

The Southern Congress was quite right; an overturn was coming, and it was precisely the sort of overturn that the men who had created the Confederacy could not at any price accept. No peace based on reunion (the only sort of peace that was really conceivable) could be contemplated, because reunion, by now, inevitably meant the end of slavery. The more hopeless the military outlook became . . . the more bitterly would Southern leaders insist on fighting.

In this fact lay the real horror of 1864. The end of the war could not be hastened, even though it might become visible; it would have to go on until the last ditch had in fact been reached. The peculiar institution was at last taking its own revenge; taking it by the singular dominance it exerted over the minds of men who had gone to arms to perpetuate it.

Six weeks before Sherman made his raid on Meridian there was a singular little meeting one evening in the headquarters tent of General Joe Johnston, commanding what had been Bragg's hard-luck army, at Dalton, Georgia. All corps and division commanders, with one exception, were present; among them, Irish General Pat Cleburne, who had fought so stoutly against Sherman's troops at Chattanooga. General Cleburne had been considering the plight of the South, and he had a paper to present. With Joe Johnston's permission (although not, it would appear, with his outright approval) he read it to the other officers.

The Confederacy, said Cleburne, was fighting a hopeless struggle. It had lost more than a third of its territory; it had lost many men and had "lost, consumed or thrown to the flames an amount of property equal in value to the specie currency of the world." It was badly outnumbered and the disparity was getting worse instead of better, and the Confederate soldier was "sinking into a fatal apathy" and was coming more and more to "a growing belief that some black catastrophe is not far ahead of us." Worst of all, at the beginning of the war slavery was one of the Confederacy's chief sources of strength; now, from a military point of view, it had become "one of our chief sources of weakness."

In any area that had been touched by Northern armies, said Cleburne, slavery was fatally weakened, and with this weakness came a corresponding weakness in the civilian economy. The Confederacy thus had an infinite number of vulnerable spots: there was "one of these in every point where there is a slave to set free." The burden could not be carried any longer. Therefore—said Cleburne, reaching the unthinkable conclusion—the South must boldly and immediately recruit Negro troops, guaranteeing in return freedom to every slave who gave his support to the Confederacy. In substance, what Cleburne was asking for was emancipation and black armies. If the peculiar institution was a source of weakness, Cleburne would abolish the institution and turn its human material into a source of strength.

The war, said Cleburne, was killing slavery anyway. From one source or another, the Negro was going to get his freedom; as clearly as Sherman, Cleburne saw that the old relationship belonged in the grave with departed grandfathers. Make a virtue of necessity, then (said this foreign-born general), "and we change the race from a dreaded weakness to a position of strength."

Cleburne's proposal had certain support. It was signed by two brigadiers and a number of field officers from his own division, as well as by a stray cavalry general; and the first signature on the list, of course, was that of Cleburne himself. But the net effect of this modest proposal, dropped thus into a meeting of the commanding generals of the Confederacy's Western army, was about the effect that would be produced in a convention of devout churchmen by the unexpected recital of a grossly improper joke. It was received with a shocked, stunned, and utterly incredulous silence. Cleburne had mentioned the unmentionable.

One of the generals who had heard him hastened to write to good Bishop [and Confederate General] Polk. He began with a simple confession: "I will not attempt to describe my feelings on being confronted by a project so startling in its character—may I say so revolting to Southern sentiment, Southern pride and Southern honor." He went on: "If this thing is once openly proposed to the Army the total disintegration of that Army will follow in a fortnight, and yet to speak and work in opposition to it is an agitation of the question scarcely less to be dreaded." Secretary of War Seddon wrote earnestly to General Johnston, expressing Jefferson Davis's conviction that "the dissemination or even promulgation of such opinions under the present circumstances of the Confederacy . . . can be productive only of discouragement, distraction and dissension." General Johnston passed the word down the line, Cleburne put his paper away and agreed not to press it any farther, and the matter was buried.

It had to be buried, for what Cleburne had quite unintentionally done was to force his fellow officers to gaze upon the race problem which lay beneath the institution of slavery, and that problem seemed to be literally insoluble. It did not, in that generation, seem possible to most men that white and black folk could dwell together in one community in simple amity. There had to be a barrier between them—some tangible thing that would compel everyone to act on the assumption that one race was superior and the other inferior. Slavery was the only barrier imaginable. If it were removed, society would be up against something monstrous and horrifying.

A great many men of good will felt that way. Lincoln himself had hoped that the business might be settled by some scheme of colonization, with freed Negroes transplanted bodily to some other continent in order that a free society might not have to admit them to full membership. Davis, addressing the Confederate Congress at the beginning of 1863, had denounced the Emancipation Proclamation as "the most execrable measure recorded in the history of guilty men"; it was a program, he said, "by which several millions of human beings of an inferior race, peaceful and contented laborers in their sphere, are doomed to extermination." A junior officer in the Confederate War Department, addressing himself to Secretary Seddon about the time Cleburne was putting his own thoughts on paper, had spoken feelingly of "the difficulties and conflicts that must come from exterminating the Negro, which upon this continent is the only mode of exterminating slavery."

None of these folk who talked so lightly of extermination really meant it, of course. It would be left for a much more ruthless society in a far more brutal age to try the actual experiment of genocide. All anyone actually meant was that to make human brotherhood a working reality in everyday life seemed too big a contract for frail human beings. The privilege of belonging to an admittedly superior race—the deep conviction that there actually were superior and inferior races—could not be wrenched out of human society without a revolutionary convulsion. The convulsion was unthinkable, yet it was beginning to take place, even though hardly anyone had consciously willed it; it was coming down the country roads with the swaggering destructive columns in weathered blue, lying across the landscape behind the haze of smoke that came down from the ridges around Gettysburg and Chattanooga, and there was no stopping it. The bugle that would never call retreat had been heard by people who had not previously been allowed to look upon themselves as persons possessing any rights which other people were bound to respect. To end slavery was to commit the nation permanently to an ideal that might prove humanly unattainable. The inner meaning of the war now was that everything which America had done before—its dreams and its hopes, its sacrifices and its hard-bought victories—was no more than prologue to a new struggle that would go on and on for generations, with a remote ideal lying dim but discernible beyond the dust of the coming years.

Here was the real revolution: here was the fundamental and astounding conclusion, which had been implicit in the first crash of the marsh guns around Fort Sumter, which had followed Old Glory and Palmetto Flag down so many streets amid so many gaily cheering crowds. Here was what was being bought by infinite suffering, tragedy, and loss. Here was the showdown, not to be understood at once, not to be accepted for generations, but nevertheless wholly inexorable. Mr. Lincoln was worried and Mr. Davis was desperate, and General Cleburne was quietly snubbed; and down the dusty roads came ten miles of Negroes, bags packed for a journey longer than any man could understand, marching toward a future that could never again be built in the image of the past.

. . . If people could not see it or say it, they could sing it. There was a tinny, jingling little song in the air that year across the North: a Tin Pan Alley ditty, mocking and jeering and pulsing somehow with a *Ça Ira* sort of revolutionary drumbeat. It spoke for the colored folk in a queer inverted way, although it had not yet reached them, and in a ten-cent manner it voiced what the year meant. It was called "The Year of Jubilo":

> Say Darkies has you seen old Massa
> Wid de muffstache on his face
> Go long de road sometime dis mornin'
> Like he gwine to leave de place?

It went on, shrill and imperious, the song of the great overturn, the cheap little tune to which a great gate was beginning to turn painfully on creaking hinges:

> De massa run, ha-ha!
> De darkey stay, ho-ho!
> I tink it must be Kingdom Coming
> And de year ob Jubilo!

It would be that sort of year: year of Jubilo, year of overturn and disaster and ruin, year of infinite bloodshed and suffering, with the foundations of the great deep broken up; hard tramp of marching military feet, endless shuffle of splay-footed refugees running away from something they understood little better than they could understand what they were running toward; the significance of their march being that it led toward the unknown and that all America, like it or not, was going to follow.

This Hallowed Ground

X

Twilight, 1865

The ruins of Richmond, 1865

When the days of a city, a cause or a nation are numbered, and the actors in the drama know that fate is closing in, a special kind of sadness suffuses those moments that remain. No one who was there could ever forget the last, defiant, useless hours of the Confederacy; or the fine spring day before the Yankee army entered Richmond; or the last, furious victories of Mr. Lincoln's army; or the quiet drama in a farmhouse at Appomattox Courthouse, Virginia. It was part of Catton's special gift for entering into the spirit of other times that he could make these twilight hours so vivid. And it was another that he could write his way through these final events of the war in no fewer than five books, without ever seeming to repeat himself. The selections that follow, in a kind of rough chronology, are taken from four of the five.

It had been going on for nearly four years, and there would be about four more months of it. It had started at Fort Sumter, with officers on a parapet looking into darkness for the first red flash of the guns; now Fort Sumter was a mass of rubble and broken masonry, pounded to fragments by the hammering of repeated bombardments, but it still flew the Confederate flag, a bright spot of color to take the morning light that came slanting in from the sea—symbolic, a flag flying over wreckage and the collapse of a dream. Elsewhere, in many states, winter lay on the hills and fields that had been unheard of four years earlier but that would live on forever now in tradition and national memory— Shiloh, Antietam, the Wilderness, Chickamauga, and all the rest. Here and there all over the country were the mounded graves of half a million young men who had been alive and unsuspecting when all of this began. There would be more graves to dig, and when there was time there would be thin bugle calls to lie in the still air while a handful of dust drifted down on a blanketed form, but most of this was over. A little more killing, a little more marching and burning and breaking and smashing, and then it would be ended.

Ended; yet, in a haunting way, forever unended. It had laid an infinity of loss and grief on the land; it had created a shadowed purple twilight streaked with undying fire which would live on, deep in the mind and heart of the nation, as long as any memory of the past retained meaning. Whatever the American people might hereafter do would in one way or another take form and color from this experience. Under every dream and under every doubt there would be the tragic knowledge bought by this war, the awareness that triumph and disaster are the two aspects of something lying beyond victory, the remembrance of heartbreak and suffering, and the moment of vision bought by people who had bargained for no vision but simply wanted to live at peace. A new dimension had been added to the national existence, and the exploration of it would take many generations. The Civil War, with its lights and its shadows, its unendurable pathos and its charred and stained splendor, would be the American people's permanent possession.

This Hallowed Ground

TRUCE

In the lines facing Richmond, Union pickets one night heard a great hallooing and cursing from a swamp out in front, and they crept out and rescued an indignant Rebel conscript who had got stuck in the mud while trying to desert. They took him to their campfire and found that he was fat and sixty, a man who ordinarily wore a wig, spectacles, and false teeth, but who had lost all three while floundering in the swamp. They dried him off and gave him coffee; he drank, looked about the circle, and then began to curse the Confederacy:

"He cursed it individually, from Jeff. Davis and his cabinet down through its Congress and public men to the lowest pothouse politician who advocated its cause; he cursed its army, from General Lee down to an army mule; he cursed that army in its downsittings and uprisings, in all its movements, marches, battles and sieges; he cursed all its paraphernalia, its artillery and its muskets, its banners, bugles and drums; he cursed the institution of slavery, which had brought about the war, and he invoked the direst calamity, woe and disaster upon the Southern cause and all that it represented; while the earnestness, force and sincerity with which it was delivered made it one of the most effective speeches I ever heard, and this together with his comical appearance and the circumstance of his capture made the men roar with laughter."

The Union man who told about all of this added, perhaps unnecessarily, that "the best element in the Southern army" did not desert.

A New England private said that each evening the men in his company would speculate about the number of deserters who would come in that night: "The boys talk about the Johnnies as at home we talk about suckers and eels. The boys will look around in the evening and guess that there will be a good run of Johnnies." Heavy firing on the picket lines was always taken to mean that the enemy was trying to keep deserters from getting away. Many deserters were willing to enlist in the Union army, and before 1864 ended it was ordered that all such should be sent West to fight the Indians—it would go very hard with them if the army from which they had deserted should recapture them. When these men talked about the Southern cause, it was said, they would remark that it was a rich man's war and a poor man's fight. . . .

At the end of January there was an odd, revealing incident.

Over the Rebel parapet near the old mine crater came a white flag, with a bugler to blow a parley, and a message came over for General Grant. As it happened, Grant was away just then, and there was a twenty-four-hour delay before the message reached him. During the delay, by the mysterious army grapevine, word went up and down the rival lines: the Confederacy was sending a peace commission to meet Lincoln and Seward to see whether they could not agree on terms to end the war.

The peace commissioners were men of note. One was John A. Campbell, former justice of the United States Supreme Court, now the Confederacy's Assistant Secretary of War. Another was Senator R. M. T. Hunter, former Confederate Secretary of State. The third was the Vice-President of the Confederacy, wizened Alexander Stephens, who had been in Congress with Lincoln and who, in 1848, made a speech which caused Lincoln to write to his law partner, Herndon, that "a little, slim, pale-faced consumptive man" had just made the best speech he had ever heard, a speech which moved him to tears. He and Stephens had been drawn to each other, somehow. Members of the Whig party, they had worked together in 1848 to help nominate Zachary Taylor. . . .

By the time Grant got the message, consulted Washington, and made arrangements to get the commissioners through the lines, it was the afternoon of January 31. Both armies knew what was up, and when the carriages came out the Jerusalem Plank Road from Petersburg, bearing the three dignitaries and any number of anxious private citizens, the parapets of Union and Confederate trenches were jammed with soldiers as far as the eye could see.

There was an expectant hush. The commissioners' carriage turned and made for an opening in the Confederate lines—and suddenly all of the soldiers who could see it, blue and gray alike, swung their hats and raised a tremendous cheer. A gunner who looked on remembered: "Cheer upon cheer was given, extending for some distance to the right and left of the lines, each side trying to cheer the loudest. 'Peace on the brain' appeared now to have spread like a contagion. Officers of all grades, from lieutenants to major generals, were to be seen flying in all directions to catch a glimpse of the gentlemen who were apparently to bring peace so unexpectedly."

Slowly the carriage came through, jolting over the uneven ground. The cheering died down. Having yelled, the men seemed to be holding their breath in nervous anticipation. The Federal soldiers now saw something which they had never seen before, or dreamed of seeing—a large number of ladies, dressed in their frilly best, standing on the Confederate parapet.

The carriage stopped and the commissioners got out, tiny Stephens weighed down and made almost helpless with an enormous overcoat. The Confederates began to cheer again, and the three civilians walked across no man's land to the place where Grant had ambulances waiting for them. As they reached these a couple of soldiers helped Stephens climb in, and the Northern troops cheered. The ambulances drove away, and as they passed from sight a Confederate picket sprang out, turned to face his comrades, and proposed three cheers for the Yankee army. These were given, after which a Union man led his side in three cheers for the Confederates. When this shouting died down somebody proposed three cheers for the ladies of Petersburg and both sides joined in, and the ladies fluttered their handkerchiefs prettily. Then the winter day ended, and the ladies went back to town, and the men climbed down from the parapets, and there was a quiet buzz of talk all up and down the lines. No soldier on either side seems to have asked what sort of peace terms were apt to come out of the conference. On this one afternoon, nobody was thinking of victory or defeat. It was enough to think that perhaps the war could end with no more killing.

For anti-climax, the conference came to nothing.

A Stillness at Appomattox

FLIGHT TO THE WEST

The break came at the end of March, 1865. Sherman was far up in North Carolina now, watched again by Joe Johnston, who had been restored too late to command of an army which, as Johnston himself confessed, could do no more than annoy its antagonist. Far in the South a great army of Union cavalry armed with repeating rifles and led by young General James H. Wilson was slicing across Alabama, destroying the last of the South's war industries there, too powerful for even Bedford Forrest to drive away.

In the lines before Petersburg, Lee made a last despairing effort to break the Union grip and failed, and then Sheridan took cavalry and infantry in on Lee's extreme right, smashed the force that was sent out to stop him, and cut the railroad that linked Petersburg to what was left of the South. Meade struck Lee's thinned trench line with the 6th Army Corps and made the break-through the Federals had been hoping for so long—and by April 3 the Army of Northern Virginia had abandoned Richmond and Petersburg and was in full flight, hoping against hope that it might reach Johnston's forces and somehow, somewhere, whip either Sherman or Grant or perhaps both of them together and so keep the war going a little longer.

It was hope born of delirium. Grant moved out in pursuit, as swift and as sure in movement now as in the Vicksburg campaign. He swung around in front and drove Lee west instead of letting him go south, closing all avenues of escape, striking the fugitive army as it moved and cutting down what was left of its fighting power. And the pleasant little courthouse town of Appomattox moved into American legend forever when Lee at last was at bay there, overpowering enemies on all sides, no food left for his men, half of the soldiers that remained too weak and dispirited to carry weapons or to form line as organized troops.

U. S. Grant and the American Military Tradition

LAST DAY IN RICHMOND

Richmond people remembered how that last Sunday [April 2, 1865] came in as a special sort of day. It was warm, with a mild breeze stirring the early blossoms on the capitol grounds; the city's churches were crowded, not because national affairs were at crisis but simply because it was a good day to go to church, with high spring in the air and Easter only two weeks away. One woman recalled it as "one of those unusually lovely days that the spring sometimes brings, when delicate silks that look too fine at other times seem just to suit." A Massachusetts soldier out in the siege lines confessed that spring reaches Virginia "with greater splendor" than New England ever sees, and felt that there had not been a finer day than this one since the creation. Secretary of the Navy Mallory wrote that in all the war the city had never looked more serene and quiet, and the woman who had put on her best silk said that she never saw a calmer Sunday morning—or a more thoroughly confused and alarming Sunday evening.

The news from Petersburg came up shortly after the eleven o'clock services had begun, and an aide with a telegram from General Lee extracted President Davis from St. Paul's just as Dr. Minnigerode intoned the words: "The Lord is in His holy temple: let all the earth keep silence before Him." The congregation took Mr. Davis' departure calmly enough—after all, the President might get called out of church at any time, by almost anything—but other dignitaries were called out later, from this church and from others, and by early afternoon the tidings had gone all across the city: Lee was going to retreat, the government was to move out tonight, the Yankees would take over in the morning. Those who could leave the city were comparatively few; for most people there could be nothing now but a restless, fruitless stirring-about in the face of approaching catastrophe.

Richmond's fate was strange. Other cities, like Atlanta and Columbia, were burned and sacked by their enemies; Richmond was burned and sacked by her own people, and when the hated conquerors at last entered they came in as rescuers and protectors.

Ancient military protocol requires a retreating army to burn the supplies it cannot carry off, lest they be of use to the enemy. The army that had to leave Richmond now was taking the shortest road to extinction and it was leaving behind nothing that the Yankees especially needed, but the old ritual prevailed: possibly, for somebody, it eased the agony of dissolution. President and cabinet, clerks and servants and others of more or less consequence—all of these, amid much confusion, much jostling and running about, and a gabble of frantic orders on gas-lit station platforms, got on the last trains of the Richmond & Danville line and went south out of Richmond. By midnight their exodus was over. Then the Richmond defense troops began to come back through the city, the men who had been holding the fortifications so long, going across the James now to meet, as they hoped, General Lee's troops from Petersburg somewhere on the road to Burkeville. As they left, dutiful officers went about setting fire to the rations and warehouses and warships and bridges that could not be taken along, and when the last of the cavalry patrols went out of the city Richmond was in flames, with all of its defenders bound elsewhere.

When the sun came up on April 3 it was a red ball, shining dully through heavy layers of smoke. In the murky streets there were thousands of men and women, breaking into army depots to get the bacon and flour and other things the army could not carry away, following this before long by breaking into stores and residences to take anything else of value; consuming barrels of whiskey that had not been dumped in the gutters soon enough. There was no chance to control the flames, and no chance to control the mob, which gleefully disabled the few fire engines that appeared. Like all wartime capitals, Richmond had drawn itself much human refuse, including, at an estimate that will do until someone makes a better one, at least 5,000 deserters from the now-absent armies. Until today these had been kept under restraint, because the city authorities could always call on the military; but now, with calamity dawning, the military was gone, all restraint had been removed, and the lawless had a field day. The day was frightening enough even without them. Just after dawn a new ironclad at the builders' dock, C.S.S. *Richmond,* blew up with a noise like the sky cracking open; then a government arsenal took fire, and when the flames reached its magazines the air was full of exploding shells, the crackle of the spreading fire blended with the crackle of thousands of rounds of small-arms ammunition, and a dense cloud of black smoke hung over the center of the city.

Somewhere around eight in the morning the United States Army came in—combat patrols, conquerors-on-parade and life-saving fire brigades arriving all at once. First, scattered cavalry details trotted into Capitol Square, with bright officers running into public buildings to hoist flags; then came more cavalry, followed by rank upon rank of infantry, whose bands played "The Girl I Left Behind Me" and "Dixie." Smoke from burning buildings lay across their shoulders, and the looters went scurrying at last for cover. Presently there came regiments of Negro soldiers, and men and women who had been slaves until this moment ran out to greet them with hysterical cries, seeing the substance of things hoped for in these black men who wore Federal blue. (The officer in command of these occupation forces was General Godfrey Weitzel, . . . who two years earlier in New Orleans had told Ben Butler that no good would ever come of putting Negroes into the army uniform.) Some of the soldiers stood guard over homes and stores, and others stacked their arms and went to work to fight the fire, blowing up buildings that stood where the flames were going so as to make gaps the flames could not cross. Some time that night the city became comparatively quiet. Most of the fires were out, although smoldering ruins still sent wispy smoke into the April night. The streets were crowded, but the looting had been stopped, and Capitol Square was piled with bundles of things the Federal soldiers had taken away from marauders on the chance the proper owners could some day claim them.

The next morning—Tuesday, April 4—Abraham Lincoln came to Richmond.

It was not really necessary for him to be here, and the way his visit was handled would have given a modern security officer the vapors. He came upstream in the *River Queen,* with Admiral Porter cruising just ahead in his flagship, U.S.S. *Malvern,* and the narrow river had not yet been swept clear of mines. Some distance below the landing, obstructions in the river kept the steamers from going farther, so Admiral Porter's 12-oared barge came alongside and President, Admiral, and three or four army and navy officers got in it and finished the trip that way. A tug carrying a guard of marines to escort the President through the city went astray en route, and when the party at last got ashore there were no guards except for ten sailors carrying carbines. For a mile and a half the President walked up the streets to the Confederate White House, where General Weitzel had his headquarters, his way obstructed by ecstatic crowds of colored people shouting "Glory, Glory, Glory!" and striving to get close enough to touch the hand or the garments of the man who was the embodiment of their freedom. Somehow the trip was made without mishap, and at last Abraham Lincoln sat down to rest in the office where Jefferson Davis had worked so long.

Never Call Retreat

By April 9, the relic of the Army of Northern Virginia was boxed in on all sides, with no escape possible. But once again the two armies met as if to fight.

APPOMATTOX

The blue lines grew longer and longer, and rank upon rank came into view, as if there was no end to them. A Federal officer remembered afterward that when he looked across at the Rebel lines it almost seemed as if there were more battle flags than soldiers. So small were the Southern regiments that the flags were all clustered together. . . . The two armies faced each other at long range, and the firing slackened and almost ceased.

Many times in the past these armies had paused to look at each other across empty fields, taking a final size-up before getting into the grapple. Now they were taking their last look, the Stars and Bars were about to go down forever and leave nothing behind but the stars and the memories, and it might have been a time for deep solemn thoughts. But the men who looked across the battlefield at each other were very tired and very hungry, and they did not have much room in their heads for anything except the thought of that weariness and that hunger, and the simple hope that they might live through the next half hour. . . .

Off toward the south Sheridan had all of his cavalry in line again, mounted now with pennons and guidons fluttering. The Federal infantry was advancing from the west and Sheridan was where he could hit the flank of the Rebels who were drawn up to oppose that infantry, and he spurred over to get some foot soldiers to stiffen his own attack. General Griffin told Chamberlain to take his brigade and use it as Sheridan might direct. Men who saw Sheridan pointing out to Chamberlain the place where his brigade should attack remembered his final passionate injunction: "Now smash 'em, I tell you, smash 'em!"

Chamberlain got his men where Sheridan wanted them, and all of Ord's and Griffin's men were in line now, coming up on higher ground where they could see the whole field.

They could see the Confederate line drawing back from in front of them, crowned with its red battle flags, and all along the open country to the right they could see the whole cavalry corps of the Army of the Potomac trotting over to take position beyond Chamberlain's brigade. The sunlight gleamed brightly off the metal and the flags, and once again, for a last haunting moment, the way men make war looked grand and caught at the throat, as if some strange value beyond values were incomprehensively mixed up in it all.

Then Sheridan's bugles sounded, the clear notes slanting all across the field, and all of his brigades wheeled and swung into line, every saber raised high, every rider tense; and in another minute infantry and cavalry would drive in on the slim Confederate lines and crumple them and destroy them in a last savage burst of firing and cutting and clubbing.

Out from the Rebel lines came a lone rider, a young officer in a gray uniform, galloping madly, a staff in his hand with a white flag fluttering from the end of it. He rode up to Chamberlain's lines and someone there took him off to see Sheridan, and the firing stopped, and the watching Federals saw the Southerners wheeling their guns back and stacking their muskets as if they expected to fight no more.

All up and down the lines the men blinked at one another, unable to realize that the hour they had waited for so long was actually at hand. There was a truce, they could see that, and presently the word was passed that Grant and Lee were going to meet in the little village that lay now between the two lines, and no one could doubt that Lee was going to surrender. It was Palm Sunday, and they would all live to see Easter. . . .

A Stillness at Appomattox

General Philip Henry Sheridan, U. S. A.

Before he went to this meeting Lee quietly spoke a few words that were both a judgment on the past and an omen for the future. To him, as he prepared to meet Grant, came a trusted lieutenant who urged him not to surrender but simply to tell his army to disperse, each man taking to the hills with his rifle in his hand: let the Yankees handle guerilla warfare for a while and see what they could make of that. Lee replied that he would have none of it. It would create a state of things in the South from which it would take years to recover, Federal cavalry would harry the length and breadth of the land for no one knew how long, and he himself was "too old to go bushwhacking"; even if the army did break up into die-hard bands of irreconcilables, "the only course for me to pursue would be to surrender myself to General Grant." This was the last anybody heard about taking to the hills. The officer who suggested this course wrote that Lee "showed me the situation from a plane to which I had not risen, and when he finished speaking I had not a word to say."

The unquenchable guerilla warfare this officer had been hinting at was perhaps the one thing that would have ruined America forever. It was precisely what Federal soldiers like Grant and Sherman dreaded most—the long, slow-burning, formless uprising that goes on and on after the field armies have been broken up, with desperate men using violence to provoke more violence, harassing the victor and their own people with a sullen fury no dragoons can quite put down. The Civil War was not going to end that way (although it was natural to suppose that it might, because civil wars often do end so) and the conquered South was not going to become another Ireland or Poland, with generation after generation learning hatred and the arts of back-alley fighting. General Lee ruled it out, not only because he was General Lee but also because he had never seen this war as the kind of struggle that could go on that way. He understood the cause he served with complete clarity. His South had meant neither revolution nor rebellion; it simply desired to detach itself and live in its own chosen part of an unchanging past, and Mr. Davis had defined it perfectly when he said that all his people wanted was to be let alone. Borne up by that desire, the Confederacy had endured four years of war, and it was breaking up now because this potential for inspiring the human spirit had been exhausted. With unlimited confidence the Confederacy had fought an unlimited war for a strictly limited end. To go on fighting from the woods and the lanes and the swamps might indeed plague the Yankees and infect a deep wound beyond healing, but the one thing on earth it could not do was give the South a chance to be left alone with what used to be.

Never Call Retreat

General Robert E. Lee, C. S. A.

THE MEETING

Lee rode to the house of a man named McLean to have a talk with Grant. He wore his best uniform and he had a sword buckled at his side, and there should have been lancers and pennons and trumpets going on before, for he was the last American knight and he had a grandeur about him, and when he rode out of the war something that will never come back rode out of American life with him.

Great moments provide their own dramatic contrast. Grant came to the meeting in the coat of a private soldier, with tarnished shoulder straps tacked on, and his boots and uniform were spattered with mud. He had forgotten to wear his sword—as an eminently practical man he hardly ever bothered with it; during the great Battle of the Wilderness his side arm had been a jackknife, with which he pensively whittled twigs while the fighting raged—and there was nothing at all imposing about him as he sat down, for the third time in this war, to write the terms of surrender for an opposing army. The beaten man looked the part of a great soldier; the victor looked perhaps like a clerk from a Galena leather store, unaccountably rigged out in faded regimentals, scribbling on a scratch pad in the front room of a little house in southern Virginia.

The terms were simple. The beaten army would not go off to prison camp, any more than had been the case after Vicksburg. The men would lay down their weapons and then they would go home; and since most of them were small farmers, and the war was about over, Grant directed that each one who claimed to own a horse or a mule be allowed to take one home with him from the stock of captured Confederate army animals. The men would need these beasts to get in a crop and work their farms, said Grant. No one knew better than he the heartbreak of trying to get a living from the land with inadequate equipment.

And he wrote into the terms of surrender one of the great sentences in American history. Officers and men were to sign paroles, and then they were to go home, "not to be disturbed by the United States authority so long as they observe their paroles and the laws in force where they reside."

Grant looked at the beaten army and he saw his own fellow Americans, who had made their fight and lost and now wanted to go back and rebuild. But the war had aroused much hatred and bitterness, especially among those who had done no fighting, and Grant knew very well that powerful men in Washington were talking angrily of treason and of traitors, and wanting to draw up proscription lists, so that leading Confederates could be jailed or hanged.

The sentence Grant had written would make that impossible. They could proceed against Robert E. Lee, for instance, only by violating the pledged word of U. S. Grant, who had both the will and the power to see his word kept inviolate. If they could not hang Lee they could hardly hang anybody. There would be no hangings. Grant had ruled them out.

It did not strike the eye quite as quickly, but U. S. Grant had a certain grandeur about him, too.

U. S. Grant and the American Military Tradition

THE LOST CAUSE

It would of course be easy to make too much of the general air of reconciliation. Lee's soldiers were hard, passionate fighters, they did not enjoy defeat, they were not ready to start loving their enemies with sentimental fondness, and there were wounds that would be a long time healing. And yet by any standard this was an almost unbelievable way to end a civil war, which by all tradition is the worst kind of war there is. Living for the rest of their lives in the long gray shadow of the Lost Cause, these men were nevertheless going on toward the future. General Lee, who had set the pattern, had given them the right words: ". . . unsurpassed courage and fortitude . . . steadfast to the last . . . the consciousness of duty faithfully performed." Pride in what they had done would grow with the years, but it would turn them into a romantic army of legend and not into a sullen battalion of death.

Here is how the legend worked. Fifteen years after the surrender, one of Lee's veterans—a soldier from South Carolina, who had been in the worst of it from beginning to end—sat down to write his memoirs, a little job of writing that did not get published until many years after its writer was dead. Looking back, he seemed to see something that was worth everything it had cost him, something indeed that a man would almost like to get back to if he only could. He wrote, remember, as one who had been through the mill and not as a starry-eyed recruit, and this is how he put it:

"Who knows but it may be given to us, after this life, to meet again in the old quarters, to play chess and draughts, to get up soon to answer the morning roll call, to fall in at the tap of the drum for drill and dress parade, and again to hastily don our war gear while the monotonous patter of the long roll summons to battle? Who knows but again the old flags, ragged and torn, snapping in the wind, may face each other and flutter, pursuing and pursued, while the cries of victory fill a summer day? And after the battle, then the slain and wounded will arise, and all will meet together under the two flags, all sound and well, and there will be talking and laughter and cheers, and all will say: Did it not seem real? Was it not as in the old days?"

The worst experience on earth could be remembered that way, with a still-youthful veteran dreaming about foes meeting under two flags and one all-embracing sky. No civil war ever ended quite like this. The men who lost at the Boyne or at Culloden did not write memoirs in this vein.

Never Call Retreat

XI

Veterans

Veterans' reunion at Gettysburg, 1910;
survivors of the 143rd Pennsylvania

As an old newspaperman, Bruce Catton admired the professionals—veterans in any line, men who knew their jobs, who, in a crisis, could deliver whatever the occasion required. As a boy in Michigan he got to see a little of the hard life of that disappearing breed, the loggers. Throughout life he enjoyed the swift, saucy expertise of old-time baseball. And his admiration for old soldiers was boundless.

The story at the beginning of this chapter he told at Galesburg, Illinois, in 1958, to a convention of historians. As the new editor of a new history magazine, American Heritage *(founded in 1954), he felt a little abashed, he said, among the certified academics, and he was reminded of an old Civil War soldier who also felt a little out of place.*

This veteran was born in Pennsylvania but while still a boy moved to Mississippi with his family and became a thorough-going Southerner. When the Civil War came he joined the Confederate army, in which he served bravely to the very end, acquiring a wound at Shiloh and taking his parole, at last, when Joe Johnston's army surrendered in North Carolina in the spring of 1865.

A long time after the war this man moved to New Hampshire and there he spent the rest of his days. He became tolerably well reconstructed, and toward the end he even used to hoist a United States flag in front of his house on Lincoln's birthday. And one day, when he was quite old, the local post of the Grand Army of the Republic invited him to address a Decoration Day meeting of Union veterans.

The old Confederate explained that he felt just a little out of place in that gathering—one wearer of the gray, among all the men who wore blue—and he recalled an incident of his own boyhood.

Back around 1850, he said, a little Pennsylvania town was preparing to celebrate the Fourth of July, when someone brought in word that a veteran of the Revolution was still living, on a farm back in the mountains a little way from town. By 1850, of course, authentic veterans of the Revolution were getting very scarce, so nothing would do but that the old gentleman must be brought into town to be guest of honor at the Independence Day celebration.

They sent a carriage up to the mountains and brought old Uncle John into town, and after a big parade with the local brass band leading the way they wound up at the speaker's platform in the public square; and there, presently, Uncle John found himself pushed forward to the edge of the rostrum to make a speech.

He began bravely enough:

"I remember when we surrendered at Yorktown . . ."

Then, of course, someone on the speaker's stand tugged at his coattails and reminded him, in a stage whisper:

"Uncle John! You've got it wrong! It wasn't *you* that surrendered at Yorktown!"

Uncle John cleared his throat, straightened his tie, and began again:

"I remember the day when we laid down our arms at Yorktown . . ."

Someone in the audience called out:

"Hey, old man! You didn't lay down your arms!"

"Well, I guess I ought to know. I was one of Cornwallis's Hessians!"

It is when I reflect that as a lifelong newspaperman I am now the editor of a magazine of history—which, I suppose, by logical extension, makes me a historian myself—that I begin to feel uncomfortably like that old Hessian.

American Association for State and Local History Conference
Galesburg, Illinois, 1958

THE GREAT AMERICAN GAME

By the carefully repeated definition of men who stand to make money out of its acceptance, baseball is the Great American Game. The expression was invented long ago and it has been rammed home by talented press agents ever since, even in times when most Americans seemed to be interested very largely in something else. But what has given the phrase its sticking power is not the fact that a big industry has kept plugging it, or the allied fact that unceasing repetition has dinned it into an unreflecting public's ears for generations, but simply the fact that in its underlying essence it is perfectly true.

Baseball is the American game, great or otherwise, because it reflects so perfectly certain aspects of the American character that no other sport quite portrays.

It has few of the elements of pure sportsmanship, as that dubious word is commonly accepted, and it is not notably a game for gentlemen. But it does embody certain native-born fundamentals, including above all others the notion that the big thing about any contest is to win it. It also is built upon the idea that anything you can get away with is permissible, and it is the only sport (at least the only one since the Roman populace sat in the thumbs-down section at the gladiatorial games) that puts an invitation to homicide in one of its enduring sayings: "Kill the umpire!" (The thing has actually been attempted, too, more than once.) It is pre-eminently the sport for the professional rather than for the amateur, the sport in which the well-intentioned duffer neither is given nor especially wants a part.

Almost everyone in the country has played it at one time or another, but almost nobody except the professional dreams of going on playing it once full manhood has come. It is a spectator sport in which each spectator has had just enough personal experience to count himself an expert, and it is the only pastime on earth that leans heavily on the accumulation of page upon page of inherently dry statistics. It is also an unchanging pageant and a ritualized drama, as completely formalized as the Spanish bullfight, and although it is wholly urbanized it still speaks of the small town and the simple, rural era that lived before the automobile came in to blight the landscape. One reason for this is that in a land of unending change, baseball changes very little. There has been no important modification of its rules for well over half a century. The ball in use now will go farther when properly hit, and the gloves worn on defense are designed to do automatically what personal skill once had to do, but aside from these things the game is as it was in the early 1900's. Even the advent of night baseball, which seemed like pure sacrilege when it was introduced two decades ago, has made little difference; the pictorial aspect of the game—which is one of its most important features—has perhaps even gained thereby. The neat green field looks greener and cleaner under the lights, the moving players are silhouetted more sharply, and the enduring visual fascination of the game—the immobile pattern of nine men, grouped according to ancient formula and then, suddenly, to the sound of a wooden bat whacking a round ball, breaking into swift ritualized movement, movement so standardized that even the tyro in the bleachers can tell when someone goes off in the wrong direction—this is as it was in the old days. A gaffer from the era of William McKinley, abruptly brought back to the second half of the twentieth century, would find very little in modern life that would not seem new, strange, and rather bewildering, but put in a good grandstand seat back of first base he would see nothing that was not completely familiar.

But that is only the surface part of it. Baseball, highly organized, professionalized within an inch of its life, and conducted by men who like dollars better than they like sport, still speaks for the old days when nine young men in an open park somehow expressed the hot competitive instincts of everybody and spoke for home-town pride.

And perhaps the central part of all of this is the fact that in its essence baseball is still faintly disreputable and rowdy. Its players chew tobacco, or at least look as if they were chewing it; many of them do not shave every day; and they argue bitterly with each other, with their opponents, and with the umpires just as they did when John McGraw and Ed Delehanty were popular idols. They have borrowed nothing from the "sportsmanship" of more sedate countries; they believe that when you get into a fight you had better win, and the method by which you win does not matter very much. Anything goes; victory is what counts.

This John McGraw, for example. When he was playing third base and there was a runner there, and someone hit a fly to the outfield, McGraw would unobtrusively hook his fingers in the player's belt so that the take-off for the plate, once the ball was caught, would be delayed by half a second or so. He got away with it, too, and no one thought the worse of him, until one day a base runner unbuckled his belt in this situation and, legging it for home, left the belt dangling in McGraw's hand, tangible evidence of crime. Note, also, that baseball knows about the bean ball—the ball thrown at the batter's head to drive him away from the plate and hamper his hitting process. A big leaguer was once killed by such a pitch; it has been condemned by everybody ever since then, and it is still a regular feature of the game.

In its essentials, then, baseball is plebeian, down-to-earth, and robustious. Even half a century ago it was dwindling to the rank of secondary sport in the colleges. Professors who have adjusted themselves to the presence on the campus of *soi-disant* students who are paid to attend college so that they may play football have a way of considering the football player one cut above the baseball player. The former may be a hulking behemoth of pure muscle, wholly incapable of differentiating between Virgil's *Eclogues* and Boyle's law, but he does not seem quite as uncouth as the baseball player—who, in his own turn, may also be on the campus as a paid hand, the difference being that he is being paid by some major-league team that wants to see his athletic skills developed, while the football player gets his from ardent alumni who want to see the college team beat State on Homecoming Day next fall. There has never been any social cachet attached to skill on the diamond.

The reason, obviously, is that baseball came up from the sand lots—the small town, the city slum, and the like. It had a rowdy air because rowdies played it. One of the stock tableaux in American sports history is the aggrieved baseball player jawing with the umpire. In all our games, this tableau is unique; it belongs to baseball, from the earliest days it has been an integral part of the game, and even in the carefully policed major leagues today it remains unchanged. Baseball never developed any of the social niceties.

In the old days, when (as we suppose, anyway) most of us lived in small towns, or at least in fairly small cities, the local baseball team represented civic pride, to say nothing of representing at the same time the dreams of a great many young men who wished to be much more athletic than they actually were. In very small towns, its games were usually held in Farmer Jones's pasture, where the difficulty, in a hot moment of split-second play, of distinguishing between third base and some natural cow-pasture obstacle sometimes led to odd happenings; and in slightly larger places the county fairground or a recreational park at the end of the streetcar line provided the arena. In any case, muscular young men, wearing the singularly unbecoming uniforms that were standardized 75 years ago, presently took their positions on the grass, and the game was on.

It was, and still is, hotly competitive, and within reasonable limits anything goes. If the umpire (there was just one, in the old days) could be suborned to give all vital judgments in favor of the home side, all well and good; no one ever blushed to accept a victory that derived from an umpire's bias. If he could be intimidated, so that close decisions would go as the spectators wanted them to go, that also was good. This often happened; an umpire who decided a crucial play against the home team was quite likely to be mobbed, and few pictures from the old-time sports album are more authentic or more enduring than the vision of an umpire frantically legging it for the train, pursued by irate citizens who wished to do him great bodily harm. It took physical courage to render impartial judgments in old-time small-town baseball, and not all umpires were quite up to it.

If the umpire could be deceived while the game was on, that also was good. A man running from first to third on a base hit would cut twenty feet short of second base if he thought he could get away with it, and no one dreamed of censuring him for it. If an opposing player could be intimidated, so that he shirked his task, that was good, too. Not for nothing was the greatest baseball player who ever lived, Ty Cobb, famous for sitting on the bench just before the game sharpening his spikes with a file. An infielder, witnessing this, and knowing that Cobb was practically certain to ram those spikes into his calf or thigh in a close play, was apt to flinch just a little at the moment of contact, and out of that split second of withdrawal Cobb would gain the hair's edge of advantage that he needed. It was considered fair, too, to denounce an opponent verbally, with any sort of profane, personal objurgation that came to mind, on the off-chance that he might become unsettled and do less than his best. (This still goes on, like practically all of the other traditional things in baseball, and the "bench jockey"—the man who will say anything at all if he thinks it will upset an enemy's poise—can be a prized member of a big-league team even now.)

Baseball is conservative. What was good enough in Cap Anson's day is good enough now, and a populace that could stand unmoved while the federal Constitution was amended would protest with vehemence at any tampering with the formalities of baseball. It looks as it used to look; the batter still grabs a handful of dust between swings, the catcher still slams the ball over to third base after a strike-out, and the umpire still jerks thumb over right shoulder to indicate a putout. (Dismayingly enough, some umpires now grossly exaggerate this gesture, using an elaborate full-arm swing, but possibly the point is a minor one.)

An inning begins; the pitcher takes his warm-up tosses, now as in the days half a century ago, and after three, four, or five of these he steps aside and the catcher whips the ball down to second base. The second baseman tosses it to the shortstop, two yards away, and the shortstop throws it to the third baseman, who is standing halfway between his own base and the pitcher's box; the third baseman, in turn, tosses it over to the pitcher, and the inning can get started. To vary from this formula is unthinkable; from the little leaguers up to Yankee Stadium, it is as one with the laws of the Medes and the Persians.

Then action: players shifting about, pounding their gloves, uttering cries of encouragement (which, like all the rest, are verbatim out of the script of 1900); and the batter approaches the plate, swinging two bats (another ironclad requirement), tossing one aside, planting his feet in the batter's box, and then swinging his single bat in determined menace. The fielders slowly freeze into fixed positions; for a moment no one anywhere moves, except that the pitcher goes into his stretch, takes a last look around, and then delivers—and then the frozen pattern breaks, the ball streaks off, men move deftly from here to there, and the quick moments of action are on.

In all of this there is unending fascination, coupled with the knowledge that wholly fantastic athletic feats may at any moment be displayed by any one of the players. Even an easy fly ball to the outfield or a simple grounder to short can call forth a nonchalant, effortless expertness that a man from another land would find quite incredible. (I once took an Englishman to see his first baseball game, and he was dumfounded by the simplest plays, marveling at what all the rest of us took for automatic outs.) In no other contest can the split second be so important. A routine double play can make both outs with no more than half a second to spare, and if the half second is lost anywhere, the player who lost it will be derided for a clumsy oaf.

Primarily a team game, baseball is also the game for the individualist. The team play is essential, and when you watch closely you can see it, but the focus is usually on one man. A base runner streaks for second with the pitch, falls away while in full stride, and slides in in a cloud of dust, baseman stabbing at him with gloved hand, umpire bending to peer through the murk and call the play; an outfielder runs deep and far, arching ball coming down—apparently— just out of his reach, trajectories of fielder and baseball coming miraculously together at the last, gloved hand going out incredibly to pick the ball out of the air; a pitcher who has been getting his lumps looks about at filled bases, glowers at the batter, and then sends one in that is struck at and missed . . . always, some individual is trying for an astounding feat of athletic prowess and, now and then, actually accomplishing it.

Hence baseball celebrates the vicarious triumph. The spectator can identify himself completely with the player, and the epochal feat becomes, somehow, an achievement of his own. Babe Ruth, mocking the Chicago Cubs, pointing to the distant bleachers and then calmly hitting the ball into those bleachers, took a host of Walter Mittys with him when he jogged around the bases. (There is some dispute about this, to be sure; he was jawing with the Cubs, but purists say he did not actually call his shot. This makes no difference whatever.) It was the same when old Grover Cleveland Alexander, the all-but-washed-up veteran of many baseball wars, came into the seventh inning of a decisive World Series game, found the bases filled with Yankees, and struck out Tony Lazzeri, going on to win game and Series; and this was after a wearing night on the tiles, Alexander having supposed that his work was over until next spring. Many an aging fan shared in Old Alex's triumph.

These things are part of baseball's legend, for the game never forgets its gallery of immortals. That it actually has a tangible Hall of Fame, with bronze plaques to commemorate the greatest, is only part of the story; the noble deeds of the super-players are handed down in bar-side stories, year after year, losing nothing in the telling. Some of the heroes have been supermen, in a way, at that. There was, for instance, Shoeless Joe Jackson, barred from baseball in midcareer because he let himself be bribed to help lose a World Series. (He did not do very well at losing; even under a bribe, he batted .375 in that Series—a natural hitter who just couldn't make himself miss even when paid to do so.) A sand-lot pitcher tells of a day, a whole generation later, when, pitching for a textile-mill team in the Carolinas, he found on the opposing team none other than Jackson—a pathetic, fat, doddering wreck in his late fifties, with a monstrous belly like some disreputable Santa Claus, still picking up a few odd bucks playing semi-pro ball under an assumed name. The young pitcher figured Jackson would be easy; a low inside curve, coming in close to the overhang of that prodigious paunch, was obviously the thing to throw. He threw, Jackson swung, and swung as he used to thirty years earlier, and the ball went far out of the park, one of the most authoritative home runs the young pitcher ever witnessed. Old Jackson lumbered heavily around the bases, and halfway between third and home he turned to accost the young pitcher. "Son," he said, "I always could hit them low inside curves."

There were others cast in similar molds. . . . Rube Waddell, the wholly legendary character who, when cold sober, which was not often, may have been the greatest pitcher of them all: the man who now and then, on a whim, would gesture the entire outfield off the premises and then retire the side without visible means of support; Walter Johnson, who once pitched fifty-odd consecutive scoreless innings, and who to the end of his days had nothing much in his repertoire except an unhittable fast ball; Tris Speaker, who played such a short center field that he often threw a batter out at first on what ought to have been a legitimate down-the-middle base hit; and lean Satchel Paige, who in his great days in the Negro leagues had a way of pointing to the shortstop and then throwing something which the batter must hit to short, and who then would go on around the infield in the same way, compelling the opposition to hit precisely where he wanted to hit it. The legends are, in some ways, the most enduring part of the game. Baseball has even more of them than the Civil War, and its fans prize them highly.

Under the surface, baseball is always played to a subdued but inescapable tension, because at any second one of these utterly fabulous events may take place. The game may be distressingly one-sided, and the home team may come up in the ninth inning five runs behind, and in a clock game like football or basketball the margin would be physically unbeatable; but in baseball anything can happen, and the tiniest fluke can change everything. (Remember the World Series game the Yankees won when a Brooklyn catcher dropped a third strike with two men out in the ninth?) A commonplace game can turn into a hair-raiser at any moment, and things do not actually need to happen to create the suspense. A free-hitting, high-scoring game may be most eventful, but few strains are greater than the strain of watching a pitcher protect a 1–0 lead in the late innings of a routine game. Nothing, perhaps, actually happens—but every time the ball is thrown the game may turn upside down, and nobody ever forgets it.

All of this is built in, for the spectator. Built in, as well, is the close attention to records and statistics. Batting averages and pitchers' records are all-important; to know that a Rogers Hornsby, for instance, could bat more than .400 in three different years—that is, could average getting two hits for every five times he came to the plate, 154 games a year, for three years—is important. It has been suggested, now and then, that big-league playing schedules be reduced from 154 games to some smaller figure, and the suggestion has always been howled down: it would upset all the averages. Unthinkable; how do you compare today's pitcher with Walter Johnson or Lefty Grove if today's pitcher plays in fewer games every year?

The circumstances under which baseball is played nowadays have changed greatly, to be sure. Less than half a century ago, every town that amounted to anything at all was represented in some league of professional players, and these leagues—the minor leagues, of hallowed memory—have been dissolving and vanishing, as more and more spectators get their games by television or by radio and ignore the local ball park. The Little Leagues have come up, and semi-subsidized sand-lot leagues, and even college baseball is here and there enjoying a new lease on life—after all, the new players in the big leagues have to come from somewhere, and besides, young Americans still like to play baseball; but the old pattern is gone, and even the major leagues themselves have undergone profound changes and, to a purist from the old days, are all but unrecognizable. Where are the St. Louis Browns, or the Philadelphia Athletics, or the Boston Braves—or, for the matter of that, even the magnificent New York Giants, and the Brooklyn Dodgers? Gone forever, to be sure, with new cities taking over, and with a few old-timers muttering that the last days are at hand.

Actually, the last days are probably a long, long way off, for baseball even in its modern guise has not changed in its essentials. It is a rough, tough game, encased by rules that were made to be broken if the breaking can be accomplished smoothly enough, a game that never quite became entirely respectable, a game in which nobody wants to do anything but win. It will undoubtedly be around for a good time to come, and it will continue, in spite of its own press agents, to be in truth the great American game.

Or so, at least, believes one old-time fan.

"The Great American Game," American Heritage, *April 1959*

THE LOGGERS

A lumber camp would stand or fall on the food it provided. The men who worked there were exploited as ruthlessly as any workers in American history—the work was hard, often it was dangerous, the hours were long, the pay was low and there were no fringe benefits whatever. The one compensation was that there was always plenty to eat. The quality might vary, from camp to camp, although the men knew good cooking from bad and a firm that was known to use inexpert cooks generally had trouble recruiting its working crew. One of the biggest companies logging the Manistee River got a bad name because it served baked beans three times a day, with everything else regarded as trimmings. The men made up an irreverent jingle about it, and to this day there are people around Manistee who can sing it for you, to the tune of "Maryland, My Maryland":

> Who feeds us beans until we're blue?
>> Louie Sands and Jim McGee.
> Who thinks that nothing else will do?
>> Louie Sands and Jim McGee.
> Who feeds us beans three times a day,
> And gives us very little pay?
> Who feeds us beans, again I say?
>> Louie Sands and Jim McGee.

The lumberman lived mostly on meat, potatoes, bread and pastry. One historian of the logging era estimated that a hundred-man camp would consume six barrels of flour every week, plus two and one-half barrels of beef and an equal amount of pork, eight bushels of potatoes, three bushels of onions, a barrel of sugar and forty pounds of lard, along with incidentals like canned tomatoes, pickles, prunes and sausage. The chief breakfast staple was the pancake, covered with molasses or pork gravy and accompanied by whole pans full of fried potatoes and fried salt pork. A cook who served a sixty-five-man camp in the Grand Traverse Bay area baked thirty-five loaves of bread and three hundred and fifty buns twice a week, got eighteen pies out of the oven every morning before the sun was up and produced two kegs of cookies each day. A cook in an upper peninsula camp complained—or boasted—that he had to make a barrel of doughnuts daily. Besides the salt meat a good deal of fresh beef and pork was eaten. In the early days, when game was plentiful, a camp sometimes hired a hunter to provide a supply of venison. All in all, the woodsman got plenty to eat.

He needed it, because his life was hard. In the early days, conditions were downright rugged. The bunk shanty originally was simply a rectangular building of chinked logs, with no floor but the packed earth. Bunks were ranged along the walls, and the heat came from an open fire in a shallow pit in the middle of the room. There was no chimney; overhead there was a slot in the roof, and most of the smoke went out there. Windows there were none, and the bunk shanty was as smoky, ill-ventilated and generally smelly as any living quarters man has ever used. As a matter of fact, in its essentials a shanty like this was much like the traditional long house of the Iroquois Indians, except that the long house was probably more comfortable. The point to remember is that the Indians were a stone-age people giving themselves the best housing they could devise; the lumbermen were nineteenth-century Americans occupying the worst quarters their society had to offer.

As years passed, of course, conditions improved. The bunk shanty was given proper flooring, and a stove with a regular chimney replaced the open fire pit. The bunks remained about as they had been—oblong wooden boxes, with evergreen branches and a sack of straw for mattress and springs, and woolen blankets for covering, the whole offering a secure refuge for the vermin that were a plague of every camp. Except for the fact that there was no smoke in the air, ventilation remained about as it had been. The shanty was usually crisscrossed with clothes lines, on which wet socks and boots were hung up to dry, and by bedtime the air was thick enough to float a canoe. . . .

To the men who occupied it this shanty gave the name to the entire trade. The man who worked in the woods rarely spoke of himself as a lumberjack, because he considered that a city man's expression. Sometimes he called himself a logger, but most of the time he spoke of himself and his fellows as shanty boys. . . .

Though the housing improved, the life remained hard. The men were out in the woods as soon as the sun came up—the get-'em-up cry in the bunk shanty was a chanted "Daylight in the swamp!"—and the foreman went about indicating the trees that were to be felled. (Until fairly late in the game the lumbermen wanted nothing but tall, straight white pines; lesser pines, and all of the hardwoods, were left standing. Before the logging era ended, to be sure, they took everything, but as long as there was plenty of pine it was the only tree that really mattered.) When a tree had been chosen, two ax-men came up,

A log drive in the 1860's

standing facing one another, one of them swinging his double-bitted ax from the right shoulder, the other swinging from the left; it was their job to cut an eight-inch or ten-inch notch on one side of the tree to control the direction in which the tree would fall. Before they began to cut, the axmen took pains to clear away any undergrowth that might be standing by the trunk; to strike a limb or a sapling by accident, either on the back-swing or on the cutting stroke, would produce an out-of-control glancing blow that might maim a man for life, and these men took no chances. When everything was ready the men began to swing their axes, striking alternate blows in a remorseless rhythm, cutting a deep triangular notch whose edges were as smooth as if they had been planed; an ax was a precision instrument in the pineries.

Once the notch was deep enough to determine the direction in which the tree would fall the axmen laid aside their axes and took another weapon, with which they actually brought the tree down. The new weapon was a cross-cut saw seven feet long—limber, with sharp jagged teeth, bowed out along the cutting edge, thicker at the back than it was where the teeth were, with a handle at each end. The sawyers attacked the tree on the side opposite to the notch; they drew the blade back and forth lightly a few times, to provide a guiding groove, then settled down to work in a steady rhythm like the one made by the axes, and the blade made a musical zing-zing as it cut deeper and deeper into the wood, spurting a handful of sawdust with each stroke. This part of the work went fairly fast. If pitch from the raw pine clogged the teeth of the saw the men used a rag and a bottle of kerosene to clean the blade, and if the weight of the tree pressed down on the blade as the back edge went in out of sight, a hardwood wedge would be driven into the cut to relieve the pressure. And at last the top of the pine, far above, would quiver and give a sudden movement, and there would be a sharp cracking sound from the trunk, at which moment the sawyers would remove the blade, step backward, and raise the warning cry of the pinewoods— "Tim-m-ber-r-r!"

When this cry was raised everybody within range took cover, because a tall pine came down with a mighty crash and nobody was quite certain what might happen. Sometimes the heavy trunk rebounded when it hit the ground, sometimes it struck another tree on the way down and fell off, unpredictably, sideways, and now and then it bore an unexpectedly long branch, sticking out at right angles to the trunk, to strike a man who had thought himself out of danger. (A long branch of that kind was known, significantly, as a widow-maker.) Usually, of course, the tree came down the way it was supposed to come, and as soon as it had come to rest, work on the other trees went on as before.

Once the tree was on the ground, men with axes attacked it, cutting off the branches and the too-slender tip; then the trunk was marked off into sixteen-foot lengths and the sawyers returned to cut the trunk into logs. The sawyers were veterans, owning that finely wrought skill that makes a hard job look easy. The rule was that a sawyer simply pulled the saw toward himself; he did not press down on it, because the weight of the saw itself was enough to keep the teeth biting into the wood, and he did not push it away from him at the end of the stroke because that made his partner's job harder. (To push on the return stroke was known as riding the saw, and it was enough to get a man demoted.) A pine tree two feet thick could be reduced to logs in short order.

Now the first step in the destruction of the forest and the creation of useful building material was over. From this point to the moment the logs entered the sawmill the lumber business was a matter of transportation. That does not mean that it was simple. Logs are hard to move, moving them is subject to all manner of evil strokes of chance, an aspiring lumber baron could go broke if his luck was bad, and year in and year out the business killed a few of the baron's hired hands no matter how the boss's luck was running.

The initial move in this business of transportation was to get the logs out of the trackless timber and over to the roadway the lumbermen had created. Teamsters came in, a device much like an oversized pair of ice tongs was attached to one end of a log, and a pair of stout horses—oxen, in the early days, but usually horses toward the end—dragged it off through the trees to the skidway, a pile of logs by the roadway. This roadway was an affair of packed snow, turned to ice by water that was sprayed on it at night from a tank cart in zero weather, and it was built for just one purpose: to make it possible to move the ponderous logs over to the river that would carry them off to market once spring came and the ice was out. The roadway snaked its way through and around the stand of timber that was under attack, it avoided uphill drags as much as possible, and it could be used only in the wintertime. No wagon ever built could carry the incredible loads that could be moved by sleigh on an icy road; a mild winter without enough snow or freezing weather to keep the roads well iced offered the boss lumberman a sure route to bankruptcy.

Naturally the lumber camp sleigh was a heavy-duty affair. It consisted chiefly of two pairs of steel-faced runners, in tandem, bound together by ponderous beams, the forward pair of runners of course working on a pivot. Each runner was set some eight feet away from its partner, and the pair carried a heavy transverse beam, known as a bunk, twelve or fourteen feet in length, and the two bunks, one on each pair of runners, were what the sixteen-foot logs rested on. The sleigh was loaded at the skidway, and the record of the weight a sleigh could carry would be unbelievable if there were not plenty of photographs of loaded sleighs to prove it. A load of logs piled three times the height of a man's head and weighing thirty tons was not especially unusual.

The first logs were rolled onto the sleigh's bunks from the skidway; the rest were hoisted up by horse power, while men with cant hooks guided them into place. The cant hook was the indispensable tool here. It had a handle of tapered ash or rock maple, from four to six feet long, iron-shod at the base, with a sharp steel hook a foot long swinging from a hinge ten inches above the base. It gave a man a grip on a log so that he could turn it over, hold it in place, inch it over into the spot where he wanted it to go, and in general keep it under control. He could do these things, that is, if he knew precisely what he was doing and had the strength, skill and nerve to do it properly; inert logs tended to be cranky, and a cant hook man could get mashed if a log got away from him. (Given a sharp spike at the business end, a cant hook became a peavey; the cant hook was the favored instrument in the woods and the peavey was used after the logs had been put into the river.) When the sleigh was fully loaded the logs were bound in place with chains, and the teamster took over.

It was up to the teamster to drive the sleigh along the glare ice of the roadway two or three miles to the banking grounds, an open place on the bank of the nearest river where the logs were stacked in enormous piles that would be tumbled into the water when spring came. The teamster was another man who had to know what he was doing. His horses were shod with calked shoes so that they could work on the ice, but the sleigh had no brakes whatever and on a downhill drag the load could take charge if the teamster was the least bit careless. As a safety measure, one or two men went out at night and spread horse manure on the icy ruts on all descending grades; a man who held this job was known, for some reason, as a chickadee. If a thirty-ton load once picked up speed on a downgrade the horses could not hold it back, and the result was a wild smashup, sleigh running over the team, heavy chains snapping like thread, logs scattered all about, teamster and horses buried under everything as likely as not. If the teamster survived he was in danger of being either fired outright or turned into a chickadee, but his chance of survival in a downhill wreck was not good. It was bad enough to lose a teamster, but the loss of the horses was what really hurt. A good team of Percherons represented a cash investment of six hundred dollars or more.

In one way or another the winter's cut of logs was finally stacked up along a river, and when spring came the camp's work was over. Until near the end of the lumber era in Michigan, the work was strictly seasonal. The men were hired late in the fall, when a new camp was built, and they were paid off in the spring, and what they did in the warm-weather months was entirely up to them. Many were farmers, raising potatoes and beans and anything else the thin soil of the lumber country would produce from spring to mid-autumn, and then going back into the woods for another winter of it. Most of them were subsistence farmers, although they would not have recognized the expression if they had heard it. When the lumbering era was over, a great many discovered that their hardscrabble farms would not support a family unless the farmer could earn money on the side, and in the first quarter of this century they abandoned their farms by the dozen and by the score, letting unpainted houses and barns fall in, letting the fields grow up to weeds and sumac, letting the state take over for unpaid taxes. Many a county in the lumber country has a smaller population today than it had fifty years ago. . . .

Meanwhile, as the lumber camps paid off their men and closed, the business of transporting the logs to the mills got under way. Originally everything went by water, and right down to the end a lot of it did, and now it was the riverman who was all important. A crew of rivermen was usually composed of the coolest and handiest veterans of the lumber camp. They carried peaveys and pike poles—long poles with a metal spike and crosspiece at the end, like oversized boat hooks with sharpened points—and they wore spiked boots so that they could keep their footing on the floating logs; and it was their job to bring the logs downstream from the banking grounds to the log booms at the river's mouth, where the logs were sorted out and sent on to the different mills that were waiting for them.

This called for hard work, on a dawn-to-dusk basis, and at times it was extremely dangerous. When logs grounded on a sand bar or some other obstruction, or got into some other sort of tangle through the natural cussedness of logs adrift in moving water, a log jam developed, with logs at the rear of the drive piling upon the logs in front, the force of the current packing them together, the whole thing acting like a dam, with the river's flow downstream reduced to a trickle while the water level upstream rose higher and higher so that many logs floated off and became stranded in the swamps or undergrowth some distance away from the ordinary banks. The sheer weight of the logs impounded in a big jam could be prodigious. A log drive that contained one and one-half million board feet of lumber, a winter's cut for an average camp, would fill a major river, bank to bank, for two miles.

Naturally, a log jam had to be broken as quickly as possible, and it was the riverman who had to break it. He did it usually by going out along the downstream face of the jam with his peavey, prying and poking and tugging to get the logs loose. He started at the riverbank, and often enough careful work there would do the trick; the pent-up water would come surging through, loosened logs would go floating downstream, and the jam would fall apart. (Afterward, some of the men would have to go back upriver and get the stranded logs back into the water, but this was not dangerous; it was just drudgery.) Sometimes work along the bank was not enough, and it was necessary to attack the jam in midchannel. Here the logs might be piled up in a jackstraw heap twelve feet high, and the riverman had to keep his wits about him. There was always the chance that when a key log was moved the whole jam would start tumbling down with explosive force, like a water-borne avalanche, and a man who could not see this coming and get ashore with all speed did not have long to live.

Behind the logs came the wanigans—rafts or scows, one carrying the cook shanty and another bearing sleeping quarters: tents, sometimes, to be put on the bank. The rivermen came to the wanigans when the sun went down, ate the traditional outsized meal, smoked their pipes and yarned briefly, and then tumbled into bed. Men frequently finished the day in wet clothing—it was common to have to stand waist-deep in icy water, dislodging logs that had piled up on some submerged obstacle and seemed likely to cause a jam if not removed—and these men rarely changed to dry clothing when they reached camp. It was the riverman's belief that if he did this he would catch cold, so he simply went to bed soaking wet and let his clothing dry on him.

Sending logs downstream called for careful organization. No single drive had the river to itself, especially on a large stream like the Muskegon or the Manistee. A dozen separate drives might be afloat at the same time, and the lumber companies usually arranged things so that each river crew was responsible for a certain part of the river, receiving everything that floated down to its beat and sending the logs on to the next crew downstream. Since one pine log looks much like another, this was an invitation to chaos when all the logs reached the sorting grounds at the river's mouth and each company had to collect its own logs. The companies met this problem just as the Western cattlemen met a similar problem arising from common use of an open range: each one put its brand on its own stock. . . .

Duly measured and stamped, then, the logs went down the river in care of the rivermen, and they were workers who took immense pride in their calling. They had to be daring and skillful, with stamina enough to bear up under exposure that would have sent the ordinary mortal to a hospital with pneumonia in short order, and they gloried in their own toughness. When the drive ended, and the rivermen collected their pay and descended on the barrooms and other places of amusement at the end of the line, many fights resulted. Put a few slugs of whiskey under the belt of one of these men and he was likely to find himself in a state of grace; in which condition, as he lounged with his elbows on the bar and a shot glass of this or that in his fingers, he was apt to reflect that he could lick any man in the house, perhaps any man in the state, and sooner or later he would mention it, not to brag but just as an interesting item for conversation. Put a dozen such men in one saloon, with whiskey giving everybody the gift of tongues, and interesting things were bound to happen. In the encounters that resulted, no holds were barred. When one man got another down he would choke him, gouge him, or (by preference) stamp on him with his spiked boots. Veterans of such brawls usually had sinister pockmarks on their faces. They had suffered, it was said, from logger's smallpox.

But hard living and hard fighting were not the whole story. There were easy stretches on every drive—times when the logs floated smoothly down a steady current, with no tangles, no jams and nothing to worry about. At such moments a riverman would jab the spike of his peavey into one end of the log he was riding, stretch out on his back along the length of the log, light his pipe, look up at the clouds, and let all of tomorrow's problems take care of themselves. This was the time when he saw the glamor of his own existence, and reveled in it.

Waiting for the Morning Train

That, said U. S. Grant during the war, was how long he would "fight on this line." Years later, after his presidency, after his personal financial disaster, he showed again, in one last battle, the iron in his soul.

IF IT TAKES ALL SUMMER

He had had about all that any American can get—the four stars of a general and two terms in the White House, plus enough gifts, testimonials and public functions to crowd half a dozen lifetimes—and somehow most of it had been a cloak for ill fortune. A shadow lay across his fame. To millions of people his name had come to mean everything that he himself was not, as if the Whiskey Ring and the bloody shirt carried a deeper meaning than Vicksburg and Appomattox.

And then, at the very last, after a few empty years that meant nothing in particular, fate give him good fortune in the disguise of absolute and final catastrophe. He lost all of his money and he was sentenced to die by slow torture; and through these things he once again found a task he could do superlatively well, and his old virtues of courage and determination blazed up to light his way down the valley of final shadows.

Leaving the White House in 1877, Grant was on his own for the first time since Governor Yates asked him to help with the muster of the Illinois volunteers, sixteen years earlier.

Ever since his Ohio boyhood he had liked to travel, and now he gratified that liking to the full. He started off on a transatlantic cruise, taking ship from Philadelphia, accompanied down Delaware Bay by whistle-tooting tugs and excursion steamers, and he wandered from England to the Continent and back to England again in an erratic zigzag without goal or program. He was received by kings and by parliaments, and he was looked at by millions of ordinary folk. He received the freedom of various cities and he listened to any number of addresses of welcome. And finally he went all the way around the world, and he did not get back to America until the autumn of 1879. His world tour had lasted a little less than two and one half years. Incidentally, it had consumed most of his cash savings.

It was a planless sort of wandering, because in truth Grant was at a loose end. There is seldom anything very significant for an ex-President of the United States to do, and it was harder for Grant than for most of that select breed to

Grant as President, with his wife and son, from a stereograph

find an occupation for himself. Without plan or prospects, he simply drifted about the world as an unattached famous personage.

The years had changed him a little, and his photographs show it. There is a lean hard look on the face that was photographed during the war, as if the man behind the face knew exactly where he was going and could not be kept from getting there. The civilian in frock coat and top hat visible in the pictures made a dozen years later is a little stouter and a little softer, better groomed and cared for but somehow slightly at a loss, with the look of a man who does not quite know where he has been. It was noted on the world tour that the Grant who had once disliked ceremony and adulation seemed to get genuine pleasure out of them. It was as if the medals and speeches and cheering crowds gave him a welcome reassurance; and yet in the old days, even when everything was going very badly, this man had never needed reassurance.

No matter. He came back to America, landing in San Francisco, and they made a big occasion out of it, with flags tossed into the wind and a committee of eminent citizens to meet his ship. (He had left this city a quarter century earlier, out of the army and on his uppers, lacking the price of a steamship ticket to New York.) As he traveled east there were whistle-stop receptions of high and low degree, and when he reached Chicago the city was all bunting and cheers and there was a big parade, with Phil Sheridan out of the past riding at the head of it and any number of old soldiers in the ranks.

People seemed honestly glad to see him again. A little perspective had been gained during his years out of office, and it could be seen that he had given the country ever so much more than the partisan highbinders had been able to take away. Yet the welcomes were not entirely spontaneous, for the Republican old guard was helping to pump them up. If his popularity revived enough, he might have a third term. The old guard was not happy with President Hayes. The lush pickings of the reconstruction era were gone and reform was the word, and it would be nice to turn the clock back a decade.

Grant seemed willing. He had always had a slightly fatalistic attitude toward promotion, from the day when he first got a brevet in Mexico, and from beginning to end the step from general to President had seemed to him to be essentially a promotion, differing only in degree from the step from colonel to brigadier. Besides, he had nothing to do these days. By the time the Republican convention of 1880 met, a full-scale Grant boom was under way.

The attempt was hopeless. When the balloting began Grant had a plurality but his managers could never turn it into a majority, and after a long deadlock the nomination at last went to James A. Garfield. Garfield went on to become President, and the long row over reform produced an infuriated place-seeker who killed him after he had been in office a few months; and private citizen Grant was still trying to find a proper niche for himself in civilian life.

Inevitably, he drifted to New York. (Galena he had tried again, but somehow his horizons had changed and the place was no longer quite wide enough for him.) He tried this and that and nothing quite panned out, and at last he went into business with a Wall Street broker named Ferdinand Ward, with whom his elder sons had had some profitable dealings. The investment firm of Grant and Ward came into being, and into it Grant put all of his capital, together with a hundred and fifty thousand dollars borrowed from William K. Vanderbilt.

It seemed, for a time, that solid prosperity had been attained, and as far as Grant knew he was a comparatively wealthy man, partner in a well-established business.

Then came disaster.

Ward was no more a fit person to lead Grant through the business world than Ben Butler had been fit to lead him in the world of politics; in each case, a trickster used the general's name and confidence for his own ends. The firm of Grant and Ward went broke with startling suddenness, in the middle of 1884, and in the course of one day Grant learned that every last cent he owned (plus all the money he had borrowed) was gone forever and that his partner was nothing more than a swindler.

The partnership was bankrupt for a prodigious sum, a great deal of which had been lost by people who had invested because they trusted the great name of Grant; and the man whose one solid pride had always been in his own good name was compelled to see, at last, how that name had been sullied and misused by men to whom he had given his trust.

His own financial pinch was acute. To a friend, just after he got the bad news, Grant summed it up: "When I went down town this morning I thought I was worth a great deal of money, but now I don't know that I have a dollar." Actually, he was hard pressed for ordinary housekeeping money. A friend loaned him a thousand dollars to tide him over; and one day a letter came from a total stranger, enclosing five hundred dollars with a note saying that this was a payment on account "for my share of services ending April 1, 1865."

That was heart-warming, but the fact remained that the disaster was all-embracing. Grant had no money, the taint of the bucket shop hung over him, and he seemed no more able now to provide for his family than he had been back in the hardscrabble days in Missouri.

And it was imperative that he think about providing for his family, because in the middle of all of this misfortune Grant learned that he had cancer of the throat.

So now the end of the road was nearly in view. It had been a long strange road, winding across mid-America from dark valley to mountain peak, leading through battle smoke and the wild uproar of combat to an oath taken in front of the Capitol and a long view of America through White House windows. In it there had been tremendous success and great fame and bewildering tragedy, and now it was going to end this way—with the mocking ghost of old Jesse

Grant somewhere in the background, shaking his head and repeating his ancient complaint that West Point had spoiled his oldest son for business.

There was not much of the road left, but there was room in it for one more fight, and it was a fight Grant could win. The man who had taken many cities would at last fight a battle with his own spirit, and with death at his elbow and pain rising to its unendurable crescendo he would put despair and discouragement under his feet and do the last job there was for him to do . . . and make his exit, at last, like a victor.

The job itself was simple enough. Grant would write his memoirs.

The country was re-examining its Civil War experience, and books by men who had fought in the war were in demand. As the most famous old soldier of all, Grant would find a ready market, and his memoirs would make a modest fortune and leave a comfortable estate for his family—if he could just get them written. He was not exactly a writing man by nature, although he did own the priceless ability to express himself very clearly in simple language. He was popularly supposed to be rather inarticulate, as if he were intellectually muscle-bound.

But he had had great years and he had had time to sort out his thoughts about them, and in any case what mattered now was that his life had once more—after so long a time—given him the kind of challenge that he could meet. Courage and determination were of use to him now, for life was suddenly reduced to its elementals, and in a way he was back where he had been when he wrote: "I propose to fight it out on this line if it takes all summer."

It took more than all summer, as it turned out. It took all the rest of Grant's life, which lasted a little more than a year, so that he finished his book a scant day or two before he died, and the pages of his original manuscript are eloquent in a way Grant did not intend, for they tell their own story of his last battle.

In the beginning these pages are very neat, with regular lines of inked script marching across good paper, corrections and interlineations carefully made in the proper order, penmanship regular and easily legible. The corrections show a man rereading what he had written, striking things out here and there, looking for words and phrases that would more exactly express his thoughts, sometimes knocking out whole paragraphs—and, occasionally, feeling apparently that after all these years some of his judgments might as well be withheld from print.

But toward the last, physical weakness and sheer agony begin to leave their unmistakable traces. (Grant might have died sooner, if he had permitted it, and at times his doctors resorted to elaborate expedients to keep him alive. Every added day of life was an added day of torture, and death now was a friend; but he had to live until he got this job done . . . *if it takes all summer.*) The rough paper of a schoolboy's tablet replaces the smooth bond used earlier, and instead of pen and ink the general is using a pencil, and at times the writing becomes a desperate scrawl, very hard to decipher.

You can see him, no longer able to sit at a desk, holding a scratch-pad in his lap, driving away at it with gripped pencil. There are hardly any more corrections; now the man is fighting to get the job done while the light lasts, and there is no time for trimming and polishing. The narrative no longer flows in smooth, well-thought order. From page to page the subject changes abruptly, as if the writer wants to get his ideas down and trust his editor to put things into sequence.

Toward the very last the writing becomes skeletonized, as if pain and the rising mist made it impossible to get every word in. Yet he would keep at it, he would finish this job in spite of everything, and if at times successive pages become no better than a collection of unrelated notes for insertion at different places in the narrative, there is no mere gibberish and confusion. Down to the very end Grant knew just what he wanted to say and, very largely, how he wanted to say it, but as he fought off unimaginable pain he left a little more to his editor.

Three times he scribbled off a section under the heading "Conclusion." (In the published book the chapter so marked is a blend of the three versions. It appears that Grant did have a very able editor. Be it noted, though, that no part of his book was ghostwritten.) The race problem bothered him, and at different times he wrote: "I do not know now how it is to terminate . . . problem yet to be solved as to how two races will get along together in future . . . our duty to inflict no further wrong on the Negro." Those last ten words, written in the hour of the last backward glance, when every written word was bought at the price of endured agony, contain the key to everything he was driving at in the reconstruction program.

One of the final pages, curiously, is half covered with doodles: a flat-roofed house, a series of squares and triangles, a little aimless crosshatching. Time might be running out, but U. S. Grant was not going to be rushed out of all countenance. After all, this was the general who sat on a stump and casually whittled during the great Battle of the Wilderness.

Toward the end his mind roamed back through many battles, and the last pages are an unclassified set of paragraphs meant to be inserted somewhere earlier: a critique of what Thomas did at Nashville, some notes on Chattanooga, a rehash of Grant's old plan to capture Mobile and how Halleck blocked it. On the back of the very last page is a two-sentence reference to the way Colonel Joshua Chamberlain of the 20th Maine was wounded in action at Petersburg, and how for his valor Grant made him a brigadier general on the spot. Then, having made sure that he had paid proper tribute to a brave soldier, Grant stopped writing. Within forty-eight hours he was dead—on July 23, 1885.

What he had set out to do, Grant had done. He wrote his story and he climbed back out of poverty, and he left a decent estate for his family when he died. (He had licked the eternal world of the Jesse Grants, after all.) But while he was doing all of this, Grant did a great deal more. Going back along the old road he somehow found himself, and a good many of the things that had stuck to him during the might-have-been years seem to have scaled off.

For although the manuscript pages which Grant left may show the most excruciating physical suffering, the book itself has a glow and a shine that could only come from a contented spirit. In its essence, the book is a record of what Grant saw when he looked back on things from his deathbed, and apparently what he saw was very good.

. . . the old days in Ohio, when the land was open and the world was young, and a boy could ride a horse down an infinite sandy road with a dapple of sunlight and shadow resting on his shoulders; Mexico, where youth had been a stack of golden coins to be spent prodigally amid the dangers and romance of a marvelous drowsy land of beauty and flowers; the West Coast, with green forests and white surf and blue sky making an enchantment that no memory of failure or malice could spoil; Missouri and Illinois before the war, where life had been good even when it was dark and hard, and where tough times had brought happiness because Julia and the children were there and everything one did was done for them and with them.

And always the army: not the thin companies of regulars at lonely frontier posts, but the army that was a nation on the march—endless columns of men in faded blue swaying forward on the eternal road, glimpsed like figures in a red mist, always going toward some unseen goal that could neither be attained nor given up . . .

All of this was what could be seen when Grant looked back from the final bend in the road: his own life, and the national life which it symbolized, tragedy touched by remembered moments of hope. Victory and death were forever bound together; and over all of it, the sunlight on a broad land brimming over with life and forever on the move.

U. S. Grant and the American Military Tradition

XII

Handwritings on Walls

Pearl Harbor, 1941, USS California *in foreground*

In his first book, The War Lords of Washington, *Catton described a Washington dinner party given by Donald Nelson, a name to conjure with in the days just before and during the Second World War, in which Nelson headed the powerful War Production Board. Some two dozen very important persons were there, beginning with the Vice President, Mr. Henry Wallace. The sixth chapter of the Book of Daniel was clearly on Catton's mind.*

Upon invitation of the host, Frank Knox stood up. The Secretary of the Navy was in no mood for light banter. . . . Knox performed his social duty by paying his respects to his host, remarking that he thought this kind of get-together was a good idea, and mentioning that he was glad to be present. Then, darkly serious, he looked down the long table for a moment in silence.

"I feel that I can speak very frankly, within these four walls," he said. "I want you to know that our situation tonight is very serious—more serious, probably, than most of us realize. We are very close to war. War may begin in the Pacific at any moment. Literally, at any moment. It may even be beginning tonight, while we're sitting here, for all we know. We are that close to it."

He paused, and the silence was impressive. Then he went on, his voice rising confidently.

"But I want you all to know that no matter what happens the United States Navy is ready! Every man is at his post, every ship is at its station. The Navy is ready. Whatever happens, the Navy is not going to be caught napping."

He sat down, and there was a hum of comment. Nelson leaned over toward him.

"Are things really as bad as that, Frank?" he asked quietly.

"Every bit as bad," said Knox, nodding vigorously. "It can start at any minute."

Nelson meditated for a moment.

"You know," he said, "if we do have to fight the Japs, I can't see that there'd be much for our Army to do. Won't it be pretty much a Navy show?"

Knox nodded again.

"Oh, yes, of course. We're all ready for them, you know. We've had our plans worked out for twenty years. Once it starts, our submarines will go in to blockade them, and sooner or later our battle fleet will be able to force an action. It won't take too long. Say about a six months' war."

But there is always somebody around to spoil a good effect. Belshazzar gave a big dinner in Babylon once, and right at the height of the festivities a mysterious hand appeared and traced some words upon the wall, the general purport being that the dam had busted and that good men should take to the hills. Tonight the spoil-sport, or moving finger, was a black-haired, bullet-headed man named Robert Wyman Horton, who rejoiced in the cumbersome title of Director of Information in the Office for Emergency Management of the Executive Office of the President.

Horton was a misfit at this party. He was the official mouthpiece, so to speak, for the defense program—for OPM, SPAB, and all the rest of it—and he had watched the entire process at close range ever since the formation of the original Defense Commission at the time of the fall of France, and he was not impressed by what he had seen. He was a Vermonter, exemplifying to a marked degree every characteristic of that rugged state; at all times and places he believed in saying exactly what he thought, and what he thought was usually rather acrid. He had thoughts, now, for which he craved utterance, and he passed up to Nelson a note which said, in effect, "How about calling on me for a few remarks next?"

Fortified by the all-is-well assurances of the Secretary of the Navy, Nelson glanced at the note, rose to his feet, and remarked that they would now hear from Mr. Horton, the Director of Information. He sat down, not without a faint misgiving or two about what might be coming next, and Horton got up. It was not long before Nelson realized that his faint misgiving was amply justified.

"I have been very interested," said Horton, "in the little talk which the Secretary of the Navy has just made. It has been very encouraging to be assured that the Navy is ready for whatever may happen. But somehow, some of the things I've seen recently make me wonder if the Secretary of the Navy may not be mistaken."

He fixed his cold blue eyes on Knox's face and went on.

"The other afternoon," he said, "I had to go over to the Navy Department to attend a conference. It was a little before four o'clock when I got over there. I was almost trampled underfoot in the lobby by captains and admirals, rushing out with golf bags over their shoulders. It seemed to me that the high-ranking people in the Department were knocking off work rather early, if we're so close to a war."

(Knox leaned over to Nelson and whispered savagely, behind his hand: "Who *is* this son of a bitch?")

"But the thing that really bothers me," Horton went on, "is something that happened last week. I had occasion to take a little trip down Chesapeake Bay on a little Coast Guard patrol boat. We were down around Norfolk, and late in the day the skipper of the boat—a chief petty officer—decided it might be interesting to cruise up to the Navy yard and see what we could see. So up we went. We not only cruised up to the yard, but we cruised all through it. Nobody challenged us, nobody stopped us, nobody did anything to find out if we were really in a Coast Guard boat or just in a cabin cruiser painted gray.

"Now I've heard a lot about Navy security measures lately. Some of the news we've tried to get out, over at OPM, has been held up because the Navy objected that it would violate security. Okay; if we're close to war we have to be careful about giving away military information. But as I understand it, one of the top military secrets right now is the fact that the British aircraft carrier *Illustrious* is in the yard at Norfolk for repairs. Well, we cruised right by her dock. There she was, standing up like a ten-story building, with an enormous Union Jack flying over her. If we could cruise in like that and see her, I should think any German agent who wanted to could do the same.

"Anyhow, we left the yard after a while and went out through Hampton Roads, and pretty soon it got dark and we wanted to tie up somewhere and make a phone call. So we headed into the nearest place, which happened to be one of those big new Navy installations—I think it was a mine base. We came in, after dark, and tied up at a pier where there were three or four minesweepers tied up. Nobody challenged us. Nobody tried to find out whether we were really in a Coast Guard boat, or whether we had any business in there. Nobody paid any attention to us at all. We got off the boat and walked along the pier, looking for some place where we could find a telephone. We didn't find any, so we walked on to dry land and pretty soon we came to a guard house or sentry box of some kind. We hammered on the door, and by and by a sailor stuck his head out, and we asked him where there was a public telephone. He pointed vaguely up the road and said it was about half a mile. So we walked up there. The guard didn't pay any attention to us. He didn't know who we were, but he didn't ask for a pass and he didn't want to see any credentials. For all he knew we might have been Hitler's grandsons.

"Sure, the CPO I was with had a uniform on. But there are at least thirty places in Norfolk where you can walk in and buy a CPO's uniform. All it takes is a little money. We could have been spies, saboteurs, anything—but the Navy, which is so touchy about the press releases that come out of OPM, let us wander all over that base, after dark, for upwards of half an hour, without once bothering to find out who we were or what our business was. We could have blown the whole place to pieces, for all the obstacles the Navy put in our way."

Horton paused, and looked coldly at Knox, who by now was painfully close to apoplexy.

"Mister Secretary," he said, "I don't think your Navy *is* ready."

This was the night of December 4, 1941.

The War Lords of Washington

VIEW FROM THE FRONTIER

First there was the ice; two miles high, hundreds of miles wide and many centuries deep. It came down from the darkness at the top of the world, and it hung down over the eaves, and our Michigan country lay along the line of the overhang. To be sure, all of the ice was gone. It had melted, they said, ten thousand years ago; but they also pointed out that ten thousand years amounted to no more than a flick of the second hand on the geologic time clock. It was recent; this was the frontier, where you could stand in the present and look out into the past, and when you looked you now and then got an eerie sense that the world had not yet been completed. What had been might be again. There was a hint, at times, when the dead winter wind blew at midnight, that the age of ice might some day return, sliding down the country like a felt eraser over a grade school blackboard, rubbing out all of the sums and sentences that had been so carefully written down; leaving, barely legible, a mocking *quod erat demonstrandum.*

Now and then it was a little confusing. The contrast between the old and the new was too great. There was nothing for the mind to get hold of; what probably had been was hardly more real than what possibly might yet be. We lived less than three hundred miles from Detroit, which seemed to be a door looking into the future, showing unimaginable things; and three hundred miles in the other direction, off into the desolate north country, lay the bleak spine of the upper peninsula of Michigan, a reef of the oldest rocks on earth—pre-Cambrian rocks, laid down before there were any living creatures to be fossilized, rocks dead since the hour of creation. There was no way to comprehend that reef. The geologists said that it was two billion years old, or perhaps three billion—a measure of the age of the earth—and there is no way to digest any such figures. The mind cannot grasp a time span like that. The scientist's book is as far beyond our comprehension as the book of Genesis, which simply asserts that the entire job was done in six days, with a seventh day for rest. Take it either way you please, you wind up with something you have to accept on faith. Real understanding is impossible.

In any case, the north country is very old. It is also very empty. Take a two-hundred-mile tape measure, long enough to span the lower peninsula of Michigan from east to west, and move it northward, broadside on; once you pass Lake Superior your tape strikes nothing at all except primitive wilderness, clusters of stubby firs, tamarack bogs and barren tundra, with the left-over fragments of the old age of ice lying beyond. Take the tape on to the North Pole and go down the far side of the globe; you will be deep in Siberia before you strike anything more than a trading post or a mining camp, or—visible symbol of the age of fear—an outpost of national defense.

It was and is all empty, a land that could not be lived in except by a few understanding stone-age tribes, and across its emptiness lies the gray shadow of a profound unease. The ice age, if it comes back, will come from up here; and if that, after all, is a thin chance, a crippling wisdom has reached us in this century; the Enemy may some day come down from the north, aiming at Detroit and Chicago and everything they stand for, including ourselves, bringing fire instead of cold. That is why I can look out of the window in the room where I write and see unobtrusive white domes on the skyline—radar domes, scanning the north country with unsleeping attention. To be sure, we do not give them much thought. Life in Michigan north of the industrial zone is easy and pleasant, with fish to be caught and clear lakes for swimming, lonely streams for canoes and the big lake itself for larger craft; here it is possible to escape from the steamy, overcrowded, overactive Middle West and get back to something we knew long ago, when it was good enough just to breathe the clean air and feel sunlight and wind on your shoulders. But the white domes are there, and it is not quite possible to forget what they stand for. This is the frontier, a place for looking before and after, where we try to think what we shall do with the future only to discover that we are conditioned by what we have already done with the past. The frontier! Three quarters of a century have passed since we announced that America's last frontier was gone forever. We were wrong. In spite of ourselves we have moved on into an undiscovered world. We shall always have a frontier, because we are not facing a finite North American continent whose menaces and surprises must some day all be tabulated; we are facing an infinite universe, and the last challenge has yet to be formulated. Possibly we shall encounter it tomorrow morning.

Waiting for the Morning Train

In the cities of the Mayas, more inscrutable writings moved Catton to a comparison with his own native state.

MASTER OF HIS FATE?

It is one state out of fifty, but somehow its story helps to sum up the whole. Here, perhaps more clearly than in most places, can be seen the enormous increase in the speed of society's movement, the pressures that come when a society adjusted to one era is suddenly compelled to shape itself to an entirely new one, the torment of modern man torn by the astounding discovery that the things he makes have taken charge of his life. Living in memory of an interesting past and imagining himself to be relaxing in the warmth of a long afternoon, man finds himself facing a terrifying dawn—and it seems to be a little too much for him. Without intending anything of the kind, he discovers that he is involved in an enormous revolution, simply because the power in his hands is so vast that its mere existence turns the world upside down. Michigan certainly did not cause this to happen, but it shows a good deal about *how* it happened. Here is the slice of modern life, ready to go to the lab for the biopsy. . . .

The automobile, of course, was not invented in Michigan, and its development might easily have come somewhere else. It remains true, however, that the development did take place here and that the great case history of what happens to a people dedicated to the automobile has been recorded here. It is not possible to tell the story of this state without putting the internal combustion engine, the rubber tire, and the white desert-ribbons of the concrete highway on to the center of the stage for the grand finale. . . .

The concrete ribbons grew longer and wider every year, and their loops became more and more convoluted, and the only thing that mattered was to create more of them and extend them past every hill and across every valley. The railroads were driven into bankruptcy and began to vanish utterly, and highway-building became almost a religious observance. It seemed advisable to throw a highway bridge across the Straits of Mackinac, although an earlier generation would have considered this both impossible and unnecessary; it was done, at a cost of a hundred million or thereabouts; autos rolled across it, and in increasing thousands, the bridge itself became an object of adoration, with thousands of people driving up just to have a look at it. . . .

The society that did all of this had obviously committed itself to movement regardless of cost. The oceans of fuel used come from half the world away, and it may be time to reflect on their eventual exhaustion and on social anarchy that may result when a highly mobile society abruptly finds that it cannot move.

The problem is characteristic. The whole organization of society is keyed to a means of transportation that must, some day, in the familiar phrase, run out of gas. And Michigan, where the age of the automobile came to its fullest flowering, is a state that grew up in the belief that abundance is forever. Men gabbled about inexhaustible forests and unlimited ores, right up to the moment when further self-deception became impossible. They adjusted their whole social structure to a force whose life span was similarly limited and kept from worrying unduly by increasing reliance on the faith that sustains the modern world—a faith not in the goodness of God, but in the endless ingenuity of man. . . .

The automobile is catalyst for a series of forces that are destroying the established social order. Fittingly enough, this is clearly visible in that fabulous city of magnificent beginnings, Detroit itself.

Detroit is of the essence of the twentieth century. And yet, if a reflective person sits down to ponder about it, he is likely to find himself meditating about the deserted cities of the ancient Mayas, far down in Mexico.

These cities have been in ruins since time was young, and the descendants of the people who built them know nothing much about them, except that they vaguely suspect that they are haunted. They contain survivals of a mighty architecture, with shining towers rising above the green surf of a shoreless jungle, monuments to a faith that once led stone-age men to test themselves apparently, just a little beyond their capacity. These cities pose a riddle that goes beyond mere puzzlement over the astounding skills that went into their construction. It is hard for a modern man to understand why they were built at all. They appear to have been ceremonial centers, elaborate places for rites of worship or government, but it does not seem that they were places where very many people lived. They contain temples but no houses, statues and paintings and memorials to the mighty ones (of this world or the next) but no shops or markets. If they drew multitudes in, now and then—as they unquestionably did: some of them are large, and somebody went to great trouble to design and build them—they sent them all away again after a short time. Sooner or later, the student finds himself wondering what they were for and suspecting that the sheer immobile weight of them finally dragged the people who built them down to defeat. For all of these cities, sooner or later, were deserted.

A long way off, to be sure, and Yucatan is not much like Michigan, except for the coincidence that both are peninsulas. But at this moment, Detroit cannot really be defined or described. In one sense, it is a hollow shell; in another, it is a state of mind; in still another, it is a growing section of the state of Michigan, spraddling out over what very recently was good farming country, planting the most startling skyscrapers and modernistic factories where nobody had ever planted anything but corn, up to a year or so ago. Where the heart of the city is depends on who you are, what your job is, and where you sleep; it is likely to be miles away from anything men would have recognized a few years earlier as part of Detroit. Over and over again, crossing level green fields to find a cluster of soaring towers reaching for the distant sky, you find yourself thinking: Magnificent—but of course no one really lives here.

The Mayas at least had something in mind, even though we do not know what it was, when they built their cities. Today's cities, in the very heart of automobile land, were built while men were thinking about something else. They built the automobile; and the automobile has become the instrument through which the whole face of the earth is changed. It changes because men can go where they will. Men who can go where they will look for more comfortable places to work and play and live; in the finest tradition of this land of milk and honey and riches-for-the-taking, they use up what they have, throw the husk away, and go on to fairer fields.

Nowhere is this so frighteningly visible as in Detroit. There is a certain pattern handed down from earlier generations. The forests were used hard and at last used up, and the sawmill towns that grew so great fell ill and some of them died outright, so that the former lumber country is spotted with ghost towns, where blank windows look out of decaying, paintless houses, and weeds grow on docks and in empty railroad yards. The mines were used in the same way, and the mining country has ghost towns of its own, with the gaunt buildings that once housed pit-head machinery standing over the deep shafts that go down to darkness. And now there are the great industrial cities with blank windows and empty houses of their own.

Detroit is not really a ghost town, of course, because many hundreds of thousands of people still live there. In a sense, they have to live there. Some of them are tied down by jobs. Others have invested their savings in homes or small businesses and will lose if they sell out to move elsewhere. And a great many have simply lost or never gained the mobility that is modern man's great acquired characteristic. To all intents and purposes, public transportation has died, and the man who cannot afford transportation of his own has to stay put. When everyone else goes off to some place where life is nicer, he has to make the best of what cannot be carried off, and the best may not be very good. A city that contains so many people who would move out if they could is not likely to have a robust community spirit, and so crime rates go up, and there is a great increase in homicides, the traffic in drugs thrives, the relief rolls are all scabby with people who have given up, and, under the surface, the city suffers progressive physical and spiritual decay. It becomes a less pleasant place to live and work, and so more of the people who can move out do so, and the gap between those who move and those who stay becomes wider and wider, the mutual estrangement, more and more bitter.

Tocqueville saw American democracy when it was younger and simpler, and back in the 1830's, he remarked that, before long, "Man will be less and less able to produce, of himself alone, the commonest necessaries of life." A society whose lusty tradition of individualism and firm belief in the equality of all men were both based on that frontier ability is likely to flounder when conditions change, and Tocqueville went on to draw a somber conclusion: "Among the laws which rule human societies there is one which seems to be more precise and clear than all others. If men are to remain civilised, or to become so, the art of associating together must grow and improve in the same ratio in which the equality of conditions is increased."

Hazen Pingree saw it the same way and feared that a revolution was coming "because of the present system of inequality."

It is neither the increased mobility nor the ingrained prodigal wastage that causes the real trouble. Under everything else, there is a loss of "the art of associating together," and an increase in "the present system of inequality," and from these comes darkness. So perhaps there are fixed grades and classes of men, after all, even in the land of promise, with eternal enmity dividing the halves of society; and perhaps it was a long whisper such as this that caused everyone to let those Mayan cities go back to the jungle.

Michigan: A Bicentennial History

THE THUNDERING WATER

In the beginning Niagara was surrounded by wilderness, as wild and free and unspoiled as something in the Garden of Eden, and now it is in the heart of the world's busiest continent, chained by superhighways, soaring bridges, high-tension power lines, and a nexus of hotels, motels, and curio shops. But the surpassing wonder of the cataract itself is unspoiled. It still speaks with the voice of the forest primeval, it is the green water of the old north country running out to the ocean just as it did when the last ice sheet melted, and although it lies on the edge of the world's most highly industrialized area, its spray carries the tang of the long-gone wilderness. There is nothing quite like it anywhere.

One trouble with Niagara, of course, is that practically everybody has seen it but nobody can refrain from trying to describe it as if it were quite new. On writing people it has had a bad effect; it moves them into unbridled prose, and there seems to be something about it that causes writers to flap their wings and try to soar. Father Hennepin, for instance, wrote: "The Waters which fall from this horrible Precipice do foam and boyl after the most hideous Manner imaginable, making an outrageous Noise, more terrible than that of Thunder." This is true enough, but as good a writer as Charles Dickens felt compelled to rhapsodize as follows:

"What voices spoke from out the thundering water; what faces, faded from the earth, looked out upon me from its gleaming depths; what Heavenly promise glistened in those angels' tears, the drops of many hues, that showered around, and twined themselves about the gorgeous arches which the changing rainbows made!"

Harriet Beecher Stowe, ordinarily given to deep thoughts about slavery, was moved to write thus:

"I thought of the great white throne; the rainbow around it; the throne in sight like unto an emerald; and oh! that beautiful water rising like moonlight, falling as the soul sinks when it dies, to rise refined, spiritualized and pure. . . ."

These are rather special thoughts to come out of a few minutes' study of a waterfall, but that is the way Niagara affects people. Mark Twain, being somewhat more sardonic, moved off in the other direction. He once remarked that although it was wonderful to see all of that water tumbling *down,* it would be even more wonderful to see it tumbling *up.*

Lesser people have written worse things about the spectacle, but almost everybody writes something. People carry away their own memories of the place, which tend to be quite various.

It is the privilege of the elderly to believe that everything was better in the old days, and this writer's fondest memory of Niagara goes back to the

The mighty cataract in Mark Twain's time

pre-automobile age. (Well, there *were* automobiles then, but there weren't very many, and they had not yet begun to remodel American life.) Anyway, in those days one rode about the river above the Falls, and the islands, in carriages and took the trolley car down the gorge on tracks that ran just along the frightening water's edge. Since the things that can impress a small child are sometimes unpredictable, let it be added that the high point of this particular visit to Niagara was a tour through the factory—upstream from the Falls, somewhere, near the river before the river becomes so scary—where people made shredded wheat biscuits. This was especially memorable because at the end of the tour we were all taken into a nice lunchroom and were given, for free, a nice dish of cereal with strawberries and cream.

"The Thundering Water," American Heritage, *June 1964*

INDIANS

There is a story, probably apocryphal but significant none the less, about a United States Senator [from Michigan] who was running for re-election a few years ago. According to this story, the Senator got to a small north country town one evening to make a campaign speech, and just before he was led into the hall where the speech was to be delivered the local party chairman gave him a briefing about the issues that were on people's minds locally.

"You'll notice, at the back of the hall, quite a few Indians," he said. "It would be helpful if somewhere in your speech you could say that you are fully aware of their problem and that you will do your best to solve it."

The Senator promised that he would do this. Then—moved by simple curiosity—he asked: "By the way, what is their problem?"

The local man looked at him wide-eyed.

"What's their problem?" he repeated. "God damn it, they're *Indians!*"

Yet the Indian was incidental. It was the earth and the fullness thereof that mattered. It passed into American hands just as the tools to exploit it were being perfected—the tools and the driving urge to use them—and the men who held the tools moved in as if they had to get the job finished before nightfall. They succeeded (at any rate, recognizable nightfall has not yet come) and in about a century the job was done. The trees had gone to build homes for half of America, the copper had gone to serve the new age of electricity, and if the iron lasted longer it had been moved south by millions of tons, in a progress as inexorable as the Sleeping Bear's ponderous drift to the eastward, to make railroads and machinery and skyscrapers and weapons; and the land was left bruised and scarred, with the radar domes to indicate that the age of applied technologies advances by geometrical progression.

So we live as the Indians of Lewis Cass's time lived, between cultures, compelled to readjust ourselves to forces that will not wait for us. There is no twentieth-century culture; the twentieth century is simply a time of transition, and the noise of things collapsing is so loud that we are taking the prodigious step from the nineteenth century to the twenty-first without a moment of calm in which we can see where we are going. Between nineteenth century and twenty-first there is a gulf as vast as the one the stone-age Indians had to cross. What's our problem? We're Indians.

Waiting for the Morning Train

IS SOMETHING GAINING ON US?

Maybe they ought to call this the Uneasy Decade. As we move on toward the twenty-first century (and it really is not so far away, when you stop to think about it), we seem to spend a good part of our time looking back over our shoulders. Satchel Paige, the black baseball star, advised people never to look behind "because something may be gaining on you," but we are doing it persistently and perhaps we are beginning to understand what Mr. Paige was talking about. *Something* back there seems to be overtaking us. Naturally, we are nervous.

Out of this nervousness there has developed an odd resignation. We are being offered a credo that embeds a whole chain of gloomy expectations in a matrix of unrelieved pessimism; it is possible to become fairly ecstatic in one's acceptance of approaching disaster. These horrors so clearly foreseen are inevitable. They cannot be averted no matter what we do. The only question is which one hits us first.

Consider these articles of faith:

Nuclear fission will destroy us all, and possibly the living globe along with us. This is certain. We can do nothing about it.

The energy crisis is beyond remedy and will cause all the machines to run down and all the wheels to stop turning; at which point the human race, like some immense demented scorpion, will sting itself to death.

Our pollution of the atmosphere with indigestible gases will create a "greenhouse effect" under which the earth's temperature will get stabilized at something like 500 degrees Fahrenheit. A pleasant variant is that this will bring on a universal ice age which will be equally lethal. I know people who accept both of these points at one and the same time.

If all else fails, the modern world of push-button electronics and the art of thought control will turn human society into an anthill that *ought* to be destroyed even if it does turn out to be viable.

It is not necessary to believe all of these things, but to believe none of them—to believe, that is, that we have a future and that we have some control over the form it will take—is held practically equivalent to believing in a flat earth. The enlightened man, we are told, goes around with a litany of disaster in his vest pocket.

Fortunately, the irreverent skepticism that somehow got built into the American spirit a long time ago begins to come to the rescue. People in this country don't scare easily, and if in the valor of benighted ignorance they try to do the impossible they now and then succeed in doing it. They have never yet marched under a banner inscribed "It can't be done."

In spite of Mr. Paige's excellent advice, we do need to look behind us. Something is indeed gaining on us, and it is nothing more or less than the unhappy fact that what people have been encouraged to want is somehow a good deal less than what they actually have. On that baffling fact we have got to build our plans for meeting the future.

It points us, that is, in the right direction. The dismaying world we confront was given its vast intricacy and its perilous speed by human beings for the benefit of human beings. The one basic resource we have always had to rely on is the innate intelligence, energy and good will of the human race. It is facing an enormous challenge, but then it always has; and it meets each one only to confront another. If now we give way to the gloom of the apostles of catastrophe we are of course in the deepest sort of trouble. The old reliance is at our service. It can bear us up if we put our full weight on it.

Unpublished essay

XIII

Night Train

Each man who mourns his father mourns also for himself. This sad and affectionate remembrance of George Catton's last years, with its powerful final image, is taken from the concluding chapter of Waiting for the Morning Train. *It is not impossible to think that Bruce Catton, climbing into the same sleeper, may have had hopes too.*

Father had his full share of that profound conviction which lies so close to the headwaters of the American spirit: the conviction that if in the end the world is saved from disaster the saving will be done in America and by Americans. As a people whose ideas about the cosmos have at least in part an Old Testament base, we have a deep suspicion that we are the chosen people. We may not actually be the ones specifically mentioned in Scripture, but we feel that we are fairly close; maybe Providence made a supplementary choice somewhere along the way. (After all, no less a man than Abraham Lincoln, trying to nerve his countrymen for the shock of civil war, spoke of them as the *almost* chosen people.) This feeling is in fact one of the most powerful forces in American life, and now and then it leads to interesting happenings. It frequently makes us hard to live with, and it bewilders a great many people—including, often enough, ourselves. For every so often it impels us to take drastic action, and a subconscious belief in mission is not always accompanied by the sense to make a sound choice of the sort of action that is required. Sometimes we act with wisdom and at other times we do not. The same impulse that led us to destroy Hitler's obscenely contrived Nibelungen Reich, composed in equal parts of the fantasies of Teutonic chivalry and grisly shapes from the far side of midnight, led us a few years later into Southeast Asia where we made obscene contrivances of our own.

But whether we act wisely or foolishly, we always feel that what we do is important to the whole wide world and not just to ourselves, and the responsibility runs all the way down to the conscience of the individual. We are mindful of the text which, telling the chosen ones that they were the salt of the earth, asked what the world would do if the salt ceased to be salty. A man who feels so will make no small decisions. Thus it happens that the elderly principal of an unimportant school in one of the remote parts of the earth, reflecting that time was short and anxious to make good use of the thin years that remained to him, might conclude that he owed to mankind a larger debt than he had yet tried to pay. What he did might mean nothing to anybody in particular, but by what he was and what he believed he would do it as if the fate of the world depended on it. By the end of the summer of 1916, I am sure, Father had made up his mind to leave the academy.

Of all of this I at that time knew nothing. I was thinking about myself, and about the great things that lay ahead of me; the place that had been all the world was about to become nothing more than a receding milestone, growing ever smaller with increasing distance but not actually changing. The institution that had shaped me (and in a sense it was simply an extension of my own home) would remain just as it always had been: always, that is, for the last ten or twelve years. Changes that took place would happen to me, not to what I left behind. My background was immutable, and when I finally went off to Oberlin I felt no need to take a fond backward glance.

A college freshman was as far from maturity then as he is today, but it did seem to me that I was just about grown up. Boyhood certainly was ended. Youth indeed remained, to be squandered as blithely as if it came from an inexhaustible store, but the mere fact that I could be prodigal of it if I wished made a difference. I felt that by getting to college, exchanging a small campus for a large one, I was being set free. . . .

The academy would always be there, and someday I would return, probably as a famous foreign correspondent on furlough, and tell the impressionable young people graphic tales about gathering the news in places like Paris and London.

The one thing I did not dream of at that time was that the academy was not going to wait for me. My own class of 1916 was second from the last class ever to be graduated there. At the end of the 1917 school year Father resigned his post, and one year later, in the summer of 1918, the academy closed its doors forever. . . .

A graduate of the academy, meeting Father in the fall of 1918, asked him why the academy had disintegrated. Father replied that any small, undernourished institution of that sort was simply the reflection of one man's activity: when the man ceased to be active the institution ceased to exist. Whether he was consciously adapting Emerson's remark that an institution is the lengthened shadow of one man or worked the thought out for himself I do not know, but he had the right explanation. Benzonia Academy, founded by dedicated men to light an educational lamp in a wilderness which, left to itself, would remain in darkness, had outlived the condition that called it into being. The wilderness had been destroyed and the academy had become an anachronism. Once it existed because a state needed it and a community willed it; in the end, no longer really essential, it existed because one man willed it. When America went to war in the spring of 1917 he focused his will on another objective. It took the academy just a year to die. . . .

Father was a dedicated Theodore Roosevelt man, a card-carrying member of the Bull Moose Party. He had campaigned for Roosevelt, on the village and county level, in 1912, and in 1916 he had been elected a delegate to the national convention of the Progressive Party, and down to Chicago he went, to see the great leader in person and get inspiration for the approaching presidential election.

What he got, of course, was profound disillusionment. Like hundreds of other delegates, he had keyed himself up (in Roosevelt's own words) to stand at Armageddon and to battle for the Lord, and these were words he could rise to because he was both a devout Roosevelt man and a good Biblical scholar. But the emotional build-up led to nothing but a let-down. Roosevelt was not going to run for President after all, the Progressive Party had served its purpose and would be dismantled; instead of standing at Armageddon, rallying to a banner held high in a clanging wind, they were to go home quietly, vote for Charles Evans Hughes, and resume their places in the Republican Party which they had spent four years learning to distrust. Father never said much about it, but I am convinced that in the fall of 1916, for the only time in his life, he voted the Democratic ticket. Woodrow Wilson—precise, professorial, full of hard passions but apparently having no zest for living—might seem an unlikely heir for the Bull Moose legacy but he got a lot of Bull Moose votes that fall. . . .

When America went to war Father saw the war through Woodrow Wilson's eyes and heard the summons in Wilson's voice; if Theodore Roosevelt, in the showdown, had failed to call him to Armageddon, Wilson sounded the call and Father responded. He left the academy to support the cause as a free lance, believing that his eloquence and his knowledge of world history ought to be of service. His knowledge of world history was limited and may have led him at times to unsound judgments; but men in a position to know far more than he knew did no better with what they knew, and all in all he did a good, serviceable job. He wrote analytical articles for various Michigan newspapers, and he set up a series of lectures explaining the causes and the meaning of the war and traveled up and down the state delivering them to a considerable variety of audiences. These talks seem to have gone over well in the high schools—an enthusiastic educator in Saginaw wrote that they "should be presented in every high school in the United States"—and a former academy student, finding himself early in 1918 wearing khaki with other trainees at Camp Custer, was marched with his battalion into the mess hall one day to listen while Mr. Catton explained the true significance of the war. He had one lecture on "spiritual conscription" designed for church groups, explaining how Christians could sustain the young men who were being taken into the army; and in a notebook wherein he jotted down points to be made in his talks he scribbled this sentence: "The one inevitably oncoming thing, in politics, industry, commerce, education and religion, is *Democracy*."

All of this, of course, was a venture that had no tomorrow. He had cut loose from his job and had in fact destroyed the base on which the job had rested, and once the war was over nobody was going to want articles or speeches about why we fought and why we had to win. Furthermore, he was sixty-two years old, and his prospects in a postwar job market were not good. Presumably he was well aware of this, and privately, where no one could hear him, he did a little whistling for his courage's sake. In his notebook there is a yellowed newspaper clipping, worn by much handling: a poem entitled "At Sixty-Two," which apparently he had read many times. One stanza gives the tone of it:

> Just sixty-two? Then trim thy light
>   And get thy jewels all reset;
> 'Tis past meridian, but still bright,
>   And lacks some hours of sunset yet.
>   At sixty-two
>   Be strong and true,
> Scour off thy rust and shine anew.

Excellent words, but it did not lack as many hours of sunset as might have been thought. For a long time Father had suffered an abdominal pain, with certain distressing symptoms, which he did his best to ignore. But sometime early in 1919 the matter reached a point where it could be ignored no longer, nor could it be concealed. He confided, at last, in a doctor, and learned (as I suppose he had expected to learn) that he had cancer, and that although an operation would presently be performed it was not likely to do much good. His number, in other words, was up, and now there was nothing to do but get his affairs in order, compose his mind, and wait for the end.

. . . Old age, as I said before, is like youth in this one respect: it finds one waiting at the railroad junction for a train that is never going to come back; and whether the arrival and possible destination of this train is awaited with the high hopes that youth entertains when it waits for its own train depends, no doubt, on the individual. I think Father had hopes.

But you know how it can be, waiting at the junction for the night train. You have seen all of the sights, and it is a little too dark to see any more even if you did miss some, and the waiting room is uncomfortable and the time of waiting is dreary, long-drawn, with a wind from the cold north whipping curls of fog past the green lamps on the switch stands. Finally, far away yet not so far really, the train can be heard; the doctor (or station agent) hears it first, but finally you hear it yourself and you go to the platform to get on. And there is the headlight, shining far down the track, glinting off the steel rails that, like all parallel lines, will meet in infinity, which is after all where this train is going. And there by the steps of the sleeping car is the Pullman conductor, checking off his list. He has your reservation, and he tells you that your berth is all ready for you. And then, he adds the final assurance as you go down the aisle to the curtained bed: "I'll call you in plenty of time in the morning."

. . . in the morning.

Waiting for the Morning Train